W9-BCC-638

Virgin Martyrs

Virgin Martyrs

❊ ❊ ❊ ❊ ❊

LEGENDS OF SAINTHOOD
IN LATE
MEDIEVAL ENGLAND

Karen A. Winstead

CORNELL UNIVERSITY PRESS

ITHACA AND LONDON

First Published 1997 by Cornell University Press.

Library of Congress Cataloging-in-Publication Data

Winstead, Karen A. (Karen Anne), 1960–
    Virgin martyrs : legends of sainthood in late medieval England /
Karen A. Winstead.
        p.   cm.
    Includes bibliographical references and index.
    ISBN 0-8014-3333-9 (cloth : alk. paper)
    1. Christian women saints—Biography—History and criticism.   2. Christian
martyrs—Biography—History and criticism.   3. Virginity—Religious aspects—
Christianity—History of doctrines—Middle Ages, 600–1500.   4. Legends,
Christian—England.   5. England—Church history—1066–1485.   6. England—
Religious life and customs.   I. Title.
    BX4659.G7W56   1997
    272'.082—dc21   97-9318

Printed in the United States of America.

Cornell University Press strives to utilize environmentally responsible suppliers
and materials to the fullest extent possible in the publishing of its books. Such
materials include vegetable-based, low-VOC inks and acid-free papers that are
also either recycled, totally clorine-free, or partly composed of nonwood fibers.

Cloth Printing   10   9   8   7   6   5   4   3   2   1

For Carl

Contents

Figures ix

Acknowledgments xi

Introduction 1

1 Martyrdom, Marriage, and Religious Communities,
1100–1250 19

2 Unruly Virgins and the Laity, 1250–1400 64

3 Decorous Lives: Saints and Consumers, 1400–1450 112

4 The Politics of Reading 147

Bibliography 181

Index 197

Figures

1. Mary and Child with female saints, inv. 2576, Musées royaux des Beaux-Arts de Belgique 2

2. St. Agatha brought before Quintianus, MS lat. 5594, Bibliothèque Nationale, Paris 29

3. Aphrodisia takes Agatha to her brothel, MS lat. 5594, Bibliothèque Nationale, Paris 30

4. Agatha admonishes Quintianus, MS lat. 5594, Bibliothèque Nationale, Paris 30

5. Agatha is returned to prison, MS lat. 5594, Bibliothèque Nationale, Paris 31

6. Agatha's torment, MS lat. 5594, Bibliothèque Nationale, Paris 31

7. Torturers remove Agatha's breast, MS lat. 5594, Bibliothèque Nationale, Paris 32

8. St. Peter restores Agatha's breast, MS lat. 5594, Bibliothèque Nationale, Paris 32

9. Torture of St. Agatha, Jacobus de Voragine, *Legenda aurea,* MS HM 3027, Huntington Library 87

10. Torture of St. Lucy, Jacobus de Voragine, *Legenda aurea,* MS HM 3027, Huntington Library 88

11. Execution of St. Euphemia, Jacobus de Voragine, *Legenda aurea,* MS HM 3027, Huntington Library 89

12. Execution of St. Christine, *Queen Mary's Psalter,* MS Royal 2.B.VII, British Library 90

13. Margaret tramples the dragon, Brewes-Norwich Commentary on the *Liber Sextus,* MS 4A, vol. 2, St. John's College, Cambridge 91

14. Katherine tramples Maxentius, Brewes-Norwich Commentary on the *Liber Sextus,* MS 4A, vol. 4, St. John's College, Cambridge 91

15. St. Apollonia, *Luttrell Psalter,* MS Add. 42130, British Library 93

16. Margaret and Olibrius: first interrogation, *Queen Mary's Psalter,* MS Royal 2.B.VII, British Library 94

17. Margaret and Olibrius: second interrogation, *Queen Mary's Psalter,* MS Royal 2.B.VII, British Library 95

18. Margaret and Olibrius: third interrogation, *Queen Mary's Psalter,* MS Royal 2.B.VII, British Library 95

19. Margaret and Olibrius: final interrogation, *Queen Mary's Psalter,* MS Royal 2.B.VII, British Library 96

20. Olibrius courts Margaret, *Queen Mary's Psalter,* MS Royal 2.B.VII, British Library 97

21. The execution of St. Catherine, A119B–1946, Victoria and Albert Museum, London 114

22. St. Agatha, *South English Legendary,* MS Tanner 17, Bodleian Library 115

❁ Figures ❁

23. St. Juliana, *South English Legendary,* MS Tanner 17, Bodleian Library   116

24. St. Barbara, by Robert Campin, Museo del Prado   148

25. St. Petronilla, MS 349, Queen's College, Oxford   149

26. St. Barbara, MS Auct. D. inf.2.13, Bodleian Library   151

27. St. Katherine, MS Douce 20, Bodleian Library   152

28. St. Katherine, MS W.222, Walters Art Gallery   153

29. Seal of Margaret, Lady Hungerford, Seal XCII 23, British Library   154

30. St. Katherine sitting on Maxentius, MS Gough Liturg. 15, Bodleian Library   155

❀

Acknowledgments

It is a pleasure to thank the people and institutions that contributed in various ways to this project. First, however, I must mention someone I cannot thank, the late C. Clifford Flanigan, whose courses in medieval culture kindled my interest in hagiography. An impassioned scholar and educator, he not only taught his students about the Middle Ages but also how to think about the Middle Ages, impressing on us that *any* text—even the drabbest martyr legend—is exciting if we only know what questions to ask. He is deeply missed.

Several scholars have offered valuable criticism and advice. I thank Sherry L. Reames and Pamela Sheingorn for their comments on an early draft of Chapter 2. Nicholas Howe and Lisa J. Kiser, my colleagues at Ohio State, suggested crucial revisions and, along with Xiaomei Chen, provided advice and encouragement. A most generous mentor, Paul Strohm has spent much time discussing ideas and reading drafts of my work since I began researching virgin martyrs in the mid-1980s. His scholarship has been a continuing source of inspiration. Maureen Novak has been not only a splendid critic and meticulous research assistant but an indispensable friend as well. I am grateful to Cornell University Press and its readers for their careful attention and numerous suggestions, which have greatly improved this book.

My research was supported by a Seed Grant from the Ohio State University, which provided for a research quarter and the purchase of essential materials. A Grant-in-Aid from the College of Humanities and Office for Research funded travel to British libraries and archives in the summer of 1994, and a Probationary Faculty Development Quarter allowed me to devote the spring of 1994 to research and writing. A grant from the Center for Medieval and Renaissance Studies at Ohio State and a Grant-in-Aid from the College of Humanities helped defray the cost of reproductions and permissions. I am grateful for the hospitality of the Huntington Library, where much of the research for this book was conducted.

In closing, I would like to acknowledge some personal debts. I thank my parents, Arthur and Elizabeth Welborn, for their unconditional support and love. My husband, Carl Winstead, has for fifteen years been my best, toughest, and most valued critic. I can't begin to thank him for his investment in my work and for his confidence in me.

Karen A. Winstead

Columbus, Ohio

Virgin Martyrs

Introduction

A late-fifteenth-century altar panel from the Church of Our Lady in Bruges depicts the Virgin Mary in a garden, holding the baby Jesus on her lap, with a company of fashionably dressed ladies gathered around her (figure 1). The Virgin's court is remarkably homogeneous: nine of the eleven saints in her entourage are virgin martyrs of the early Church. These women endured hideous ordeals to preserve their bodies for Jesus, their heavenly spouse. Two were boiled, another was burned, and another mangled by spiked wheels. Two others had their breasts torn off, and another, her teeth yanked out. One gouged out her own eyes to discourage an admirer, while another was butchered, along with eleven thousand fellow virgins, in a spectacular mass martyrdom.[1] Though they now sit peacefully about the Queen of Heaven, they bear the emblems of past violence: a plate of eyes, a pair of arrows, a tooth, a breast, a gown embroidered with wheels. This painting's association of feminine virtue with beauty, sexual purity, and the endurance of brutality is by no means unusual. As numerous catalogues of medieval artworks and of saints' legends attest, the overwhelming majority of medieval Christian heroines were virgins, and when we examine the legends of those virgins, we find that most of them were attractive young women who proved their love of God through their gruesome deaths.

In the Bruges altar panel, ascribed to the Master of the St. Lucy Legend, all the saints are young and richly dressed, their delicate features accented by elegant headpieces or flowing hair—a sameness that also characterized their legends. Those legends rehearse similar incidents of faith, family conflict, sexual persecution, and torture. Indeed, hagiographers sometimes created "new" virgin martyrs by reproducing existing legends, changing only the protagonist's name, while in many other cases, legends of different saints are distinguished only by minor variations in plot.[2] The similarities among the legends were quite deliberate, for hagiography as a genre aimed to suppress individualizing

---

[1] I am referring, respectively, to Saints Margaret, Cecilia, Agnes, Katherine, Agatha, Barbara, Apollonia, Lucy, and Ursula.

[2] For example, the legend of St. Regina is identical with that of St. Margaret of Antioch. Both women are courted by the prefect Olibrius, who, when spurned, subjects them to the same sequence of tortures.

1. Mary and Child with female saints, inv. 2576, by permission of Musées royaux des Beaux-Arts de Belgique, Brussels.

detail and to bring out the saints' resemblance to one another and to Christ. Thus, the sixth-century hagiographer Gregory of Tours deemed it more appropriate to speak of the *life* of the saints (*vita sanctorum*) than of the *lives* of the saints (*vitae sanctorum*), while his contemporary, Pope Gregory the Great, observed in his prototypical life of St. Benedict that the saint "was filled with the spirit of all the righteous."[3]

The allusions to suffering in the Bruges panel clash with the tranquility of the saints and their surroundings. To an extent, those allusions were conventional and even necessary, for by the fifteenth century, the virgin martyrs had come to be distinguished from one another by the ways in which they were tortured. How could one tell St. Apollonia from St. Lucy, were one woman not carrying her extracted tooth and the other her extracted eyes? Yet this conventional use of body parts and torture instruments as emblems is not merely a convenience, for the ordeal associated with a particular emblem often was not unique to the saint that it came to signify—Juliana, for instance, was tortured on a "Katherine" wheel in some accounts, while many a virgin martyr besides Agatha had her breasts torn off. Although St. Katherine could be and was identified by some combination of a book, a crown, a trod-upon Emperor Maxentius, or a sign of her mystical marriage, her wheel is almost never omitted. Thus the Master of the St. Lucy Legend, though he might have identified Katherine by her crown and wedding band, includes not only those emblems but also the conventional reference to violence. Analogously, though I will show in later chapters that writers often related virgin martyr legends in ways that emphasized the saint's serenity, faith, and good works, they never actually omitted her passion. Emblems and accounts of suffering, then, are not simply a means of distinguishing one virgin martyr from another; they are simultaneously a means of subsuming the saint into a single "life" of triumph through suffering alongside Christ and the male martyrs. The incongruous juxtaposition of mutilation and beauty also hints at the paradoxes that, I will later argue, help explain why virgin martyrs, more than any other type of saint, appear to have captured the imagination of the faithful.[4]

The timelessness and serenity that the Bruges panel evokes mask its participation in a protean tradition that proved exceptionally responsive to its cultural

---

[3] Gregory of Tours, *Life of the Fathers*, trans. Edward James (Liverpool: Liverpool University Press, 1985), 2; Gregory the Great, *Dialogues*, bk. 2, *Saint Benedict*, trans. Myra L. Uhlfelder (Indianapolis: Bobbs-Merrill, 1967), 17.

[4] Though, in keeping with what Jane Tibbetts Schulenburg has seen as an overarching sexism, male martyrs outnumber their female counterparts in calendars and legendaries, the women were more commonly chosen as the subjects of individual legends or paintings. For Schulenburg's formulation, see "Sexism and the Celestial Gynaceum—from 500–1200," *Journal of Medieval History* 4 (1978): 117–33.

environment. Following common practice, the artist removes the saints from history by assembling inhabitants of different places and centuries and suppressing all but a few tokens of their pasts. Paradoxically, however, his attempt to transcend history is rooted in history: virtually everything about the painting—from the saints' stylish dress to the landscape behind them—locates the women in the late fifteenth century. Such cultural specificity was typical of medieval representations of the saints, whose responsiveness to contemporary tastes and implication in current social and political debates has lately engaged the attention of cultural critics. In their seminal essay on St. Anne, Kathleen Ashley and Pamela Sheingorn argue that, as a vital cultural symbol in the later Middle Ages, the Virgin Mary's mother must be seen as "part of ideological constellations employed in specific institutional contexts at specific historical times."[5] The legend of St. Anne has no fixed meaning, Ashley and Sheingorn maintain; rather, different meanings became dominant in different renditions, as the legend was variously construed and appropriated by individuals and groups over time. Scholars of individual virgin martyrs have observed a similar richness of interpretation. Yet, despite the increased attention to hagiography and to virgin martyr legends in particular, the widespread assumption is still that virgin martyr legends as a genre express a more or less constant paradigm of sainthood—that it is safe to use, say, Osbern Bokenham's mid-fifteenth-century virgin martyr legends to infer what Chaucer's late-fourteenth-century audience would have expected of the genre. In this book, I take a closer look at virgin martyr legends and at the cultural work they performed by examining interpretations of the saints in late medieval England. Far from remaining static, the virgin martyr legend underwent remarkable transformations that signal a struggle over the meaning of these powerful cultural symbols.

That struggle was, of course, multifaceted. We cannot properly understand the development of the virgin martyr legend as a genre without attending to what individual hagiographers thought they were accomplishing by producing certain kinds of texts, but neither can we neglect the values, prejudices, and professional interests—often unconscious, often contradictory—that influenced them. This book is, however, less about saints and their creators than about saints and their consumers, and I consider authors not only as producers of new narratives but as readers of a larger tradition, engaged in a contest over meaning both with that tradition and with their own readers. In seeking to elucidate the re-creation of virgin martyrs in the minds of those who painted or

[5] Kathleen M. Ashley and Pamela Sheingorn, introduction to *Interpreting Cultural Symbols: Saint Anne in Late Medieval Society,* ed. Ashley and Sheingorn (Athens: University of Georgia Press, 1990), 6.

wrote, saw, read, or heard their stories, I draw on artifacts, texts, and social trends from the broader environment in which these saints' legends were experienced. By exploring the legends as part of that environment, we can perceive their intriguing and often surreptitious engagement with matters as remote from the traditional purview of hagiography as etiquette and the succession to the English Crown.

Because part of what makes the study of virgin martyr legends so absorbing is that the genre remained popular for such a long time, we should ask why virgin martyr legends were spawned and adapted more frequently than the stories of other early female saints—reformed prostitutes, transvestites, and saintly nuns. In part, the answer lies in the continuing appeal of the virgin martyr legend's subject matter. Sexuality (especially virginity), violence, and conflicts between the sexes, among family members, and, more generally, between material and spiritual values were topics of abiding interest to medieval audiences. In part, the legends also remained popular because they dramatized estimable, if banal, staples of Christian teaching—for example, that one should be willing to sacrifice all for God. As I will shortly elaborate, however, the legend's success is perhaps best attributed to the inconsistencies and ambiguities that allowed the virgin martyr legend, more than any other hagiographical genre, to mean different things to different people. If we look carefully, virgin martyr legends are rarely definitive about anything—including virginity. Rather, contradictory messages coexist, ready to be exploited to different ends. Often, then, the legends worked not to propagate enduring values of medieval Christianity but to invest partisan views on topical issues with the authority of tradition. In this respect, the virgin martyrs are like the Eucharist and other supposedly unifying symbols that are now recognized to be fraught with tension.[6]

The Generic Virgin Martyr

To appreciate how the virgin martyrs were re-created, it is essential to understand the many features that changed little from legend to legend through the centuries. Many of the standard ingredients of virgin martyr legends are found in the accounts of most early Christian martyrs, male or female: the saint refuses to participate in pagan sacrifices, debates her antagonist, affirms the fundamental tenets of Christianity, destroys idols, performs miracles, and endures excruciating torments. What distinguishes the legends of most female martyrs

---

[6] On the Eucharist, see especially Miri Rubin, *Corpus Christi: The Eucharist in Late Medieval Culture* (Cambridge: Cambridge University Press, 1991).

from those of their male counterparts is a preoccupation with gender and sexuality. Almost all virgin martyr legends dramatize some threat to the saint's virginity. Usually that threat is directly linked to religious persecution. For example, in many of the most popular legends, including those of Margaret, Juliana, Agnes, and Agatha, a pagan falls in love with the saint, woos her, then persecutes her when he finds that she will have nothing to do with him. In other cases, the official presiding over the trial of a beautiful Christian offers to marry her and is rejected, as in most legends of Martina, Euphemia, and Katherine of Alexandria. Somewhat less frequently, the saint's resistance to sexual advances forms a major episode in her legend, though it is not causally related to her martyrdom. For example, in the legends of Ursula, Cecilia, Justine, and Lucy of Rome, the saint successfully overcomes a threat to her chastity by converting her spouse or suitor; these legends generally conclude with the martyrdom of both the saint and her admirer. In at least two cases, the lives of Susanna and Eugenia, the passion of the virgin martyr is linked with another popular genre of hagiography involving sexual persecution—the legend of the "transvestite saint." In these narratives, the saint's chastity is not threatened but rather her reputation for chastity: the virgin enters a monastery disguised as a man, leads a saintly life, but is forced to reveal that she is a woman when she is accused of fathering a child. Her martyrdom, occurring shortly thereafter, is unrelated to her monastic experiences.

The themes of sexual desire and frustration that so often lead to the virgin martyr's persecution recur in the ordeals she endures. She is stripped and beaten before an audience of leering spectators. She is hauled to a brothel or otherwise threatened with rape. Her breasts or nipples are torn off. She is shaved or strung up by her hair. Rarely are the perpetrators of these atrocities remote public figures. The emperor, prefect, or judge presiding over her trial is frequently her father, her suitor, or her suitor's father. In fact, sometimes the roles of father and suitor coincide: in the legends of Barbara and Christine, jealous fathers immure their daughters in towers, away from the eyes of men, while in the legend of Dympna, the saint's father actively courts her.

At one pole, then, the creators of virgin martyr legends group virtually all men, including fathers and prospective husbands, representing them as sadistic persecutors and potential rapists; the other pole is formed by a generally positive portrayal of the women. Women are rarely persecutors but are frequently sympathetic bystanders who protest the virgins' persecution and offer emotional or material comfort during their trials. Unlike fathers, mothers play minor roles (if any) in the saints' ordeals; though they may deplore their daughters' actions, as in the Christine legend, they seldom inflict or advocate physical abuse. Occasionally, as in many legends of Apollonia and of Lucy of Syracuse, they are benevolent figures who help their daughters thwart the designs of their fathers or suitors. The opposition between good mothers and villainous fathers is especially marked in some late English versions of the Margaret legend, in which the saint's father orders his daughter to be killed at birth and her mother spirits her to safety.[7]

Some of the earliest manifestations of the conventions I have described are in the "chastity stories" of the apocryphal Acts of the Apostles, which were composed in Asia Minor and Greece during the second and third centuries. Many of the Acts, including those of Paul, Thomas, and Andrew, treat the plight of women who are moved by the teachings of the apostles to renounce sexual activity. So eloquently do these narratives present the aspirations and difficulties of early Christian women that some scholars believe they originated in communities of women.[8] The closest precursor to the virgin martyr legend among these texts is the Acts of Paul and Thecla, written in Asia Minor circa 195.[9] This work possesses the structure that would become typical of virgin martyr legends: a beautiful girl of noble birth alienates her family by making a vow of virginity; the hostility of her parents and would-be lovers results in persecution; yet God demonstrates his love for her through miracles that thwart the designs of her enemies.[10] Thecla, a beautiful Iconian aristocrat, is inspired by Paul's preaching on virginity to repudiate her engagement and to become a Christian. Her jilted suitor incites the men of Iconium to agitate for Paul's arrest. When Thecla voluntarily follows the apostle into prison, her own mother denounces her, urging that she be executed as an example to other women who spurn marriage. Though the governor orders Thecla burned at the stake, miraculous rains spare her. The scene moves to Antioch, where she encounters

---

[7] For two examples, see Carl Horstmann, *Altenglische Legenden: Neue Folge* (Heilbronn: Henninger, 1881), 225–41.

[8] See especially Stevan L. Davies, *The Revolt of the Widows: The Social World of the Apocryphal Acts* (Carbondale: Southern Illinois University Press, 1980); Jo Ann McNamara, *A New Song: Celibate Women in the First Three Christian Centuries* (New York: Haworth, 1983); and Virginia Burrus, *Chastity as Autonomy: Women in the Stories of Apocryphal Acts* (Lewiston, N.Y.: Edwin Mellen, 1987). For an alternative reading of the Acts that stresses their masculine bias, see Peter Brown, *The Body and Society: Men, Women, and Sexual Renunciation in Early Christianity* (New York: Columbia University Press, 1988), 153–59.

[9] For a translation of this text, see *The Apocryphal New Testament: A Collection of Apocryphal Christian Literature in an English Translation Based on M. R. James*, ed. J. K. Elliott (Oxford: Clarendon, 1993), 364–74.

[10] It seems that medieval readers and writers also observed similarities between Thecla's story and the legends of virgin martyrs, for despite her natural death, Thecla was referred to as a virgin martyr during the Middle Ages. Bede, for example, numbers her among the virgin martyrs (Euphemia, Agnes, Eulalia, Cecilia, Agatha) in his eulogy to St. Etheldreda (*Ecclesiastical History*, 4.20).

similar trouble: another spurned admirer tries unsuccessfully to rape her, then denounces her to the local governor, who condemns her to be torn apart by wild animals. Again a miracle preserves her. Thecla returns to Iconium, converts her mother, and lives for many decades as a recluse. Eventually she dies a natural death, but not before yet another miraculous escape, this time from a band of ruffians bent on rape.

The Thecla legend contains not only plot elements but motifs that would eventually become hallmarks of virgin martyr legends. For example, the repeated references to the virgin's nakedness during her persecutions anticipate the more frankly sexual trial scenes of later legends. The Acts of Paul and Thecla also exemplifies the polarization of the sexes that, as I observed earlier, is found in almost all virgin martyr legends: when Thecla is condemned to death for the second time, not only do the women of Antioch take her side against the governor, but a lioness battles a lion on her behalf. As Stevan Davies has observed, even Paul is portrayed ambiguously, for one of the challenges Thecla faces as a holy woman in the world of early Christianity is "to break through Paul's misapprehension of her as nothing more than a beautiful woman, weak and subject to temptation." [11]

Many of the heroines celebrated in the earliest Christian literature were neither virgins nor martyrs, though their *vitae* embodied numerous features that would later become associated with virgin martyr legends.[12] Some, including the heroines of other apocryphal chastity stories, were married women who spurned sexual relations after their conversion. The prominence of wives in early Christian hagiography may be partly attributed to the actual importance of matrons in promoting Christianity during the two centuries following the death of Christ. According to Jo Ann McNamara, Roman wives were more likely to convert to Christianity than were their husbands, whose "public lives . . . required regular participation in the liturgies of state paganism." [13] Conflict within the households of first-generation Christians may thus have inspired early hagiographers who were eager to gain a foothold within the ruling classes.

Hagiographers' emphasis on chastity rather than virginity also accords with what we know of the sexual values and practices of Christian communities in

---

[11] Davies, *Revolt*, 60.

[12] Another saint whose story contains many of the elements of virgin martyr legends is Perpetua, a Roman wife and mother who was martyred in 203. For a discussion of the Perpetua legend that elucidates Perpetua's resemblance to the virgin martyrs, see Thomas J. Heffernan, *Sacred Biography: Saints and Their Biographers in the Middle Ages* (New York: Oxford University Press, 1988), 185–230.

[13] McNamara, *A New Song*, 66.

late antiquity. Though abstinence was esteemed and continent women accorded considerable stature, celibate women tended to be widows rather than virgins. As Peter Brown notes:

> The normal continent woman was not a virgin girl, dedicated to a pious seclusion from childhood up. Rather, she was a woman who had been the head of a Christian household and the mother of Christian children. She frequently controlled property. Her wealth enabled her to impinge on the local church as a benefactress, in a manner that was normal in pagan and Jewish circles. She was no demure creature, who would sink back into her parents' house. "Passing around the houses," continent adult women, as widows, enjoyed some of the enviable mobility associated with the apostolic calling. Mature, financially independent, and already influential, the Christian widow had made a decision to embrace continence that was as formal and heroic as that of her fellow widowers, the average members of the clergy.[14]

Not surprisingly, as the early medieval Church began to promote virginity more zealously and as monasteries became the principal centers of cultural production, virgins swelled the ranks of the female saints. Indeed, by the sixth century, the Christian heroine was almost invariably a virgin; what is more, she was almost always a pretty, young virgin with a distinguished pedigree. So compelling was this stereotype of the female saint that some legends about early Christian martyrs underwent dramatic transformations to accommodate it. The development of the Apollonia legend is a case in point. The earliest report of Apollonia's martyrdom during the anti-Christian riots of 249 is this eyewitness account by Dionysius of Alexandria, which Eusebius transcribed in his *History of the Church:* "Next they seized the wonderful old lady Apollonia, battered her till they knocked out all her teeth, built a pyre in front of the city, and threatened to burn her alive unless she repeated after them their heathen incantations. She asked for a breathing-space, and when they released her, jumped without hesitation into the fire and was burnt to ashes."[15] Fourteenth- and fifteenth-century hagiographers, undeterred by either Dionysius's details or his omissions, transformed the "wonderful old lady" into a beautiful princess whose father tortures and, in some versions, kills her for her faith.[16] As the

---

[14] Brown, *Body and Society,* 150.

[15] Eusebius, *History of the Church,* trans. G. A. Williamson (New York: Penguin, 1965), 276.

[16] For a more detailed account of this legend and an edition of one text, see Maurice Coens, "Une 'Passio S. Apolloniae' inédite suivi d'un miracle en Bourgogne," *Analecta Bollandiana* 70 (1952): 138–59. One example of the presentation of Apollonia as a beautiful young princess in vernacular hagiography occurs in the popular fifteenth-century collection *Der Heiligen Leben.* See the edition by Severin Rüttgers, *Der Heiligen Leben und Leiden, anders genannt das Passional,* 2 vols. (Leipzig, 1913), 1:370–71.

patron saint of toothache sufferers, Apollonia was well represented in late medieval art—and always as an exquisite young noblewoman.[17] Another such metamorphosis is that of Anastasia: in early accounts a pious wife, in later legends she became a proper virgin martyr who had avoided consummating her marriage.[18]

The Late Medieval Virgin Martyr

One might expect legends of heroic virgins to flourish in religious communities whose inhabitants were committed to a life of celibacy. More surprising is the unabated appeal of virgin martyr legends during the late Middle Ages, when, as André Vauchez, Caroline Walker Bynum, Richard Kieckhefer, and others have established, changing social conditions engendered definitions of saintliness that differed profoundly from those that had prevailed when the virgin martyr legend took shape as a hagiographical genre.[19] Late medieval piety was increasingly private and introspective, as attested in devotional literature, including the vitae of late medieval men and women who were venerated for their holiness. The virgin martyr legend, with its emphasis on spectacle, confrontation, and transcendence of the particular, would seemingly hold little appeal for admirers of Francis of Assisi or Catherine of Siena, vivid personalities whose vitae celebrated contemplation and patience. Moreover, because late medieval hagiographers were, to an increasing extent, addressing a lay audience, we might look for them to promote stories of holy parents and spouses, whose lives could provide more direct models than those of the virgin martyrs, who, after all, spurned marriage, family, laws, and property. What could their lives mean to lawyers, merchants, and craftspeople, householders and parents, immersed in the very world the saints rejected?

[17] For example, Apollonia appears in this manner on the far left side of the Bruges altar panel, where she is holding pincers with a tooth. Discussions of the cult of Apollonia with an emphasis on iconography include Gian Battista Poletti, *Il Martirio di Santa Apollonia* (Rocca S. Casciano, 1934); and José de Paiva Boléo, *O Martírio de Santa Apolónia* (Porto, n.d.).

[18] The most comprehensive discussion of the Anastasia legend is Hippolyte Delehaye, *Étude sur le légendier romain: Les saints de Novembre et Décembre,* Subsidia hagiographica 23 (Brussels: Société des Bollandistes, 1936), 151–66.

[19] See especially André Vauchez, *La sainteté en occident aux derniers siècles du moyen âge, d'après les procès de canonisation et les documents hagiographiques* (Paris: École Française de Rome, 1981); Michael Goodich, *Vita Perfecta: The Ideal of Sainthood in the Thirteenth Century* (Stuttgart: Hiersemann, 1982); Donald Weinstein and Rudolph M. Bell, *Saints and Society: The Two Worlds of Western Christendom, 1000–1700* (Chicago: University of Chicago Press, 1982); Richard Kieckhefer, *Unquiet Souls: Fourteenth-Century Saints and Their Religious Milieu* (Chicago: University of Chicago Press, 1984); Caroline Walker Bynum, *Holy Feast and Holy Fast: The Religious Significance of Food to Medieval Women* (Berkeley: University of California Press, 1987).

Yet in most late medieval legendaries, virgin martyrs continue to outnumber other female saints, including not only reformed prostitutes, saintly nuns, and transvestites but holy wives and contemplatives as well. In fact, many late collections contain more legends of virgin martyrs than of all other female saints together.[20] Though the number of holy laywomen did increase dramatically during the late Middle Ages, their legends were, for the most part, not translated into English until the fifteenth century.[21] Even fifteenth-century hagiographers, who were especially sensitive to the needs and interests of lay readers, apparently preferred the challenge of making virgin martyrs more like prosperous housewives over the task of generating biographies of actual holy wives. Osbern Bokenham, for example, composed ten virgin martyr legends, against two lives of married saints and a legend of Mary Magdalene, for his predominantly lay provincial audience. Virgin martyr legends became, in the hands of Bokenham and his ilk, both worldly and subjective.

Of course, the clergy retained a professional interest in propagating legends of holy virgins, for those legends reinforced the barrier between the laity and a celibate elite of saints and clerics. Though a fifteenth-century mother might see herself in the image of a well-dressed St. Barbara reading in her parlor, Barbara's virginity would subtly remind her of the distance that separated her from God's aristocracy. Maintaining some barrier—no matter how fragile—between clergy and laity must have seemed all the more important during the later Middle Ages, when an enthusiastic and informed lay public threatened the clergy's hegemony over the dispensation of religious and moral truths. Yet we cannot attribute the continued popularity of virgin martyrs solely to the personal preferences and political interests of the clergy, for, from all indications, not only friars such as Bokenham but bureaucrats and courtiers favored

[20] For example, six of the seven lives of female saints included in the *North English Legendary* are virgin martyr legends, and according to Manfred Görlach's table, thirteen of the twenty-two legends of female saints in major manuscripts of the *South English Legendary* were virgin martyr legends. See Görlach, *The Textual Tradition of the "South English Legendary"* (Leeds: University of Leeds, School of English, 1974), 306–9. For further evidence of the popularity of virgin martyrs in England, see Charlotte D'Evelyn's catalogue of Middle English saints' lives, "Saints' Legends," in *A Manual of the Writings in Middle English, 1050–1500*, ed. J. Burke Severs, vol. 2 (Hamden, Conn.: Archon, 1970), 561–635. D'Evelyn lists more legends of virgin martyrs than of any other kind of female saint. To judge from her inventory, only Mary Magdalene enjoyed a popularity comparable with that of Margaret and Katherine.

[21] For a survey of the growing number of holy wives and the increasingly positive portrayal of marriage in late medieval hagiography, see Marc Glasser, "Marriage in Medieval Hagiography," *Studies in Medieval and Renaissance History*, n.s., 4 (1981): 3–34. D'Evelyn indicates that the earliest surviving legends of the Virgin Mary's mother, Anne, were composed during the fifteenth century ("Legends," 567). At that time, the legends of Elizabeth of Hungary, Mary of Oignies, and Bridget of Sweden were also first translated into English.

virgin martyrs over other saints. Chaucer's only saint's life was a virgin martyr legend, while nineteen of the twenty-eight saints in Christine de Pisan's *Cité des dames* were virgin martyrs (not counting Ursula's eleven thousand martyred companions). The references to virgin martyrs in conduct books written by and for laypeople and the abundant representations of virgin martyrs in Books of Hours further suggest a genuine enthusiasm for those saints among people whose vocations did not demand sexual abstinence.

One obvious source of appeal is the virgin martyr legend's emphasis on sex, violence, and sexual violence. It is not necessary to equate medieval and modern tastes to conclude that these elements were popular; any survey of popular genres—from miracle stories and exempla to romances and fabliaux—will so attest. As I discussed earlier, the virgin martyr legend offers a heroine who is invariably young, beautiful, and endangered by sexual predators. Her narrow escapes from brothel and boudoir provide moments of suspense, while the torments she does not evade are rendered palatable—possibly even enjoyable— by their necessity and by the certainty of her body's ultimate miraculous restoration. The virgin martyr legend thus affords a safe distance from which to indulge "innocent" escapism as well as less innocent fantasies of "harmless" violence against women.

A deeper reason why the legends of virgin martyrs reverberated so powerfully through the centuries is that those legends embodied the kinds of paradoxes that were central to Christianity—the paradoxes expressed in such symbols and mysteries as the virgin birth, the Incarnation, the Eucharist, and the Tree of Life and Death. As the most vulnerable and carnal of human beings— women—the virgin martyrs testify that the flesh can indeed triumph over corporeal desires, that weakness can prevail over strength. As women who transcended their gender to become manly, the virgin martyrs evoke the mystery of a God made man. Their bodies, torn and made whole, replicate the miracle of the Eucharist. The paradox of the virgins' triumph is distilled in their emblems, where instruments of torture designed to erase identity are used to proclaim identity.[22]

Like so many paradoxical symbols, virgin martyrs lent themselves to the exploration of tensions and contradictions within medieval culture.[23] On a host of issues—political, social, cultural, and economic—these legends could be construed simultaneously in radically different ways and thus serve conflicting

---

[22] See Elaine Scarry's discussion of torture and identity in *The Body in Pain: The Making and Unmaking of the World* (Oxford: Oxford University Press, 1985).

[23] For discussions of how such symbols expressed ideological tensions, see, for example, Sarah Beckwith, *Christ's Body: Identity, Culture, and Society in Late Medieval Writings* (London: Routledge, 1993); and Rubin, *Corpus Christi*.

interests. Consider, for instance, material wealth. When forced to choose between the world and their faith, virgin martyrs exhibit a contempt for earthly possessions that would gratify the most zealous ascetic. Yet, until their persecutors force the issue, the virgin martyrs demonstrate that being holy does not preclude possessing and enjoying worldly goods. (In the legends of reformed prostitutes, by contrast, the saint's religious epiphany is followed immediately by a renunciation of all material comforts.) The virgin martyrs thus provided congenial examples for nobles, entrepreneurs, and the denizens of affluent religious houses. Conflicting messages about marriage also coexist; read literally, of course, the legends deprecate the institution, yet the martyr's relationship with Christ is depicted as a marriage and could be used to model earthly marriages, as indeed it was in many late medieval texts. Most conspicuously, virgin martyr legends encapsulate the disparate and sometimes contradictory views of sexual violence that prevailed through the centuries. Threatened with rape, the saint serenely expresses the common piety that she will remain chaste in the eyes of God, regardless of what happens to her body; yet she never is raped.[24] Her inevitable miraculous escape contains a powerful implication: although being raped would not, in theory, tarnish a virtuous woman, in practice virtuous women are not raped.

Individual renditions of virgin martyr legends bring out certain meanings and obscure others. One text will kindle outrage at the saint's victimization by dwelling on her vulnerability; another will discourage compassion for the saint by dwelling on her persecutor's anger and frustration rather than on her suffering. Some texts expatiate on the virgin's contempt for marriage and say little of her as Christ's bride, while others celebrate the virgin's devotion to an artfully humanized, divine bridegroom. Even as the hagiographer promotes certain readings, however, latent alternatives remain open to the reader.

In late medieval England, we can detect three distinct trends in the representation of virgin martyrs, which I will explore in the following chapters. In Chapter 1 I consider the portrayal of virgin martyrs in texts that were, for the most part, composed by and for monks, nuns, anchoresses, and other professional religious. To establish a foundation for understanding the later development of the virgin martyr legend in England, I first survey the features that recur most frequently in Latin *passiones* written during the early and high Middle Ages. I argue that, by the early thirteenth century, the predominantly monastic

[24] The view that a rape victim still retains her chastity is developed most fully in book 1 of Augustine's *City of God.* For a discussion of the ambivalence about rape in early Christian thought, see Jane Tibbetts Schulenburg, "The Heroics of Virginity: Brides of Christ and Sacrificial Mutilation," in *Women in the Middle Ages and the Renaissance: Literary and Historical Perspectives,* ed. Mary Beth Rose (Syracuse: Syracuse University Press, 1986), 29–72.

writers of hagiography had developed a strongly didactic and devotional mode of narrating saints' lives. Lavish passages of prayer and exposition direct the readers' or listeners' attention away from the sensational events being related, inviting them instead to contemplate the significance of those events within salvation history. Hagiographers thereby muted the potential subversiveness of their material: the martyrs appear less as radicals than as fragile brides of Christ whose experiences exalt the most cherished values of monastic life—chastity, flight from the world, and love of God. The earliest Middle English virgin martyr legends (the legends of the so-called Katherine Group) grew out of this tradition of meditative Latin hagiography. Writing primarily for anchoresses, the authors of the Katherine Group legends were as concerned as their Latin predecessors with providing material for prayer and contemplation, but they also tailored their narratives to the perceived needs and interests of a female audience. With their greater emphasis on the martyrs' gender and in particular on the saints' brash defiance of male authority, the Katherine Group writers aimed to provide inspiring models of heroism for women. At the same time, however, they wished to regulate the aspirations and conduct of religious women—and especially of anchoresses—whose relative independence from the Church's supervision and whose ambiguous situation on the threshold between secular and religious life disturbed many early thirteenth-century clergymen.

Though the writers of the Katherine Group legends expected their narratives to circulate among the laity, they do not appear to have composed their narratives with the needs of a lay audience in mind. During the late twelfth and early thirteenth centuries, however, the clergy grew ever more concerned with lay religious instruction, while laypeople became more active participants in their faith. Propelled by the Fourth Lateran Council (1215), hagiographers of the later thirteenth and fourteenth centuries increasingly addressed themselves to laypeople. In so doing, they produced legends that differed markedly from the Latin and vernacular legends I treat in Chapter 1, both in their representation of the saints and in the responses they invite from their audiences. Instead of encouraging identification with the virgin martyrs, as earlier hagiographers had, writers of the late thirteenth and early fourteenth centuries distanced the saints from the rank-and-file faithful by emphasizing their miraculous powers, their virginity, and their contempt for the institutions of marriage, family, and state. Chapter 2 surveys the widespread representation of virgin martyrs as powerful and often disorderly women in English art and literature. I argue that portrayals of the saints as zealous critics of the state became popular because they served the professional interests of a clerical elite which was anxious to preserve its authority over an increasingly informed lay public and which promoted the martyrs as emblems of ecclesiastical prerogative. Yet these legends of rebellion and defiance lent themselves to interpretations that their authors probably did not anticipate or approve. I examine evidence of such appropriation of the virgin martyrs by laypeople, including Geoffrey Chaucer and Margery Kempe, showing how the saints' legends participated in contemporary social debates.

By the early 1400s, concerns about the uses that people such as Kempe were making of virgin martyr legends may have prompted hagiographers to tone down the themes of conflict and confrontation that dominated earlier legends and to portray secular institutions, such as marriage and family, more positively. Worries about Lollardy and misdirected lay learning, rife during the first third of the fifteenth century, motivated a trend toward exemplary narratives whose heroines could be "safely" emulated. In fifteenth-century texts, we find none of the carnivalesque battles of the sexes that delighted Chaucer's generation. Instead, writers and artists transformed the saints into decorous gentlewomen who best their adversaries through heroic good manners rather than invective. Their protagonists demonstrate the courtesy, refinement, eloquence, and piety admired by the burghers and gentlepeople who had become avid consumers of saints' legends. Emphasizing faith rather than defiance, hagiographers returned to early monastic passiones and restored the long passages of prayer and exposition that their predecessors had systematically excised. Chapter 3 focuses on two representative hagiographers of the period, Osbern Bokenham and John Lydgate. Through analysis of their writings and their readership, I demonstrate how, as the century progressed, the exemplary virgin martyr suited to the conservative purposes of hagiographers increasingly suited the conservative tastes of middle-class readers.

The trends affecting fifteenth-century virgin martyr legends find their extreme expression in two popular lives of Queen Katherine of Alexandria that I treat in Chapter 4: an anonymous legend in prose, circa 1420, and John Capgrave's eight-thousand-line verse life, circa 1445. Both texts offer extensive accounts of Katherine's life before her martyrdom, describing her family, her reading habits, and her governance of Alexandria. Despite their common features, the narratives diverge in their views of Katherine. The prose life presents her as a pious laywoman who, without abandoning her worldly responsibilities, comes to enjoy an intimate relationship with Christ through study and contemplation. In Capgrave's telling, by contrast, Katherine's learning prompts her to flout tradition, and her unconventional acts harm her subjects and lead to her deposition and death. In Chapter 4 I examine these works as they address the vexed issue of lay learning. To achieve its unproblematic model, the prose life ignores conflicts between Katherine's piety, her love of scholarship, her traditional role as a woman, and her role as a ruler. Teasing out those same conflicts is Capgrave's main enterprise; he clearly sees them as relevant to his readers, caught in similar conflicts between Church teaching, tradition, and personal aspirations in a rapidly changing and unstable world. I show that we may deepen our understanding of these legends' treatment of lay learning and lay piety by reading them in context: the prose life as a product of post-Agincourt optimism during Henry V's successful reign, and Capgrave's as embodying the anxiety that burgeoned under Henry VI.

As this overview indicates, I do not undertake the meticulous comparison of texts with their sources that once occupied a central place in the study of hagiography. Scholars traditionally examined sources in order to establish a particular text's lineage or to discover what about that text was unique. Departures from a source, critics felt, revealed the artistry and the concerns of a particular hagiographer, while adherence to a source indicated little more than scrupulous translation. As interest in authorship and aesthetics has given way to a preoccupation with culture and ideology, source studies have declined. Comparisons of particular narratives with earlier renderings (not necessarily direct sources) do have much to tell scholars of culture, for departures from tradition can signal cultural change. Yet it is important not to assume that traditional elements, where found, persisted through inertia; rather, we should attempt to understand how old elements functioned in new contexts.[25]

Osbern Bokenham provides a prime example of how even relatively conservative translations take on new meanings when we consider the *milieu* in which they were written and read. Until recently, Bokenham was routinely dismissed as a mere translator of earlier works. His legend of Cecilia exemplifies his purported lack of originality, for it is a faithful English versification of a monastic *passio*. Yet knowing Bokenham's source precipitates other questions: Why did Bokenham choose to translate a passio, given that passiones had little appeal to the previous generation of Middle English hagiographers? And why were so many of Bokenham's contemporaries also rediscovering the passiones? We can understand the shape of Bokenham's legend not by identifying the text on which it was based but rather by examining the piety and reading habits of provincial gentlepeople and the convergence of the spiritual and political interests of the clerical and secular elite during the fifteenth century. The same can be said for Bokenham's Katherine legend, an English versification of Jacobus de Voragine's legend, supplemented with passages from a monastic passio. Though little is "new" in Bokenham's narrative, his legend points to an intriguing disagreement among East Anglian hagiographers over just how to present the blessed

[25] See Paul Strohm's discussion of sources and textual environments in "Introduction: False Fables and Historical Truth," in *Hochon's Arrow: The Social Imagination of Fourteenth-Century Texts* (Princeton: Princeton University Press, 1992), 6–7.

to a well-informed public eager for saints' lives. Compared with Lydgate's docile virgin martyrs, Bokenham's saint comes across as an audacious and eloquent teacher whose religious instruction seems designed to satisfy the intellectual demands of his readership. Yet even as Bokenham makes concessions to his readers' intellectualism, his work stands as a conservative rejoinder to Capgrave's newly completed Katherine legend, which has the saint deriding tradition and quoting Scripture like the stereotypical Lollard wife.

Virgin martyr legends are usually thought of as "women's stories," and to an extent they are. Most obviously, of course, virgin martyr legends are about women, and they are directly concerned with feminine conduct and sexuality. Many virgin martyr legends were written for women and circulated among female audiences. Historically, the legends seem to have appealed to women, since many women wrote about virgin martyrs—Hrotsvitha of Gandersheim, Elisabeth of Schönau, Hildegard of Bingen, Clemence of Barking, and Christine de Pisan, to name a few. Moreover, the lives and writings of women who aspired to holiness during the late Middle Ages—Catherine of Siena, Bridget of Sweden, Dauphine of Puimichel, Margery Kempe, Julian of Norwich, and many others—attest that virgin martyr legends did indeed furnish role models for women.

Yet virgin martyr legends thrived among male audiences too. As I mentioned earlier, the genre flourished largely because monks wrote virgin martyr legends for other monks. Such laymen as Chaucer and William Paris also wrote virgin martyr legends, most probably for other men; indeed, men are found among the addressees of virgin martyr legends. In addition, manuscripts point to a more substantial male readership than we might expect for these legends. For example, two copies of Capgrave's Katherine legend occur in manuscripts that also contain portions of conduct books for men.[26] One of those manuscripts includes two other virgin martyr legends: Paris's life of Christine and an anonymous life of Dorothy. One goal of this book is to broaden the usual focus on virgin martyr legends and their female audiences to elucidate the appeal of saints such as Katherine and Christine for men. Likewise, without neglecting the role of virgin martyr legends in the construction of gender, I consider how these legends participated in the formation of other ideologies—examining, for example, how the legends construe social hierarchies and assessing their contribution to the debates about heresy and literacy that were being carried on in late medieval England.

Arriving at a suitable scope for this book entailed deciding what to leave out as well as what to put in, and inevitably there are regrets. In the end, I focused

---

[26] I am referring, respectively, to British Library MSS Arundel 20 and Arundel 168 (which also contains Paris's legend of Christine).

almost exclusively on Middle English narratives composed from circa 1200 to 1450, a period of especially active generic permutation, in which legends originally addressed to a predominantly cloistered audience were reconstituted for a lay public. I had once planned also to cover the rich tradition of Anglo-Norman hagiography that flourished from the twelfth through the fourteenth century. This substantial body of literature deserves a thoroughgoing study.[27] Among other things, it includes the only English virgin martyr legend known to have been composed by a woman, the life of St. Katherine by Clemence of Barking. Moreover, the Anglo-Norman (and Continental French) legends of the thirteenth and fourteenth centuries offer a sharp and intriguing contrast to their Middle English counterparts, anticipating their broad turn toward courtliness and conservatism in the early fifteenth century.[28] I decided, however, that I could not do justice to the Anglo-Norman materials and a retain a reasonable size and scope. Neither could I hope to include the vast hagiographical materials in sermons, breviaries, and prayers, much of which, being in Latin, was in any case directly accessible to few laypeople. Although I do give some consideration to the visual arts, other nonliterary manifestations of the cult of the saints—shrines, relics, amulets, and so forth—are beyond the purview of this chiefly textual study. With a few exceptions, the works I discuss circulated primarily among a "cultural elite" of middle- and upper-class readers. In choosing narratives to discuss in detail, I considered which texts were most representative, which were most popular, and which were most influential, though where possible, I selected works that were related to one another—in particular, the cluster of East Anglian legends in Chapters 3 and 4—in order to develop a sense of the community of readers and writers that produced them. And while I sought to avoid aesthetic judgments, I realize that, to some extent, my selection inevitably reflects my own taste.

[27] For one valuable study, see Jocelyn Wogan-Browne, "'Clerc u lai, muïne u dame': Women and Anglo-Norman Hagiography in the Twelfth and Thirteenth Centuries," in *Women and Literature in Britain, 1150–1500*, ed. Carol M. Meale (Cambridge: Cambridge University Press, 1993), 61–85. Also useful is the introduction by Wogan-Browne and Glyn S. Burgess to their translation of Clemence of Barking's life of St. Katherine and an anonymous life of St. Lawrence, *Virgin Lives and Holy Deaths: Two Exemplary Biographies for Anglo-Norman Women* (London: Dent, 1996), xi–lxiii.

[28] For a representative sample of how the virgin martyrs were treated in Anglo-Norman hagiography of the 1200s and 1300s, see the legends of Nicholas Bozon, which have been edited and translated by M. Amelia Klenke in two volumes: *Three Saints' Lives by Nicholas Bozon* (St. Bonaventure, N.Y.: Franciscan Institute, 1947); and *Seven More Poems by Nicholas Bozon* (St. Bonaventure, N.Y.: Franciscan Institute, 1951). For a study emphasizing the Continental French tradition, with translations of selected legends, see Brigitte Cazelles, *The Lady as Saint: A Collection of French Hagiographic Romances of the Thirteenth Century* (Philadelphia: University of Pennsylvania Press, 1991).

I

Martyrdom, Marriage, and Religious Communities, 1100–1250

The anonymous twelfth-century account of how the recluse Christina of Markyate once used a virgin martyr legend to avoid the embraces of her bridegroom, Burthred, illustrates the intersection of old and new paradigms of holiness during the later Middle Ages.[1] Though her family has bullied her into exchanging vows with Burthred, Christina immediately regrets her weakness and refuses to have anything further to do with him. Exasperated by her stubbornness, her parents let the young man into her bedroom late one night, expecting that he will easily overcome the sleeping maiden. Christina, however, has anticipated their ploy. Wide awake and fully clothed, she greets Burthred warmly, then tells him the story of St. Cecilia—a fourth-century virgin martyr who had talked her own bridegroom, Valerian, out of exacting the conjugal debt. Christina urges Burthred to follow the example of Cecilia, Valerian, and other early saints, rejecting the pleasures of the flesh for the eternal crowns of virginity and martyrdom. Dumbfounded by this unexpected catechism, Burthred departs. When his friends and in-laws learn what has happened, however, they send him back to Christina's bedroom, admonishing him to "act the man" and promising to be on hand should he require assistance. This time, Christina narrowly escapes rape by hanging from a nail behind a tapestry as Burthred and his friends search the room.

It is no surprise that the Cecilia legend figures prominently in this account of Christina's struggle to preserve her virginity. Writers of sacred biography had traditionally certified their subjects' holiness by comparing them with well-established saints; these comparisons located the newcomer's experience within

[1] *The Life of Christina of Markyate*, ed. and trans. C. H. Talbot (Oxford: Clarendon, 1959), 50–53. I am using this text for all quotations and references; the translations are Talbot's.

what Gregory of Tours described as a universal vita sanctorum, based ultimately on the life of Christ.[2] In an odd twist on standard hagiographical practice, however, Christina's biographer fixes his attention on his heroine's *failure* to imitate a famous saint. As he presents her, Christina is a hagiographical Quixote, well versed in ancient legends but unable to enlist the cooperation of people like Burthred in acting them out. From the perspective of Burthred, her parents, and other ordinary twelfth-century people, Christina's attempt to imitate a long-dead saint seems preposterous: who would dream of taking martyr legends so literally? Paradoxically, however, her nearly disastrous endeavor actually enhances her status as a modern saint, for compared with Christina's experience, Cecilia's pursuit of sainthood was easy. She didn't need to be agile or resourceful; in fact, she didn't even need to be eloquent. Had Valerian dismissed her sermonizing and tried to exercise his conjugal rights, an armed angel was on hand, ready to smite him into eternity. Cecilia never experienced the panic that grips Christina as she hides behind the tapestry, praying that Burthred and his companions will not discover her:

> What, I ask you, were her feelings at that moment? How she kept trembling as they noisily sought after her. Was she not faint with fear? She saw herself already dragged out in their midst, all surrounding her, looking upon her, threatening her, given up to the sport of her destroyer. At last one of them touched and held her foot as she hung there, but since the curtain in between deadened his sense of touch, he let it go, not knowing what it was. (53)

By evoking the world of traditional saints' legends—a world in which good women are never raped and in which God rarely allows his handmaids to be otherwise harmed or degraded—Christina's biographer underscores the very real challenges of trying to be a holy woman in twelfth-century Huntingdonshire.

Yet even as Christina's experience makes the legends of traditional saints such as Cecilia seem remote and "literary," it also attests to their continuing power. For Christina, the Cecilia legend does not simply record the struggle of a Christian heroine in a pagan world; it speaks to her own experience and prompts her to behave in ways that are as radical as sneering at a Roman magistrate and mocking the gods. Stories of heroic virgins such as Cecilia surely confirmed Christina's conviction that she could not attain her spiritual goals as a wife and mother—a conviction that upset not only Burthred and her parents but some clergymen as well. Cecilia's bold defiance of her judge may indeed

---

[2] For Gregory of Tours's formulation, see *Life of the Fathers*, trans. Edward James (Liverpool: Liverpool University Press, 1985), 2.

have inspired Christina's equally spirited defiance of the prior Fredebert, who peremptorily declared, "Nothing remains but that you accept our advice and teaching and submit yourself to the lawful embraces of the man to whom you have been legally joined in marriage" (61). With a response that "astonished" Fredebert with its "common sense," Christina defended her rejection of marriage. To Fredebert's argument that "many mothers of families are saved," she retorted, "Certainly virgins are saved more easily" (61, 63).[3]

The danger that women might interpret or apply conventional saints' lives in alarming ways only increased during the later Middle Ages, as more people—especially women—craved intimate relationships with Christ and were seeking new avenues to that end. The period of the early 1100s, when Christina fled her home to become a recluse, witnessed an extraordinary growth in enthusiasm for religious life among women.[4] The Church initially encouraged that enthusiasm, overseeing the foundation of dozens of new religious houses and endorsing adaptations of the Benedictine Rule to the special circumstances of nuns.

By the early thirteenth century, many women were becoming recluses, treading the same path to holiness that Christina of Markyate had taken.[5] Confined to a cell often adjoining a chapel or parish church, these women had the leisure to cultivate personal relationships with Christ and the saints through prayer and contemplation. But their seclusion also left them vulnerable to temptation and to demonic visitations of all kinds, as Christina found when an army of toads invaded her cell, squatted on her psalter, and ogled her with their "big and terrible" eyes (99). Books were anchoresses' weapons against such enemies, inspiring them to repel temptation by fixing their thoughts on heaven. Books were also vehicles of clerical control over anchoresses, whose behavior was not governed by a formal rule. Not surprisingly, then, the popularity of the eremitic life among thirteenth-century women encouraged the production of

[3] The importance of virgin martyrs to Christina is also suggested by the presence of three of these saints (Christina, Faith, and Juliana) within the calendar of the *St. Alban's Psalter*, which is believed to have been made for Christina. See Jocelyn Wogan-Browne, "Saints' Lives and the Female Reader," *Forum for Modern Language Studies* 27 (1991): 316.

[4] For an extensive discussion of the flowering of women's religious life in twelfth-century England, see Sharon K. Elkins, *Holy Women of Twelfth-Century England* (Chapel Hill: University of North Carolina Press, 1988); and Sally Thompson, *Women Religious: The Founding of English Nunneries after the Norman Conquest* (Oxford: Clarendon, 1991).

[5] See Ann K. Warren, *Anchorites and Their Patrons in Medieval England* (Berkeley: University of California Press, 1985), 7–52. Warren indicates that during the thirteenth century, the number of anchoresses leaped from 48 to 123. She points out that since the twelfth century, English anchoritism was "biased toward women," and during the thirteenth century, it "became sharply female in orientation." From the twelfth to the thirteenth century, the number of male anchorites increased from 30 to only 37 (*Anchorites*, 20). For a study of the anchoritic life, see also the classic work by Rotha Mary Clay, *The Hermits and Anchorites of England* (London: Methuen, 1914).

religious literature addressed to them.[6] Much of this literature was written in Middle English: because most anchoresses came from secular life rather than the convent, they would have had no more than a rudimentary knowledge of Latin; they may not have known much French, either, for anchoresses were often of lower social classes than were the women who typically joined convents.[7] The earliest Middle English virgin martyr legends, composed during the early 1200s, formed part of this body of Middle English devotional literature. These legends of Saints Margaret, Juliana, and Katherine, along with two other treatises for women—a homily entitled *Sawles Warde,* and *Hali Meiðhad,* a virginity treatise—make up what is known as the "Katherine Group."[8]

The Katherine Group legends are steeped in the tradition of meditative hagiography that had flourished for centuries in religious houses. Because a knowledge of that tradition is essential to appreciating the distinctive characteristics both of these early Middle English legends and of subsequent narratives, I will first survey the ways in which virgin martyrs were portrayed in lengthy Latin *passiones* and pictorial cycles dating from the early and high Middle Ages. To understand how the legends of Margaret, Katherine, and Juliana might have been interpreted by and for thirteenth-century religious women, we must also consider their more immediate textual and intellectual environments. Those environments can be recovered, at least in part, by study-

---

[6] Elizabeth Robertson, *Early English Devotional Prose and the Female Audience* (Knoxville: University of Tennessee Press, 1990), 13–31; and Bella Millett, "Women in No Man's Land: English Recluses and the Development of Vernacular Literature in the Twelfth and Thirteenth Centuries," *Women and Literature in Britain, 1150–1500,* ed. Carol M. Meale (Cambridge: Cambridge University Press, 1993), 86–103. For a broader survey of twelfth- and early-thirteenth-century literature written for religious women in England and on the Continent, see Barbara Newman, "Flaws in the Golden Bowl: Gender and Spiritual Formation in the Twelfth Century," *Traditio* 45 (1989): 111–46; reprinted in *From Virile Woman to WomanChrist: Studies in Medieval Religion and Literature* (Philadelphia: University of Pennsylvania Press, 1995), 19–45.

[7] On the social origins of anchoresses and the predominance of lay women among them, see Warren, *Anchorites,* 22, 25–26.

[8] For quotations from the Middle English and page references, I am using the following editions: *Seinte Marherete,* ed. Frances M. Mack, EETS.OS 193 [henceforth cited as *Seinte Marherete*] (1934; reprint, London: Oxford University Press, 1958); *Þe Liflade ant te Passiun of Seinte Iuliene,* ed. S.R.T.O. d'Ardenne, EETS.OS 248 [henceforth cited as *Seinte Iuliene*] (London: Oxford University Press, 1961); and *Seinte Katerine,* ed. S.R.T.O. d'Ardenne and E. J. Dobson, EETS.SS 7 [henceforth cited as *Seinte Katerine*] (Oxford: Oxford University Press, 1981). Translations from these texts are mine. Some, perhaps all, of the Katherine Group texts may have been written by the same author. Indeed, Bella Millett refers to the "author of the Katherine Group *Lives*" on the grounds that "even if they are not [by the same author], they are related closely enough in style to be discussed as a group"; see "The Saints' Lives of the Katherine Group and the Alliterative Tradition," *Journal of English and Germanic Philology* 87 (1988): 16. Because we cannot be certain which, if any, of the texts are of common authorship, I prefer to refer to the Katherine Group writers.

ing contemporary writings for religious women as well as somewhat earlier texts, such as Aelred of Rievaulx's widely disseminated rule for anchoresses, which helped shape clerical attitudes toward enclosed women. Reading the Middle English legends in conjunction with these related texts suggests that even though the Katherine Group texts do not depart substantially from their Latin sources, they were judiciously chosen both to inspire and to direct religious women. The legends' dramatic portrayal of feminine heroism would surely have delighted such readers as Christina of Markyate. At the same time, the narratives' lessons about sexuality, conduct, temptation, and gender relations reinforce attempts that had been promulgated since about the mid– twelfth century to restrict the conduct of religious women. Though there was no guarantee that the independent-minded anchoress would interpret the legends "properly" (they could indeed be read in ways that subverted clerical authority), these texts offered opportunities for influencing women whose unstructured lives and perceived capacity for mischief had become a source of anxiety to the clergy.

Latin Antecedents

By the time the earliest Middle English hagiographers were composing the Katherine Group legends, Latin hagiographers had developed a mode of narrating virgin martyr legends distinguished by its profoundly didactic and devotional character. The predominantly monastic hagiographers of the early and high Middle Ages were concerned, above all, with the saint's faith and with her love of God, and they conveyed her devotion through prayers and expository passages that often have little to do with the actual narrative. A prime example of this is Martina's lengthy prayer just before her execution. She begins, "I give thanks to you, lord God, who established the choir of saints; and I worship the great and glorious and terrible name of your divinity, you who illuminated the dark foe and pulverized the unfeeling and immobile idols, you who instructed your handmaid with glorious intellect in the perfection of your faith." And she follows this introduction with a lavish recitation of actions confirming God's magnitude and mercy—actions ranging from the testing of Job to the Incarnation and the harrowing of Hell. At length, she concludes:

> Lord Jesus Christ, liberator, instruct my soul in the sweetness of your mercy and number me among your faithful, who please you faithfully. I call upon you Lord Jesus Christ, deliverer of all, and I adore you, and I entreat you and beg you to liberate me from the many evils I see. True light in the true light of your divinity, save

me, heavenly lord Jesus Christ. Made perfect through the confession of your name, order me assumed into your glory so that I might escape, splendidly adorned, the evil with which I am surrounded. Turn against the truly malignant Alexander, who has thus acted against the innocent ones and against your servant. Afflict his unbelieving heart and be hard against his hardened spirit for the chastisement of those who scorn your greatness. Although I am truly a poor little woman and a sinner, I pray that you find me worthy to be near your sacred holiness; for I have suffered for your truth and for your son, our lord Jesus Christ, who reigns in glory and power forever. Amen.[9]

This lengthy prayer is representative of the devotions embedded within virgin martyr legends. Also typical is that most of it might be uttered by any Christian; only the allusion to Martina's persecutor, Alexander, directly pertains to the saint's ordeal. All readers could join Martina in contemplating God's grandeur; with her, they could acknowledge their unworthiness and beseech God's indulgence for their own weaknesses. Such elaborate prayers thus render the passiones devotional texts, inviting members of the audience to pray *with* the saint, praising God and affirming their own commitment to Christ as they read or hear the legend.

The saint's prayers serve a number of key functions within passiones, the most important being to interpret the events that are related. This use of prayer is demonstrated in the so-called Mombritius version of the *Passio S. Margaretae*, wherein a dragon attacks and devours the saint, who, by making the sign of the cross, causes the monster to burst and emerges unscathed from its belly. Though her dramatic encounter with the dragon was described in the oldest versions of the Margaret legend, some writers were understandably uneasy about reproducing it. In the tenth century, for example, Symeon Metaphrastes dismissed it as the invention of those wishing to discredit the Christian faith.[10] The writer of the *Passio S. Margaretae* relates the incident, including a vivid description of the dragon, but he reduces its potentially alarming sensationalism by introducing and concluding his account of the action with the saint's extensive prayers.[11] Margaret prays for deliverance both before and after she sees the beast, dwell-

---

[9] *Acta Sanctorum* (Brussels [etc.], 1643–) Jan., 1:17. All translations from this and other passiones are mine. Henceforth *Acta Sanctorum* will be cited as *Acta SS*.

[10] "The Legend of Saint Margaret," ed. Frederic Spencer, *Modern Language Notes* 4 (1889): 198.

[11] Boninus Mombritius, *Sanctuarium, seu Vitae Sanctorum*, 2 vols. (Hildesheim: Georg Olms Verlag, 1978), 2:192–94. A somewhat briefer version of the Mombritius Margaret legend can be found in Mack, *Seinte Marherete*, 127–42. I will use Mack's edition for references because it is most closely related to the Middle English legend. The even longer *Passio S. Margaretae* that is printed in *Acta SS.*, Jul., 5:34–39, de-emphasizes the incident by reducing it to only a few lines (37–38).

ing on her own helplessness and God's omnipotence. As soon as she has overcome the monster, she praises God and contemplates the significance of her
victory:

> I praise and glorify your name, God; I rejoice and exult, cornerstone, Jesus Christ,
> immortal king, pillar of faith, prince of wisdom, and perpetual foundation of in-
> numerable angels. Now, therefore, comfort my faith, for I have seen joy with my
> soul. Indeed, I have seen the demon, Ruforus, prostrate on the ground, the killer
> of man destroyed, his filth gone. I have seen hell brought low, and the serpent
> trampled and the departing of his putridity. I have seen my cross blossoming; I
> have seen my body resting in the odor of sweetness, and I have seen the sacred oil
> come to me; I look forward to my joyful pillar. I see joy, and I exalt, and in sweet-
> ness I stand. I have killed the dragon; I hold eternal trust. Therefore, I thank you,
> holy immortal king and eternal emperor, refuge of all sinners, governor and tower
> of strength, crown of martyrs, rod of pearls, golden throne of sustenance, precious
> stone, savior of all, blessed God forever. Amen.[12]

This prayer redirects the reader's attention from the spectacular event that has
just taken place to themes of God's power and the saint's faith. It serves both as
a celebration of God, the "refuge of all sinners," and as a spiritual interpretation of the action.

Another common function of the saint's prayers is to situate her passion
within a typological framework by recalling how God has manifested his power
in the past.[13] Thus, in the course of a long prayer, Juliana says, "Free me from
these tortures, just as you freed Daniel from the jaws of the lion and as you
freed Ananias, Azarias, and Misael from the burning oven. As you protected
them, so protect me. Lead me into the heaven of your will as you led the Children of Israel fleeing the king out of Egypt."[14] Through these and other allusions to Old Testament events, the writer of this passio provides a specific context within which to understand Juliana's own deliverance. As is typical of early
Latin virgin martyr legends, the *Passio S. Iulianae* is not merely—even primarily—the biography of a holy woman; it is the story of God's involvement with
human beings throughout their history.

In her teachings, as in her prayers, the saint expounds fundamental themes
of Christian faith in considerable detail. Long expository passages locate the

---

[12] *Seinte Marherete*, 134–35. For an even more elaborate version of this passage, see Mombritius,
Sanctuarium 2:192–93.

[13] For a discussion of the typological orientation of monastic hagiography, see Jean Leclercq,
"L'écriture sainte dans l'hagiographie monastique du haut moyen âge," in *La Bibbia nell'Alto
Medioevo* (Spoleto, Italy: Presso la Sede del Centro, 1963), 111–15.

[14] Mombritius, *Sanctuarium*, 2:78.

events of the saint's martyrdom within Salvation history. In her encounters with other characters, both hostile and sympathetic, the virgin discusses a variety of topics, such as the value of virginity, the meaning of the Incarnation, the vanity of the world, and the rewards of heaven. Her teachings do not simply impart information; frequently they develop into elaborate professions of faith, similar in tone and content to her prayers. A typical example is this passage from the *Acta S. Dorotheae*: when Dorothy's persecutor, Fabricius, asks her, "Where is Christ?" the saint responds:

> His omnipotence is such that he is everywhere; yet human judgment is so frail that he is said to be nowhere. For that reason, we confess that the Son of God ascended into heaven and sits at the right hand of his father, God almighty, who is one in his divinity with his father and the holy spirit. He invites us to the garden of his delights, where the woods are always adorned with fruit and the lilies stay white, where the roses blossom and the fields grow green and the hills are adorned and the springs are sweetened and the souls of the saints play in Christ. If you believe these things, Fabricius, you will be freed and you will enter the paradise of God's delights.[15]

As in the prayers discussed above, the narrative function of Dorothy's response is unimportant, for the hagiographer's primary goal is to remind readers of the joys of heaven. The sixth-century *Vita S. Agnetis*, wrongly attributed to Ambrose, provides an especially good example of how the virgin's words could be used to stimulate readers' love of God. Accosted by the prefect's lovelorn son on her way home from school, Agnes tells the boy to look elsewhere for a bride:

> Get away from me, tinder of sin, food of villainy, nourishment of death. Depart from me, because I am already committed to another lover, one who has adorned me with ornaments and a ring far better than yours and who has pledged me to his faith, one who is far nobler than you and greater of kin and of dignity. He has adorned my right hand with a priceless bracelet, and he has encircled my neck with precious stones; he has given me inestimable pearls for my ears and surrounded me with beautiful and glittering gems. He has placed his mark upon my face so that I admit no lover except him. He has led me in a royal robe woven of gold, and with great necklaces he has adorned me. He has shown me incomparable treasures, which he promised to give me if I am true to him.

After continuing in this vein for several sentences, Agnes concludes: "I commit myself in all devotion to him. When I love him, I am chaste; when I touch him, I am pure; when I receive him, I am a virgin. Nor after the marriage will sons

[15] *Acta SS.*, Feb., 1:782.

be wanting, where birth takes place without sorrow and fruitfulness increases daily."[16] As in my other examples, the saint's words do little to advance the plot. Their principal function is to stir readers' devotion by dwelling on the delights of heaven and the splendor of God. As they recited or listened to Agnes's words, readers, too, could renounce temptation and affirm their faith, joyfully anticipating their own heavenly weddings.

In many virgin martyr legends, expository and devotional passages are so frequent and so lengthy that the events of the narrative—the trial, tortures, and miracles—seem peripheral. The thematic orientation of these texts was, however, eminently suited to the needs and reading practices of religious communities. As Jean Leclercq emphasized, "Medieval monastic literature is, in large part, a literature of compunction, whose aim is to possess, to increase, and to communicate the desire for God."[17] This longing for God was excited not only by the texts but also by the manner in which they were read, known as rumination, "uniting reading, meditation, and prayer."[18] Readers were not merely to scan a page for information; they were encouraged to ponder, to "masticate," and to *pray* the words before them. As William of Saint-Thierry put it in his letter to Carthusian novices: "Some part of your daily reading should also each day be committed to memory, taken in as it were into the stomach, to be more carefully digested and brought up again for frequent rumination. . . . The reading should also stimulate the feelings and give rise to prayer, which should interrupt your reading: an interruption which should not so much hamper the reading as restore it to a mind ever more purified for understanding."[19] Latin *passiones*, which in extreme cases consist of a series of loosely related prayers and meditations drawn from Scripture and the liturgy, seem designed to be consumed in this fashion.

I have argued that through lengthy passages of prayer and exposition, hagiographers invited readers to identify with the saint and to reenact her passion. The representation of the virgin as a humble supplicant would surely have promoted such an identification. When hagiographers describe the virgin's qualities, they almost invariably emphasize her unassuming devotion. Martina, for example, is "simple and pleasing to God."[20] Margaret has no regard for her

---

[16] Ibid., Jan., 2:715.

[17] Jean Leclercq, *The Love of Learning and the Desire for God: A Study of Monastic Culture*, trans. Catharine Misrahi (New York: Fordham University Press, 1961), 66.

[18] Ibid., 73. For a discussion of this mode of reading, see ibid., 15–17 and 72–75. See also Paul F. Gehl, "*Competens silentium*: Varieties of Monastic Silence in the Medieval West," *Viator* 18 (1987): 138–53.

[19] William of Saint-Thierry, *The Golden Epistle: A Letter to the Brethren at Mont Dieu*, trans. Theodore Berkeley (Spencer, Mass.: Cistercian Publications, 1971), 52.

[20] *Acta SS.*, Jan., 1:11.

noble lineage: "She did not scorn to tend sheep with the other girls. She tended them, moreover, with all humility and gentleness."[21] Dorothy's biographer writes, "Every day, in chastity and sobriety and purity, she busied herself in God's service; and with humility and gentleness she persevered in fasts and prayers."[22] The embedded prayers further underscore her humility, for the saint repeatedly offers herself to God as an unworthy handmaid (*indigna famula*) and a penitent, begging forgiveness and asking for grace and strength. Anticipating the trials that await her, Margaret reminds God of the inherent helplessness of human beings who are, after all, only "earth and dust."[23] Through the protestations of their heroines, hagiographers continually assure readers that even saints stand in need of God's mercy. "Hear me, a lowly woman and a sinner," Martina prays.[24] In a similar fashion, Christine asks God to overlook her shortcomings: "I pray and beseech that in your divinity you overlook my sins, for I have often strayed through the folly of my empty mind."[25] Likewise, Juliana prays, "Pardon my sins, and if I have sinned in my words, spare me, for you are a merciful God."[26] Repeatedly, the virgin martyr describes herself in such self-deprecating terms as "little woman" or "poor little woman."

The saint's responses to her ordeals further highlight her vulnerability. For example, Margaret recoils in fright when a dragon appears in her prison cell, and Justina falters before stepping into a pan of hot wax.[27] Such moments of doubt allow writers to iterate a central theme in the passions—that God knows and accepts human weakness. "You are . . . the creator of souls and bodies: you understand human frailty," Margaret asserts as she asks God to strengthen her.[28] One of the most eloquent affirmations of God's understanding of human weakness occurs in the *Acta S. Dorotheae*. Having induced Dorothy's two sisters to renounce their faith and sacrifice to the pagan gods, the prefect Fabricius sends them to the saint, hoping that they will persuade her to do the same. But when the women urge Dorothy to give in to the prefect, she exhorts them to turn to God, assuring them, "God is truly good and copious in his mercy toward those who turn to him with all their heart." When they tell her that all hope is lost, for they have denied Christ, she replies, "It is a greater sin to despair of God's mercy than to sacrifice to vain idols." The scene ends as Dorothy's sisters fall to their knees and the saint prays: "God, who said, I do

---

[21] Ibid., Jul., 5:34.
[22] Ibid., Feb., 1:781.
[23] Ibid., Jul., 5:34.
[24] Ibid., Jan., 1:12.
[25] Ibid., Jul., 5:525.
[26] Mombritius, *Sanctuarium*, 2:80.
[27] *Seinte Marherete*, 133; ibid., 404.
[28] *Acta SS.*, Jul., 5:35.

2. St. Agatha brought before Quintianus, MS lat. 5594, fol. 67, by permission of Bibliothèque Nationale, Paris.

not want a sinner to die, but rather to convert and live; Lord Jesus Christ, who said, there will be more rejoicing among the angels in heaven over one penitent sinner than over ninety-nine just people who never sinned: show your kindness toward these women whom the devil seized from you. Recall your sheep to your flock, so that by your mercy others who strayed from you will return to you."[29] The saint's own gentleness, as well as her words, attest to God's patience and mercy. Repeatedly, hagiographers concede that the path to heaven is not easy, and it is only to be expected that even saints will stumble along the way.

The representation of the saint as a devout and vulnerable woman who courageously upholds her faith is common not only in the texts produced in religious houses but also in the illustrations accompanying those texts. One of the most eloquent pictorial expressions of this ideal of sainthood is the late-tenth- or early-eleventh-century cycle of miniatures found in the *Passio S. Agathae*, lat. 5594, of the Bibliothèque Nationale, Paris.[30] In this cycle, the illustrator portrays a saint who must have looked much like an ordinary Christian: though devout, she is not eager to die. The first scene shows Agatha being dragged from her home by three guards, and the next scene depicts the obviously frightened woman cringing before the prefect Quintianus, who proposes to make her his mistress. One guard pulls Agatha toward her would-be lover, while two others push her forward (figure 2). In the next scene, Aphrodisia, the

[29] Ibid., Feb., 1:782.

[30] For a discussion of this cycle of illustrations, see Magdalena Elizabeth Carrasco, "An Early Illustrated Manuscript of the Passion of St. Agatha (Paris, Bibl. Nat., MS lat. 5594)," *Gesta* 24 (1985): 19–32.

3. Aphrodisia takes Agatha to her brothel, MS lat. 5594, fol. 67v, by permission of Bibliothèque Nationale, Paris.

4. Agatha admonishes Quintianus, MS lat. 5594, fol. 68, by permission of Bibliothèque Nationale, Paris.

proprietor of a brothel, hauls the cowering virgin off to her establishment, planning to teach her the arts of love (figure 3). Only gradually does she gain the confidence to stand up to her enemies (figures 4–6). Even then, she is obviously not immune to pain, as the artist shows when he depicts the saint clutching her wounded chest as a guard shoves her into her prison cell (figure 7). Agatha's human reactions are as obvious in her moments of triumph as they are during her ordeals. When the apostle Peter appears in her prison cell

5. Agatha is returned to prison, MS lat. 5594, fol. 68v, by permission of Bibliothèque Nationale, Paris.

6. Agatha's torment, MS lat. 5594, fol. 69, by permission of Bibliothèque Nationale, Paris.

carrying a breast to replace the one that torturers had squeezed off her body with poles only hours earlier, Agatha is astonished (figure 8). Wide-eyed, she watches as the apostle attaches the new flesh to her chest.

Although Agatha's persecution comes about because she refuses to become Quintianus's mistress, the illustrator does not dwell on sexual conflict but rather

7. Torturers remove Agatha's breast, MS lat. 5594, fol. 69v, by permission of Bibliothèque Nationale, Paris.

8. St. Peter restores Agatha's breast, MS lat. 5594, fol. 70, by permission of Bibliothèque Nationale, Paris.

plays down the polarization of the sexes that is implicit in his material. One way he does this is to depict women among the saint's enemies. His surprising decision to portray not only Aphrodisia but all nine of the madam's daughters injects a distinctly feminine element into Agatha's persecution (figure 3). Although the passio does mention that Aphrodisia is the head of a large family of prostitutes, this detail has a greater force in the pictorial cycle: one cannot fail to notice the large crowd of hostile women that dominates one of the seven pages of illustrations. The artist also includes a scene of Agatha comparing Quintianus's wife to Venus (figure 4). Consciously or unconsciously, he affirms that the saint's struggle is not just with men but with sinners generally. Further diminishing themes of sexual conflict, he balances scenes of the saint defying Quintianus with scenes of her honoring another male authority figure, the apostle Peter. In fact, the cycle concludes with a scene of Agatha worshiping at the apostle's feet (figure 8).

Compared with the passiones of other virgin martyrs, such as Margaret or Martina, the *Passio S. Agathae* contains relatively few prayers. Yet the illustrator clearly considered the saint's devotions essential moments in the legend, for three scenes of the cycle are devoted to her supplications. One shows Agatha praying after her confrontation with Aphrodisia (figure 3). Another depicts the saint kneeling in her prison cell as Peter appears before her, and the third shows her lying prostrate on the ground after the apostle has healed her (figure 8). As she is being tortured and shoved into her prison cell, Agatha also extends her arms in supplication to God (figure 5). Indeed, as Cynthia Hahn points out, when the saint is not making some sort of prayerful gesture, her arms are usually being restrained.[31]

Prayers also figure prominently in early illustrations of another virgin martyr legend, that of St. Margaret. The illustrator of the *Passio S. Margaretae* contained in the tenth-century *libellus* from Fulda (MS 1, 189, Hannover, Niedersächsische Bibliothek) shows Margaret praying after she is approached by Olibrius's men, before and after she overcomes the dragon, while in prison, while being tortured, and before her execution.[32] An even more extreme example is the twelfth-century *Passio S. Margaretae* preserved in Munich (Bayerische Staatsbibliothek Clm. 1133). Though the pictorial cycle for this legend was not completed, space for no fewer than seven illustrations was set aside to accompany the text of the saint's long prayer before her execution.[33]

The Latin passiones were certainly read by women as well as men; women may even have composed a few of these largely anonymous texts. From all indications, however, most of the legends were produced by monks, and they were tailored to masculine needs and sensibilities. By emphasizing the saints'

---

[31] Cynthia Hahn, "The Powers of Gesture in Illustrated Saints' Lives," paper delivered at the Sewanee Medieval Colloquium, University of the South, 3 April 1993.

[32] For a facsimile of and commentary on this libellus, see *Passio Kiliani, Ps. Theotimus, Passio Margaretae, Orationes*, ed. Cynthia Hahn (Graz, Austria: Akademische Druck-U. Verlagsanstalt, 1988). Josepha Weitzmann-Fiedler has discussed this cycle and other Margaret cycles in "Zur Illustration der Margaretenlegende," *Münchner Jahrbuch der bildenden Kunst* 3, no. 17 (1966): 17–48. Weitzmann-Fiedler reproduces the illustrations in the Fulda libellus in plates 23–32.

[33] Weitzmann-Fiedler, "Illustration der Margaretenlegende," 22.

prayers and teachings, for example, male hagiographers preseited their heroines as figures with whom they might identify. Though the saint repeatedly calls
herself a "poor little woman," the emphasis she places on her gender would not
have alienated male readers. Indeed, Caroline Walker Bynum's findings suggest
that men may have been *more* likely than women to imagine themselves as the
praying virgin. Bynum has pointed out that male writers of the high and later
Middle Ages commonly referred to themselves as "weak women" to profess
humility and renunciation.[34] This form of self-deprecation, Bynum observed,
was for men a positive statement, affirming their capacity to adopt the ultimate
posture of humility before God—the posture of a woman. The praying saint,
abject yet hallowed, offered a satisfying model for religious men that surely
contributed to the extraordinary popularity of virgin martyrs within religious
communities.

The Katherine Group and Women's Religious Life

Most scholars agree that, in contrast to the passiones, the earliest Middle English virgin martyr legends were intended for religious women—most probably for anchoresses.[35] The date, language, subject matter, and West Midlands
provenance of the manuscripts containing the legends all indicate that they
originated within the same community that produced other religious texts for
women, including the *Ancrene Wisse*, a guide originally composed for three well-
born anchoresses; *Hali Meiðhad, a virginity treatise*; *Sawles Warde*, a homily;
and four prose meditations, narrated by an anchoress, known as the Wooing

---

[34] Caroline Walker Bynum, "'. . . and Woman His Humanity': Female Imagery in the Religious
Writing of the Later Middle Ages," in *Fragmentation and Redemption: Essays on Gender and the
Human Body in Medieval Religion* (New York: Zone, 1992), 151–79, esp. 165–71; and Bynum, *Holy
Feast and Holy Fast: The Religious Significance of Food to Medieval Women* (Berkeley: University of
California Press, 1987), 282–88. On Bernard of Clairvaux's use of a "feminine model" to "treat the
limitations of mortal life positively and constructively," see David Damrosch, "*Non Alia Sed Aliter*:
The Hermeneutics of Gender in Bernard of Clairvaux," in *Images of Sainthood in Medieval Europe*,
ed. Renate Blumenfeld-Kosinski and Timea Szell (Ithaca: Cornell University Press, 1991), 190.

[35] The classic study of the context of the Katherine Group legends and related texts is E. J. Dobson, *The Origins of the "Ancrene Wisse"* (Oxford: Clarendon, 1976). More recent discussions of the
audience for these legends, which have corrected some of Dobson's hypotheses, include Robertson,
Early English Devotional Prose, 1–12; and Anne Savage and Nicholas Watson, general introduction
to *Anchoritic Spirituality: "Ancrene Wisse" and Associated Works* (New York: Paulist, 1991), 7–32.
For a different view of the legends' intended audience, see Bella Millett, "The Audience of the Saints'
Lives of the Katherine Group," *Reading Medieval Studies* 16 (1990): 127–55. Millett agrees that "the
Lives were written from the start with the special interests of women in religion in mind" but argues that the hagiographers were primarily interested in providing legends to be read aloud to a
general audience of laypeople (143). I have drawn on all these studies for the following discussion.

Group.[36] Moreover, each legend appears in early-thirteenth-century collections together with works that were explicitly addressed to women and were probably compiled for anchoresses living in northern Herefordshire: MS Bodley 34, Bodleian Library, a small volume of devotional texts, contains the Katherine Group virgin martyr legends, *Hali Meiðhad*, and *Sawles Warde*; MS Royal 17.A, British Library, comprises the legends, *Sawles Warde*, and an incomplete text of the *Oreison of Seinte Marie*; and MS Cotton Titus D.xviii, British Library, includes *Seinte Katerine,* along with the *Ancrene Wisse, Sawles Warde, Hali Meiðhad,* and *Þe Wohinge of ure Lauerd.* At the very least, we can infer that the compilers of these miscellanies considered the Middle English legends of Margaret, Katherine, and Juliana well suited to the needs or tastes of women.

Indeed, internal evidence indicates that *Seinte Marherete* was specifically intended for women, for its author writes, "Hercneð, alle þe earen & herunge habbeð: widewen wið þa iweddede, & te meidnes nomeliche, lusten swiðe ʒeorliche hu ha schulen luuien þe liuiende lauerd & libben i meiðhad" (4) (Listen, all who have ears and hearing: widows and married people, and maidens especially, should eagerly listen to how they should love the living lord and live in maidenhood). Moreover, at several points he adjusts his Latin source in ways that suggest he is tailoring his text to the needs of a female audience. For example, Margaret prays for strength "swa þet alle meidnes eauer mare þurh me þe mare trusten on þe" (16) (so that all maidens ever more through me will trust in you the more), and she specifically addresses Christ as a friend to women, "weddede weole, & widewene warant, & meidenes mede" (18) (joy of married people, protector of widows, maidens' reward). The writers of *Seinte Iuliene* and *Seinte Katerine* do not specify the gender of their intended readers; in fact, the writer of *Seinte Iuliene* initially addresses himself to a general audience of "alle leawede men þe understonden ne mahen latines ledene" (3) (all unlearned people who understand the Latin language). Yet he, too, may have had female readers in mind when he expanded the devil's reference to man ("hominem") to read "mon oðer wummon" (37).

It is no surprise that clerics wishing to provide reading material for religious women should have chosen to adapt three virgin martyr legends. With their emphasis on chastity and faith and their portrayal of the saint as Christ's bride, these legends encapsulate many of the chief themes of twelfth- and early-thirteenth-century devotional literature for women. Writers of treatises for nuns and anchoresses had long encouraged their readers to take heart from the examples of virgin martyrs. For example, in his rule for anchoresses, *De*

---

[36] For a discussion of *Sawles Warde's* female orientation, see Anne Eggebroten, "*Sawles Warde*: A Retelling of *De Anima* for a Female Audience," *Mediaevalia* 10 (1988): 27–47.

institutis inclusarum (circa 1160–62), Aelred of Rievaulx advises his reader that she should, if she finds herself tempted, "call to mind the blessed virgins who so often at an early age triumphed over their godless foe," continuing:

> Think of St. Agnes, who reckoned gold, silver, expensive clothes, precious stones and all the pomp of worldly glory as so much dung. When she was summoned to the judgment-seat she did not hold back. She despised the judge's blandishments and laughed at his threats, afraid rather of being spared than of being punished. Happy she who turned a brothel into an oratory, while the angel who entered together with the virgin flooded the darkness with light and punished with death the man who sought to corrupt her. If then you also pray and take up the arms of your tears against him who incites you to impurity, you may be sure that the angel who was present in the brothel will not be absent from your chaste cell. It is hardly surprising that this material fire of ours could not burn St. Agnes; the flame of the flesh had died in her, she was consumed by the fire of charity.[37]

Likewise, the writers of both the *Ancrene Wisse* and *Hali Meiðhad* hold up virgin martyrs—Margaret, Katherine, Agnes, Juliana, Agatha, and others—as models for their female readers, using the saints' lives to drive home points ranging from the rewards of suffering to the wiles of the devil.[38] For the *Wisse* writer, indeed, the anchoress could even participate in the more spectacular events of the virgin martyrs' lives—the gruesome tortures. "Secnesse . . . eueneð to martir þene þole mode" (Illness . . . puts the patient sufferer on a level with the martyrs), he writes, later comparing the suffering anchoress more explicitly to the "laðlese meidnes" (innocent maidens) who had their "tittes itoren of" (breasts torn off) and were "tohwiðeret o hweoles, heafdes bicoruen" (torn apart on wheels, and beheaded)—a probable allusion to Katherine and Juliana.[39] Invoking St. Agatha, he goes on to berate the anchoress who calls a doctor for every little ache and pain:

> Dude swa seinte Agace? þe ondswerede & seide to ure lauerdes sonde þe brohte sonde o godes half to healen hire tittes, Medicinam carnalem corpori meo nunquam adhibui. (Tolkien, 188)

[37] Aelred of Rievaulx, *Treatises: The Pastoral Prayer* (Spencer, Mass.: Cistercian Publications, 1971), 65–66.

[38] See, for example, *Ancrene Wisse*, ed. J.R.R. Tolkien, EETS.OS 249 [henceforth cited as Tolkien] (London: Oxford University Press, 1962), 125, 185, 188; and *Hali Meiðhad*, ed. Bella Millett, EETS.OS 284 [henceforth cited as *Hali Meiðhad*] (London: Oxford University Press, 1982), 23. All translations of *Hali Meiðhad* are mine.

[39] Tolkien, 94–95, 185; and *The Ancrene Riwle*, trans. M. B. Salu [henceforth cited as Salu] (Notre Dame: University of Notre Dame Press, 1956), 80, 160. I will be using Salu's translation of *Ancrene Wisse* and Tolkien's edition throughout this chapter for quotes and page references. For the sake of clarity, I have here and elsewhere normalized the punctuation and capitalization in Tolkien's edition.

Was this what St. Agatha did? She answered Our Lord's messenger who had brought salve from God to heal her breasts, *I have never used any medicine of the flesh for my body.* (Salu, 163)

Readers of such texts as the *Ancrene Wisse* would have been predisposed to identify with the virgin martyrs, for the saints are repeatedly portrayed as people who had to struggle against their human weaknesses. "Alle þe hali halhen weren wodeliche itemptet" (All the holy saints were severely tempted), the *Wisse* writer reminds his readers.[40]

The legends of the Katherine Group were especially well suited to the spiritual needs and circumstances of enclosed women. Katherine of Alexandria made an excellent model for anchoresses, for she eschewed the frivolous pastimes that anchoresses were warned against: "Ne luuede ha nane lihte plohen ne nane sotte songes" (*Seinte Katerine*, 8) (She did not enjoy trivial games or foolish songs). Moreover, in always having "on hali writ ehnen oðer heorte, oftest ba togederes" (8) (her eyes or heart on holy scripture, often both together), Katherine displays the same abiding devotion to Scripture that Aelred urged anchoresses to cultivate:

> Nothing is better for preventing useless ideas or driving out impure imaginations than the study of God's Word. The virgin should make herself so familiar with it that she is incapable of occupying her mind with anything else even when she wishes to do so. Let her be thinking over the Scriptures when she falls asleep, let something from the Scriptures be the first thought to come to mind when she wakes up; as she sleeps let her dreams be interspersed with some verse from the Scriptures which has remained fixed in her memory.[41]

Another feature that may have made the legends of Katherine, Margaret, and Juliana attractive to clerics writing for anchoresses is that all three narratives place more emphasis than do most virgin martyr legends on the saints' activities within their prison cells. Ann K. Warren has commented on the extensive use of prison terminology in enclosure ceremonies and religious literature for anchorites.[42] The cell in which an anchoress was voluntarily imprisoned assumed a variety of values—values enabling her imaginatively to reenact the sacred paradigms of the past: "It was a version of the desert home of the first Christian anchorites, the arena of spiritual warfare, a place for contemplation, a representation of the prison of the early martyrs, a penitential prison, a refuge, a way station."[43] The prison figures prominently as a sacred locus in all three legends that

---

[40] Tolkien, 120; Salu, 103.
[41] Aelred of Rievaulx, *Treatises*, 68. See also Tolkien, 148, which I will be discussing shortly.
[42] See Warren, *Anchorites*, esp. 8–9, 92–95.
[43] Ibid., 8.

make up the Katherine Group. There saints pray; there they are nourished, healed, and comforted by angels; there they inspire others with their holiness. There, too, they are visited by demons. In fact, the struggles with devils that Juliana and Margaret engage in while in prison dramatize the battles that the writers of both *Ancrene Wisse* and *Hali Meiðhad* insist all virgins must wage.[44] The Margaret and Juliana legends illustrate the demonic tactics, both covert and overt, that these writers warn against (Margaret's devil appears as a dragon and attacks her outright, while Juliana's first appears in the guise of an angel), and they assure readers that a frail maiden can indeed triumph over the most daunting enemy. The *Wisse* writer may actually have had *Seinte Marherete* in mind when he refers his readers to "ower englische boc of seinte Margarete" (your English book about St. Margaret) for examples of the devil's tactics.[45] Certainly, his advice on how to overcome the devil strongly evokes the Margaret legend:

> Ah nim anan þe rode steaf mid nempnunge i þi muð, mid te mearke i þin hond, mid þoht i þin heorte, & hat him ut heterliche þe fule cur dogge, & liðere to him luðerliche mid te hali rode steaf stronge bac duntes. Þet is: Rung up sture þe. Hald up ehnen on heh & honden toward heouene. Gred efter sucurs. (Tolkien, 149–50)

> But seize the crucifix at once, and with the words of the sign of the Cross on your lips, the cross itself in your hand, with the thought of it in your mind, order him out sternly, foul cur that he is, and fall upon him fiercely, with heavy blows on his back from the holy crucifix. That is to say, stand up, bestir yourself. Lift your eyes and hands to heaven. Call loudly for help. (Salu, 129)

Margaret vanquishes the devil with much the same routine—she prays, makes the sign of the cross, beats her enemy into submission, and then prays some more. The scene that immediately precedes the saint's encounter with the dragon would have also prompted a thirteenth-century anchoress to see herself as another St. Margaret:

> Hire uoster moder wes an þet frourede hire, & com to þe cwalm-hus & brohte hire to fode bred & burnes drunch, þet ha bi l[iue]de. Heo, þa, & monie ma biheolden þurh an eilþurl as ha bed hire beoden.[46]

> Her foster mother was among those who supported her, and came to the prison house and brought her bread to eat and spring water to drink, so that she could live. Then she [the foster mother] and many more watched through a window as she said her prayers.

This brief scene encapsulates the prescribed relationship between an anchoress and her community: the community provides the anchoress's daily needs; she,

---

[44] Tolkien, 92–153; *Hali Meiðhad*, 7–8.
[45] Tolkien, 125; Salu, 108.
[46] *Seinte Marherete*, 20–27; quote on 21.

in turn, supports and inspires the community through her prayers, her faith, and her heroic resistance to temptation. The anchoress's contact with the out-side world, like Margaret's, is through a window.[47]

Reading is Good Prayer

Scholars who have compared the Katherine Group legends with their closest Latin analogues generally agree that the Middle English writers were hardly slaves to their Latin originals but freely embellished, paraphrased, and con-densed their materials.[48] Nevertheless, the modifications they introduced did not significantly change the tone of their originals, nor did they seriously alter the model of holiness set forth in the earlier legends. In part, these English writers may have remained relatively faithful to their sources because their own readers had needs akin to those of the readers of the Latin passions. If the in-tended readers of the Katherine Group legends were indeed anchoresses, the richly contemplative texture of the *passiones* would certainly have been appro-priate, because recluses, like members of traditional religious houses, were en-couraged to regard reading as a form of prayer. In the words of the *Wisse* author:

> Accidies salue is gastelich gleadschipe & froure of gleadful hope þurh redunge, þurh hali þoht, oðer of monnes muðe. Ofte leoue sustren ȝe schulen uri leasse forte reden mare. Redunge is god bone. Redunge teacheð hu & hwet me bidde & beode biȝet hit efter. Amidde þe redunge, hwen þe heorte likeð, kimeð up a deuotiun þet is wurð monie benen. For þi seið sein Ierome. . . . *Semper in manu tua sacra sit lectio. Tenenti tibi librum sompnus subripiat, & cadentem faciem pagina sancta suscipiat.* Hali redunge beo eauer i þine honden. Slep ga up o þe as þu lokest þron, ant te hali pagne ikepe þi fallinde neb. Swa þu schalt reden ȝeorn-liche & longe. (Tolkien, 148)

> The remedy for Sloth is spiritual joy and the comfort of joyful hope, which comes from reading, from holy meditation or from the sayings of others. Often, dear sis-ters, you ought to say fewer fixed prayers so that you may do more reading. Read-ing is good prayer. Reading teaches us how to pray and what to pray for, and then prayer achieves it. In the course of reading, when the heart is pleased, there arises a spirit of devotion which is worth many prayers. For this reason St. Jerome says: *Always keep some holy reading in your hand. Look at it even while sleep steals upon you, and let the sacred page uphold your drooping head.* Thus must you read, atten-tively and long. (Salu, 127)

The long declarations of devotion and the effusive celebrations of God's mercy and grandeur that pervade the legends of the Katherine Group were manifestly

---

[47] Warren, *Anchorites*, 31–32.

[48] The editions of the Middle English legends that I have cited above all contain extensive discus-sions of Latin sources and analogues, and each edition of the Middle English legends also provides an edition of the closest known Latin source. I am using these editions of the Latin *passiones* for references and quotations; the translations from the Latin are mine.

designed to be prayed and, in the course of being prayed, to arouse the passion that the *Wisse* writer claims comes from reading "ʒeornliche & longe." In fact, as Diane L. Mockridge has shown, the Katherine Group writers actually enhanced the devotional quality of their legends through rich nuptial imagery, frequent references to the saints as brides and lovers of Christ, and recurring meditations on God's tenderness—embellishments apposite for readers used to thinking of themselves as "Godes spuse, Iesu Cristes brude, þe lauerdes leofmon þet alle þinges buheð" (God's spouse, Jesus Christ's bride, lover of the lord who created all things).[49]

Dramas of Suffering and Triumph

Although the writers of the Katherine Group legends preserved the devotional and didactic orientation of Latin hagiography, they departed from tradition by providing more dramatic accounts of the action, thereby heightening both the saint's victimization and her triumph. This more vivid rendering of events and characters also draws attention to the gendered nature of the saints' conflicts, prompting readers to regard Margaret, Katherine, and especially Juliana as women struggling against specifically masculine enemies.

Writers of the Katherine Group legends almost invariably embellish references to torture in their Latin sources. For example, the writer of *Seinte Marherete* amplifies Olibrius's order that the saint be "suspended in the air and beaten with supple rods" to read, "Struped hire steort-naket & hongeð hire on heh up, & beteð hire bere bodi wið bittere besmen" (12) (Strip her stark naked and hang her high up, and beat her bare body with bitter birches).[50] The English hagiographer's reference to the saint's nakedness is absent in the Latin version. He further highlights her ordeal by describing the torture itself: "Þa awariede werlahen leiden se luðerliche on hire leofliche lich, þet hit brec oueral & liðerede o blode" (12) (The accursed scoundrels attacked her lovely body so savagely that it tore all over and was foamed with blood). Toward the end of the narrative, he works an even more gruesome transformation, first changing Olibrius's terse order "Strip her, and suspend her in the air, and burn her with torches" to "Struped hire steort-naket, & heoueð hire on heh up swa þet ha hongi to mede of hire hokeres, & ontendeð hire bodi wið bearninde teaperes" (Strip her stark naked, and heave her up high so that she hangs as a reward for

---

[49] Diane L. Mockridge, "Marital Imagery in Six Late Twelfth- and Early Thirteenth-Century Vitae of Female Saints," in *That Gentle Strength: Historical Perspectives on Women in Christianity*, ed. Lynda L. Coon, Katherine J. Haldane, and Elisabeth W. Sommer (Charlottesville: University Press of Virginia, 1990), 60–78; *Hali Meiðhad*, 2.

[50] The Latin reads, "in aera suspendi, et suptilibus uirgis cedi" (*Seinte Marherete*, 131).

her audacity, and burn her body with burning tapers), then expanding "They burned her tender body" to read, "Þe driueles unduhtie swa duden sone, þet te hude snawhwit swartede as hit snercte, & bearst on to bleinin as hit aras oueral; & hire leofliche lich reschte of þe leie, swa þet alle remden þet on hire softe siden sehen þet rewðe" (42) (The vile menials quickly did so, so that her snow white skin blackened as it scorched, and burst into blisters as it puffed out all over; and her beautiful body crackled with the flame, so that everyone who gazed on her soft sides cried out in pity).[51] Similarly, where the Latin version of the Katherine legend simply reports that Maxentius orders the saint to be scourged, the writer of *Seinte Katerine* provides these grisly touches: "Het o wod[e] wise strupen hire steort-naket ant beaten hire beare flesch ant hire freoliche bodi wið cnottede schurgen, ant [swa me] dude sone, þet hire leofliche lich liðerede al [o] blode" (80) (He commanded madly that she be stripped stark naked and her bare flesh and lovely body beaten with knotted scourges, and so it was done, so that her beautiful body seethed with blood). For his part, the writer of *Seinte Iuliene* contributes a meticulous account of the diabolical spiked wheel on which Juliana is tortured as well as of its spectacular effects: "Þet ha bigon to breoken al as þet istelede irn strac hire in oueral, from þe top to þe tan, áá as hit turnde, tolimede hire ant leac lið ba ant lire; bursten hire banes ant þet meari bearst ut, imenget wið blode" (51, 53) (It began to break her as the hardened iron struck her all over, from head to toe; always as it turned it dismembered her and pulled her body and skin; her bones broke and the marrow burst out, mingled with blood).[52]

While vivid descriptions of torture convey the saints' victimization and suffering, dramatic renderings of scenes of confrontation transform the virgin martyrs into more aggressive figures than they had been in the *passiones*. The increased temerity of Margaret and Juliana is especially striking in the scenes describing their encounters with the devils. For example, the writer of the *Vita S. Margaretae* gives this brief account of Margaret's fight: "The holy virgin, taking the demon [by the hair], threw him to the ground, and she placed her right foot on his neck."[53] The writer of *Seinte Marherete*, however, draws out the description: "Þet milde meiden Margarte grap þet grisliche þing þet hire ne agras nawiht, & heteueste toc him bi þet eateliche top & hef him up & duste him

---

[51] The Latin reads, "Expoliate eam, et in aere suspendite, et incendite eam cum lampadibus"; "Conburebant autem corpus eius tenerum" (*Seinte Marherete*, 138).

[52] The Latin is somewhat less graphic: "Machinas tangebant eius nobile corpus & uirgo christi omnibus menbris findebatur & medulle de ossibus eius exibant" (*Seinte Iuliene*, 50, 52) (The devices violently struck her noble body and Christ's virgin was split in all her members and the marrow went out of her bones).

[53] "Sancta itaque uirgo, demonem comprehendens [per capillos], proiecit in terram, et posuit suum pedem dextrum in ceruicem eius" (*Seinte Marherete*, 135).

dunriht to þer eorðe, ant sette hire riht-fot on his ruhe swire" (28) (The mild maiden Margaret seized that horrible thing that didn't frighten her at all, and firmly took him by his hideous hair and heaved him up and flung him down to the ground and set her right foot on his rough neck). Similarly, when the demon threatens to denounce Juliana to his master, the Latin hagiographer writes, "Saint Juliana tied his hands behind his back and put him on the ground. And seizing one of the iron chains with which she herself had been bound, she began to beat him herself."[54] The Middle English writer, however, depicts a more colorful scene in which the saint first scolds her foe, then wrestles and thrashes him:

> "O," quoð ha, Iuliene, ihesu cristes leofmon, "þreatest tu me, wrecche? Þe schal iwurðen, godd hit wat, godes þe wurse." Ant grap a great raketehe þet ha wes wið ibunden, ant bond bihinden his rug ba twa his honden, þet him wrong euch neil ant blakede of þe blode; ant duste him ruglunge adun riht to þer eorðe, ant stondinde o þe steorue, nom hire ahne bondes, ant bigon to beaten þen belial of helle. Ant he bigon to rarin reowliche, to ȝuren ant to ȝeien, ant heo leide on se luðerliche þet wa wes him o liue. (*Seinte Iuliene*, 41, 43)

> "Oh," said she, Juliana, Jesus Christ's lover, "so you are threatening me, wretch? By God, you will be the worse for it." And she seized a great chain that she was bound with, and she bound both his hands behind his back so that each nail hurt him and turned black with blood; and she flung him backwards right down on the ground, and standing on the pest, she took her own bonds and began to beat the fiend of hell. And he began to howl piteously, to bawl and to wail, and she fell upon him so fiercely that he was sorry to be alive.

Small touches—Juliana's taunts, the devil's howls—bring out the characters' personalities. Instead of drawing readers' attention from the events being described to their significance, as the writers of the *passiones* did, the Middle English hagiographer uses descriptive language to involve readers in his story. His account encourages them to wince at the devil's knotted body and blackened nails, to laugh at his surprise at being trampled by a mere girl, and to cheer as Juliana wallops her erstwhile tempter "se luðerliche þet wa wes him o liue."

The saints' pugnacity is reinforced in scornful replies to their human persecutors that have no precedent in the Latin *passiones*. When Juliana's father vows to force her to marry Eleusius, she challenges him to make good his boast: "Þu wult, þu seist, aȝeoue me to Eleusium þe luðere. Aȝef me!" (*Seinte Iuliene*, 17) (You say you'll turn me over to the loathsome Eleusius. Go ahead!). Some time later, when Eleusius threatens to hurt and humiliate her unless she changes her mind, she tells him to do as he pleases: "Doð . . . deofles limen, al

---

[54] "Sancta iuliana post tergum manibus ligauit eum & posuit super terram. & capiens unum ferrum de ligamentis de quibus ipsa fuerat ligata, cedebat ipsum demonem" (*Seinte Iuliene*, 40).

þet te deouel, hwas driueles ȝe beoð, driueð ow to donne; lutel me is of ower luue, leasse of ower laððe, ant of þes þreates riht noht. Wite ȝe hit to wisse" (23) (Do, devil's limb, all that the devil, whose servant you are, drives you to do; your love means little to me, your hatred less, and these threats nothing at all. So there!). Equally mettlesome, Margaret derides her unwanted suitor for wasting his time ("Hwar-to luste þe warpen al awei þine hwile" [*Seinte Marherete*, 12]). She later mocks his futile attempts to harm her: "Þu swenchest te swiðe, & ne spedest nawhit for te wurchen on me, meiden an þet ich am; ah wergest þe seoluen" (42) (You put yourself out and gain nothing for all your efforts against me, maiden though I am; but you tire yourself). The writer of *Seinte Katerine*, too, enlivens the debates between the saint and her persecutor with scathing retorts: "Stute nu þenne ant stew þe, ant stille þine wordes, for ha beoð me unwurð—þet wite þu to wisse" (80) (Stop now and restrain yourself and be quiet, for your words are worthless to me—know that).

In *Seinte Iuliene*, the most innovative of the three adaptations, the hagiographer's tendency to make his material more dramatic brings into focus issues that had been peripheral, at most, in the *passio* on which it is based. *Seinte Iuliene* differs from the Latin account primarily at the beginning of the narrative, in its extensive treatment of Eleusius's courtship of Juliana. The Middle English hagiographer first fleshes out the rather meager description of Eleusius as "a certain senator from the city of Nicodemus" and "the emperor's friend" by adding that Juliana's would-be husband was "akennet of heh cun, ant swiðe riche of rente, ant ȝung mon of ȝeres" (5) (a young man of noble lineage, with a very good income). He also explains how Eleusius came to know the saint: "Þes ȝunge mon Eleusius, þet þus wes wel wið þe king, hefde iunne feolah-schipe to Affrican, ant wes iwunet ofte to cumen wið him to his in ant iseon his dohter" (5) (This young man Eleusius, who was on good terms with the king, was friendly with Africanus and often came home with him and saw his daughter). Having established this foundation, he offers a full account of how the engagement came about:

> As he hefde en-chere bihalden swiðe ȝeorne hire utnume feire ant freoliche ȝuh-eðe, felde him iwundet inwið in his heorte wið þe flan þe of luue fleoð, swa þet him þuhte þet ne mahte he nanes-weis wiðute þe lechnunge of hire luue libben. Ant efter lutle stunde wiðute long steuene wes himseolf sonde to Affrican hire feader, ant bisohte him ȝeorne þet he hire ȝeue him; ant he hire walde menskin wið al þet he mahte as þe þing i þe world þet he meast luuede. Affrican wiste þet he wes swiðe freo-iboren, ant walde wel bicumen him a freo-iboren burde, ant ȝetede him his bone. Ha wes him sone ihondsald, þah hit hire unwil were. (5, 7)

> Once he had beheld so eagerly her great beauty and her noble youth, he felt so wounded in his heart with the arrows of love that he thought he could not live without the healing of her love. And after a little while, at an early date, he went to

> Africanus her father, and he asked him if he would give her to him; and he promised to honor her with all his might as his most prized possession. Africanus knew that such a well-born man was a worthy match for a well-born lady and granted his request. She was soon betrothed to him, though it was against her will.

Here and throughout the narrative, the Middle English hagiographer emphasizes the material benefits of a match with Eleusius. For example, after relating that Eleusius persuaded the emperor to make him the prefect of Rome so that Juliana would agree to marry him, the writer of *Seinte Iuliene* dwells on the tangible signs of his rank:

> He . . . lette, as me luuede þa, leaden him i cure up-o fowr hweoles ant teon him ȝeont te tun þron from strete to strete. Al þe cure wes ouertild þet he wes itohen on wið purpres ant pelles, wið ciclatuns ant cendals ant deorewurðe claðes, as þe þet se heh þing hefde to heden ant se riche refschipe to rihten ant to readen. (7)
>
> As was the custom, he mounted a chariot of four wheels and had himself taken from street to street through the city. His chariot was canopied with costly purple cloth, with scarlet cloth and silk coverings, with expensive cloths, as suited one with important matters to attend to and the rich prefecture to govern and direct.

Later, when Juliana still refuses to marry the prefect, her father reminds her of the worldly benefits of the alliance:

> Sei me hwi þu forsakest þi sy ant ti selhðe, þe weolen ant te wunnen þe walden awakenen ant waxen of þe wedlac þat ich reade þe to. Hit nis nan eðelich þing þe refschipe of Rome, ant tu maht, ȝef þu wult, beon burhene leafdi ant of alle þe londes þe þer-to liggeð. (9, 11)
>
> Tell me why you reject the advantage and the happiness, the good fortune and the joys that would arise and grow out of the marriage that I am advising. The prefecture of Rome is no small thing, and you might, if you wish, be lady of the city and of all the lands that belong to it.

As a consequence of the writer's prolonged treatment of Juliana's ill-fated betrothal, the legend becomes a story not only about religious faith but about property, possessions, status, and power. The central conflict is not merely a good Christian's refusal to marry a pagan but more specifically a daughter's refusal to bow to her father's authority. Africanus's response to his daughter's declaration that she cannot marry Eleusius because she is already betrothed to Christ clearly portrays Juliana's faith as an assault on social convention and paternal prerogative as well as on paganism: "Hwet is he, þes were þet tu art to iweddet, þet tu hauest wiðute me se forð ði luue ilenet, þet tu letest lutel of al þet tu schuldest luuien?" (13) (What is he, this man you are to marry, that you have bestowed your love without my consent, that you think little of all that you should hold dear?). Heated dialogue, such as the following exchange, transforms what had been a fairly perfunctory explanation of how Juliana's passion came about into a bitter contest of wills:

> "For mi lif," quoð hire feader, "þe schal laðin his luue; for þu schalt on alre earst as on ernesse swa beon ibeaten wið bittere besmen, þet tu [wani þet tu] were wummon of wummone bosum to wraðer heale eauer iboren i þe world." "Swa muche" quoð þet meiden, "ich beo him þe leouere se ich derfre þing for his luue drehe. Wurch þu þet ti wil is!" "ȝe,["] quoð he, "bliðeliche!" Ant het swiðe heatterliche strupen hire steortnaket ant leggen se luðerliche on hire leofliche lich þet hit liðeri o blode. Me nom hire ant dude swa þet hit ȝeat adun of þe ȝerden, ant heo bigon te ȝeien: "Beaten se ȝe beaten, ȝe Beliales budeles, ne mahe ȝe nowðer mi luue ne mi bileaue lutlin towart te liuiende godd, mi leofsume leofmon þe luuewurðe lauerd; ne nulle ich leuen ower read þe forreadeð ow seolf, ne þe mix maumez þe beoð þes feondes fetles heien ne herien for teone ne for tintreohe þet ȝe me mahe timbrin." "Na? nult tu?" quoð Affrican. "Hit schal sone sutelin, for ich chulle sende þe nu ant biteache þi bodi to Eleusium þe riche, þet reue is ouer Rome, ant he schal þe forreaden ant makie to forswelten, as his ahne wil is, þurh al þet eauer sar is." (15)

> "By my life," said her father, "you shall forswear his [Christ's] love; for you will first be beaten so hard with bitter birches that you will be sorry you were ever born." The maiden said, "I am so much dearer to him that I would suffer crueler things for his love. Do as you please!" "By all means," he said, "Gladly!" And he very angrily ordered her to be stripped stark naked and beaten until her lovely body frothed with blood. She was seized and the blows poured down, and she began to cry, "Beat away, beat away, you lackeys of Belial. You can lessen neither my love for nor my belief in the living God, my dear lover, the precious lord; nor shall I take the advice you destroy yourselves with; nor shall I honor or worship the filthy idols that are the devil's vessels no matter what you do to me." "You won't, eh?" said Africanus. "We'll soon see, for I'll send you off and turn your body over to Eleusius the rich, Reeve of Rome, and he shall bring you to whatever wretched end he chooses."

Through such exchanges, the Middle English hagiographer portrays Juliana's metamorphosis from a pawn whose compliance is taken for granted ("ha wes him sone ihondsald, þah hit hire unwil were") to a woman with goals of her own and the determination to implement them.

Although the virgin martyr's struggle against male prerogative is most striking in *Seinte Iuliene*, all three Katherine Group legends portray the saints' conflicts as gender conflicts. For example, after Katherine has confounded the fifty wisest men in his realm, the emperor Maxentius heaps abuse on the scholars, charging that they should easily have been able to handle fifty such women:

> Is nu se st[o]rliche unstre[n]ge[t] ower strengðe, ant ower wit awealt swa, þet te mihte ant te mot of a se meoke meiden schal meistren ow alle? Me, ȝef fifti wimmen,

ant þah þer ma weren, hefden wið wordes ower an awarpen, nere hit schendlac inoh ant schir scheome to alle þet ʒelpeð of lare? Nu is alre scheomene meast, þet anlepi meiden wið hire anes muð haueð swa biteuel[e]t, itemet, ant iteiet alle—italde bi tale fif siðe tene, icudde ant icorene ant of feorrene ifat—þet al ʒe beoð blodles, bikimet, [ut] of ow seoluen. (*Seinte Katerine*, 66, 68)

Is your strength so weakened and your wit so enfeebled that the strength and argumentation of such a meek maiden shall overcome you all? Why, if fifty women—or more—had overcome you with words wouldn't it be shameful enough, pure shame, to all who boast of learning? Now it is the greatest shame of all, that a single maiden with her own mouth has so befuddled, tamed, and bound you all—all fifty of you, famous, elite, and brought from afar—so that you are all bloodless, stunned, and beside yourselves.

In both *Seinte Marherete* and *Seinte Iuliene*, the devils express shock and humiliation at being overcome by mere women. As Margaret's adversary laments, "ʒet were hit þurh a mon as is nu þurh a wummon—Þis ʒet þuncheð me wurst" (*Seinte Marherete*, 37) (If only it were through a man rather than through a woman—I consider this worst of all). The saints, too, contrast their "feminine weakness" with the supposed strength of their male adversaries, as, for example, when Katherine of Alexandria reproaches Maxentius for summoning fifty scholars to debate a maiden (*Seinte Katerine*, 40) or when Margaret taunts Olibrius because he cannot hold his own against a girl (*Seinte Marherete*, 18). In fact, the writer of *Seinte Marherete* explicitly presents his heroine's struggle as a woman's struggle on behalf of women when he has Margaret pray that her example would inspire other maidens (17).

The experiences of Katherine, Margaret, and Juliana reinforce the principal messages of another of the Katherine Group texts, *Hali Meiðhad*. The writer of that virginity treatise urges women to reject marriage, even if it means defying their families, while the legends of Juliana, Margaret, and Katherine provide examples of women who do exactly that.[55] *Hali Meiðhad* describes marriage as a form of martyrdom:

Hwen he bið ute, hauest aʒein his [ham]cume sar care ant eie. Hwil he bið at hame, alle þine wide wanes þuncheð þe to nearewe. His lokunge on ageasteð þe; his ladliche nurð ant his untohe bere makeð þe to agrisen. Chit te ant cheoweð þe ant scheomeliche schent te, tukeþ þe to bismere as huler his hore, beateð þe ant busteð þe as his ibohte þrel ant his eðele þeowe. Þine banes akeð þe ant ti flesch smeorteð þe, þin heorte wiðinne þe swelleð of sar grome, ant ti neb utewið tendreð ut of teone. (15)

---

[55] Although Katherine's persecution does not initially involve a courtship, Katherine eventually rejects Maxentius's offer of marriage and dies for her audacity.

When he is out, you anticipate his homecoming with sorrow and fear. While he is at home, you consider all your vast dwellings too confined. His gaze frightens you, his hateful clamor and his wanton din horrify you. He scolds you and reviles you and shamefully humiliates you; he mistreats you as a lecher does his whore; he beats you and whips you as his slave and his worthless servant. Your bones ache and your flesh smarts; your heart swells from anger, and your face reddens with sorrow.

The Katherine Group legends support this bleak view of married life, for the atrocities that the virgin martyrs endure at the hands of their suitors illustrate the violence men are willing to inflict on women—even women they claim to love. Whereas the martyrs earn crowns of glory, the battered wife has only bruises to show for her ordeal. Given the choice between Christ and a husband, between martyrdom and an earthly marriage, a woman's course is obvious. "Þench o Seinte Katerine," the writer of *Hali Meiðhad* exhorts his readers, "o Seinte Margarete, Seinte Enneis, Seinte Iuliene, [Seinte Lucie], ant Seinte Cecille, ant o þe oþre hali mei[d]nes in heouene, hu ha nawt ane ne forsoken kinges sunes ant eorles, wið alle worldliche weolen ant eorðliche wunnen" (23) (Think of St. Katherine, of St. Margaret, St. Agnes, St. Juliana, [St. Lucy], and St. Cecilia, and of the other holy maidens in heaven, how they not only forsook kings' sons and earls but all worldly joy and earthly happiness).

In *Early English Devotional Prose and the Female Audience*, Elizabeth Robertson argues that the Katherine Group writers' vivid descriptions of characters, settings, objects, and conflicts may have stunted women's spirituality by locating it so securely in the material world. Describing the assumptions underlying *Seinte Marherete*, Robertson writes, "A woman's essentially sensual nature requires that she come to understand God through the physical world, a requirement emphasized in this work through the use of concrete details that underscore the association of a woman's spirituality with her essential sensuality." [56] It seems to me, however, that the Katherine Group legends invite more radical— and, from a clerical perspective, more dangerous—interpretations than their Latin antecedents precisely because they are so preoccupied with the material world. The concreteness of the Middle English legends makes readers less ready to look for the theological significance of the saints' struggles and more likely to read the legends as stories with lessons for the here and now. Some women may have detected parallels between the fathers and magistrates who are vilified in the Katherine Group texts and their own spiritual fathers and governors, whose authority was justified by the same arguments that were used to sanction men's supremacy in the secular world.[57]

It seems remarkable that the presumably male writers of *Hali Meiðhad* and the

[56] Robertson, *Early English Devotional Prose*, 116.
[57] Newman discusses some of these arguments in "Flaws in the Golden Bowl."

Katherine Group should have risked undermining their authority by promoting texts that so vividly portray men as sadists and potential rapists. The heightened antagonism between men and women that characterizes these texts is perhaps best understood in the context of the changing attitudes toward women's religious vocations that Sharon K. Elkins describes in *Holy Women of Twelfth-Century England*.[58] During the initial expansion of women's religious life, Elkins explains, alliances between religious women and men had burgeoned. Nuns and even eremitic women maintained close friendships with canons, monks, hermits, and lay brothers, and these men supported—both spiritually and financially—efforts to augment the religious opportunities available for women. Some encouraged the foundation of priories or of new religious orders; some even accepted women in their own establishments. Between 1130 and 1165, monasteries willingly assumed the responsibility of supervising houses for women, and the large number of double houses for men and women attests to the extent to which women and men believed themselves part of a common endeavor. During the second half of the century, however, things began to change. In part, Elkins hypothesizes, this may have been because efforts to expand religious opportunities for women had been so successful. With some eighty-five new religious houses having been founded between 1130 and 1165, women no longer had to rely on ad hoc arrangements with men in order to fulfill their spiritual ambitions. Innovations were now looked upon with some dismay, and many clerics actively discouraged the associations that had flourished a generation earlier, while seeking to regulate existing forms of religious life. Support for women's religious houses diminished, monasteries grew reluctant to take charge of daughter houses, and the wisdom of double houses was contested.[59] Clerics also placed more restrictions on the activities of anchoresses. Whereas eremitic women of the late eleventh and early twelfth centuries, such as Eve of Wilton and Christina of Markyate, enjoyed warm friendships with men (Christina actually shared a hermit's cell), clerics of the later twelfth and early thirteenth centuries insisted on a rigid segregation of the sexes and strict enclosure for anchoresses.

From the mid–twelfth century onward, didactic writings reveal a pronounced suspicion of all associations between religious women and men. "Happy the recluse who is unwilling to see or speak with a man," Aelred of Rievaulx writes,

[58] Elkins, *Holy Women*, 105–64. These changing attitudes among English clergymen themselves form part of a broader European phenomenon, which Jo Ann McNamara surveys in "The *Herrenfrage*: The Restructuring of the Gender System, 1050–1115," in *Medieval Masculinities: Regarding Men in the Middle Ages*, ed. Clare A. Lees (Minneapolis: University of Minnesota Press, 1994), 3–29.

[59] Raymonde Foreville and Gillian Keir provide an edition and translation of letters pertaining to the controversy over the association of men and women in Gilbertine religious houses in *The Book of St. Gilbert* (Oxford: Clarendon, 1987), 134–67.

as he counsels his readers against becoming familiar with any man, even a priest, an abbot, or a prior (*Treatises,* 51–53). Echoing Aelred's opinion, the *Wisse* author warns that an anchoress should be wary of removing her veil for any man—even her confessor or the bishop.[60] Armed with the examples of Dinah and Bathsheba, he argues that a woman invites trouble if she allows herself to look at or to be seen by men.[61] To the skeptic who protests that she will not leap on a man merely because she looks at him, he replies:

> Godd wat, leoue suster, mare wunder ilomp. Eue þi moder leop efter hire ehnen: from þe ehe to þe eappel, from þe eappel iparais dun to þer eorðe, from þe eorðe to helle, þer ha lei i prisun fowr þusent ʒer & mare, heo & hire were ba & demde al hire ofsprung to leapen al efter hire to deað wið uten ende. Biginnunge & rote of al þis ilke reowðe wes aliht sihðe. Þus ofte as me seið of lutel muchel waxeð. (Tolkien, 32)

> God knows, my dear sister, more surprising things have happened. Your mother Eve leapt after her eyes had leaped; from the eye to the apple, from the apple in paradise down to the earth, and from earth to hell where she remained, in prison, four thousand years and more, together with her husband, and she condemned all her children to leap after her, to endless death. The beginning and root of all this misery was a light glance. Thus, as they say, much often comes of little. (Salu, 23).

Nowhere is the clergy's mistrust of heterosexual associations more fervidly expressed than in the circa 1166 account by Aelred of a scandal that had only a few years earlier convulsed the Gilbertine double monastery at Watton, Yorkshire.[62] That scandal, like so many of the tales of disaster rehearsed in the *Ancrene Wisse,* began with a glance, when a flighty young nun became smitten with a good-looking brother who was doing chores within the convent. One thing led to another, and the nun became pregnant. Furious at what they regarded as an insult to their collective honor, her sisters had the young man waylaid and beaten, then forced the offending nun to mutilate her lover, stuffing his severed genitals into her mouth. Though Aelred blenches at the savagery of the nuns' actions, he commends the "zeal" with which they avenged the assault on their virginity, and he deplores the difficulty of supervising the behavior of men and women who live in such proximity.

The chilling drama that was acted out at Watton is replayed in the virgin

---

[60] Salu, 27–28; Tolkien, 34.

[61] Salu, 23–25; Tolkien, 31–35.

[62] Aelred of Rievaulx, "De Sanctimonial: de Wattun," *Patrologia cursus completus: Series latina,* ed. J. P. Migne (Paris: Migne, 1861–64), vol. 195, cols. 789–96. For more detailed discussions of the incident, see Elkins, *Holy Women,* 106–11; and Giles Constable, "Aelred of Rievaulx and the Nun of Watton: An Episode in the Early History of the Gilbertine Order," in *Medieval Women,* ed. Derek Baker (Oxford: Basil Blackwell, 1978), 205–26.

martyr legends of the Katherine Group. In these texts, Aelred's tale of the public mutilation of a man by women avenging a perceived insult to their sex is recast with the genders reversed. Though the virgin martyrs are tortured for *not* having sex, the stories have a common message, namely, that relationships between men and women are disastrous. *Seinte Iuliene*'s initial portrayal of Eleusius as a courtly lover demonstrates that even the most attentive and well-spoken suitor can turn into a monster. *Seinte Marherete* and *Seinte Iuliene* further show how dangerous it is for a woman to venture out where she can even be seen by a man, for the persecution of both Margaret and Juliana begins with a glance.[63] *Seinte Marherete*, moreover, includes a lengthy section in which the devil boasts that he can corrupt even the most innocent relationship between a "cleane mon" and a "cleane wummon" (32). "Ich leote ham talkin of godd & teuelin of godlec" (32) (I let them talk about God and debate about goodness), the fiend gloats. Pious words establish trust, though, and trust engenders looks, laughter, and caresses. Soon the once devout couple is tangled in a ruinous embrace. Such examples might have encouraged anchoresses to avoid heterosexual friendships now regarded as dangerous and to restrict their contact with the outside world generally. By discouraging all other associations, however, the Middle English hagiographers solidified their own influence; the element of misandry in these legends may actually have cemented the "literary" relationship between male authors and their female readers.

Whether on the page or in the flesh, spiritual advisers were possessive of their female charges. As zealous guardians of holy women, religious men achieved an intimate relationship not only with their spiritual daughters but also with Christ, one based on a peculiar blend of identification and competition with the Savior. According to his biographer, Gilbert of Sempringham demanded that his new recruits sever all ties with their former lives and with the world at large so that, "oblivious of their families and homes," they "might cause the highest King to feel desire of their beauty."[64] After enclosing them in a cell adjoining the Church of St. Andrew in Sempringham, he taught them how to

---

[63] *Seinte Iuliene* reads, "As he hefde en-chere bihalden swiðe ȝeorne hire utnume feire ant freoliche ȝuheðe, felde him iwundet inwið in his heorte wið þe flan þe of luue fleoð, swa þet him þuhte þet ne mahte he nanes-weis wiðute þe lechnunge of hire luue libben" (5) (Once he beheld so eagerly her exceedingly fair and beautiful youth, he felt wounded in his heart with the arrows of love, so that he thought that he would in no way live without the medicine of her love); *Seinte Marherete* reads, "As he wende his wei, seh þis seli meiden Margarete, as ha wes & wiste up o þe feld hire fost[er]-modres schep, þe schimede & schan al of wlite & of westume" (6) (As he went on his way, he saw this innocent maiden Margaret, as she was tending her foster-mother's sheep, the shining and brightness of her face and form). This emphasis on the persecutor's gaze is distinctive to the Middle English legends. The Latin passio does not mention the first time Eleusius saw Juliana; the *Passio S. Margaretae* says only, "He saw the blessed Margaret tending her nurse's sheep, and he immediately desired her" (*Seinte Marherete*, 129).

64. *Book of St. Gilbert*, ed. Foreville and Keir, 35.

"please their heavenly bridegroom" so that they might "always remain in his chaste embrace." Thus removed "from the world's clamour and the sight of men," the women were "free in solitude for the embrace of the bridegroom alone."[65] Christ's possession of his brides was not exclusive, however, for Gilbert acted as a stand-in of sorts for the purportedly jealous bridegroom he served: "There was a door, but it was never unlocked except by his command, and it was not for the women to go out through but for him to go in to them when necessary. He himself was the keeper of this door and its key. For wherever he went and wherever he stayed, like an ardent and jealous lover he carried with him the key to that door as the seal of their purity."[66] As John Coakley has discussed, Jordan of Saxony similarly imagined himself in the role of Christ vis-à-vis Diana of Andalo: "He compared his own letters, in their effect on her, to the 'book of life' visible in Christ on the cross, and he compared the visits she received from him to those she received from Christ."[67] We should not suppose that such comparisons were mere pastoral fantasies, for from all indications, many holy women probably regarded their spiritual fathers as Christ surrogates. "Radically dependent" (as Coakley put it) on her mentor Siger of Lille, Margaret of Ypres (died 1237) developed such a passion for her spiritual father that, according to her biographer, Thomas de Cantimpré, "there was no one so beloved by her as not to weary her with even a little talk—excepting only her spiritual father [Siger] who had led her to salvation. His words she would hang upon, and her soul took in his conversation as a body takes in the food it lives by."[68]

The writer of literature for anchoresses may have aspired to an analogous position in his reader's heart. His book would be the constant companion of the holy woman who had resolutely severed all contact with the world. She would turn to it in her spare time—"Of þis boc redeð hwen ȝe beoð eise euche dei, leasse oðer mare" (Read something, much or little, of this book every day when you are free), the *Wisse* author urges his readers—and meditate on it constantly.[69] His stories of heroic virginity would shape her fantasies; his lessons would teach her to please her bridegroom; his words would fill the emptiness of her cell; his exhortations would be her weapons against the devil.

Yet writers—and the clergy generally—had reason to worry that books

---

[65] Ibid., 33.

[66] Ibid., 35.

[67] John Coakley, "Gender and the Authority of Friars: The Significance of Holy Women for Thirteenth-Century Franciscans and Dominicans," *Church History* 60 (1991): 452.

[68] Coakley, "Friars as Confidants of Holy Women in Medieval Dominican Hagiography," in *Images of Sainthood*, ed. Blumenfeld-Kosinski and Szell, 228, 226 (Coakley's translation of Thomas). Coakley discusses other equally passionate relationships between Continental holy women and their mentors in this essay and in "Gender and the Authority of Friars."

[69] Tolkien, 221; Salu, 192.

would not be the anchoress's most cherished companions and that matters other than pious meditations might occupy her mind. In theory, of course, an anchoress's life was severely circumscribed. Confined within her cell in a ceremony that involved the chanting of the Office of the Dead and, in certain cases, the symbolic sealing of her cell door, the anchoress's only authorized contact with the outside world was through a window. In practice, however, she had quite a bit of autonomy.[70] Some anchor-holds were comfortable—even spacious—dwellings, having servants' quarters, guest rooms, a courtyard, and even a garden. The door of the anchor-hold was only symbolically sealed; in fact, anchoresses could and sometimes did leave their cells, though such mobility was vehemently discouraged. Injunctions in guides such as the *Ancrene Wisse* against keeping pets, working, teaching, storing people's valuables, writing or copying letters, entertaining, and gossiping suggest that some anchoresses enjoyed a broad acquaintance and a varied experience.[71]

The clergy's fear that anchoresses might indulge in "inappropriate" behavior was exacerbated by the complex and ambiguous position that these women occupied within their communities. Stationed, as they were, at the crossroads between life and death, between the secular world and religious life, anchoresses had unique opportunities to transgress conventional boundaries of class, occupation, and gender.[72] The anchoress's vocation, which was held in exceptionally high esteem in thirteenth-century England, invested her with an authority that ordinary women did not have. By dispensing advice, she could influence local—and perhaps even national—events, for her clientele might range from humble parishioners to aristocrats. With the right patrons (or, at least, with *enough* of them), she could become a woman of means—a benefactor in her own right, whose generosity could earn her enough of a following among the less fortunate to alarm some members of the clergy.[73] Oddly enough, the eremitic life offered the potential for social advancement to women of humble origins. Well aware of that potential, the *Wisse* writer declares:

> Muchel hofles hit is cumen in to ancre hus, in to godes prisun, willes & waldes to stude of meoseise forte sechen eise þrin & meistrie & leafdischipe mare þen ha mahte habben inohreaðe ihaued i i þe worlde. (Tolkien, 57)

> It is very unreasonable to go into an anchorhouse, to go voluntarily and willingly into God's prison, into a place of discomfort, looking for ease, the power to rule, and the status of a lady beyond anything that she would probably have had in the world. (Salu, 46–47)

[70] Warren, *Anchorites,* 15–52.
[71] Tolkien, 210–21; Salu, 182–92. See also ibid., 106–12.
[72] On this point, see also Millett, "Women in No Man's Land."
[73] Warren, *Anchorites,* 42–43.

Concerns that anchoresses might acquire "excessive" influence within their communities or transgress conventional boundaries may have given rise to the frequent stereotypes of female recluses as flighty gossips and entrepreneurs. Indeed, Christina of Markyate's biographer suggests as much when he deplores the criticism leveled against his protagonist. Of unspecified members of "a depraved and perverse generation," he writes, "Some of them called her a dreamer, others a seducer of souls, others, more moderately, just a worldly-wise business woman: that is, what was a gift of God they attributed to earthly prudence" (*Christina of Markyate,* 173). It is perhaps no coincidence that this account of how Christina is persecuted with "gossip, poisonous detractions, [and] barbed words" comes immediately after a lengthy account of how the abbot of St. Albans consulted Christina before undertaking diplomatic missions to Rome "on business concerning himself and the realm" (173, 165).

The writer of the *Ancrene Wisse* seems especially conscious of how easily the anchoress could cross the threshold separating her from the "living"—that is, from the friends, craftspeople, traders, and housewives that bustle about her cell every day. Anxious to dissuade her from stepping over that threshold, he frequently reminds her of her proper identity and place within the community. Inveighing against anchoresses who leave their quarters to dine with visitors, he declares, "Me haueð iherd ofte þe deade speken wið cwike, ah þet ha eten wið cwike ne fond ich ȝet neauer" (One has often heard of the dead speaking with the living but I have never found that they ate with the living).[74] On several occasions, he admonishes his female reader that she is not a housewife ("nawt husewif") but rather "a chirch ancre" (Tolkien, 212). For that reason, she should not give alms, and she should own no animal larger than a cat. On the subject of livestock, he writes:

> Ancre þe haueð ahte þuncheð bet husewif. . . . for þenne mot ha þenchen of þe kues foddre, of heordemonne hure, olhnin þe heiward, wearien hwen he punt hire, & ȝelden þah þe hearmes. Ladlich þing is hit wat Crist hwen me makeð i tune man of ancre ahte. (Tolkien, 213)

> An anchoress who keeps animals looks more like a housewife. . . . for in such a case she has to think of the cow's fodder and the herdsman's wages, say nice things to the hayward, call him names when he impounds the cow, and yet pay damages nonetheless! It is odious, Christ knows, when there are complaints in a village about the anchoress's animals. (Salu, 185)

An anchoress should not behave like a gentlewoman, for "of ancre curteisie, of ancre largesce, is icumen ofte sunne ant scheome on ende" (courtly manners in

[74] Tolkien, 211; Salu, 183.

an anchoress, open-handedness in an anchoress, have often resulted in the end in sin and shame).[75] Nor should she go into business: "Ancre þet is chepilt, þet is, buð forte sullen efter biȝete, ha chepeð hire sawle þe chapmon of helle" (An anchoress who is a businesswoman, that is, one who buys with a view to selling at a profit, is selling her soul to the trader of hell).[76] She should certainly not aspire to be a scholar or to teach the priest whose duty it is to instruct her:

> Sum is se wel ilearet oðer se wis iwordet þet ha walde he wiste hit þe sit & spekeð toward hire & ȝelt him word aȝein word & forwurðeð meistre þe schulde beon ancre & leareð him þet is icumen hire forte learen, walde bi hire tale beon sone wið wise icuððet & icnawen. (Tolkien, 35)

> Some anchoresses are so learned or can talk with such wisdom that they would like their visitors to know it, and when a priest talks to them, they are always ready with a reply. In this way a woman who ought to be an anchoress sometimes sets up as a scholar, teaching those who have come to teach her, and wishes to be soon recognized and known among the wise. (Salu, 28)

An anchoress should not presume even to teach children, thus turning herself into a "scolmeistre" and her "ancre hus to childrene scole" (Tolkien, 216–17).

A generation earlier, Aelred had voiced similar concerns about the "freedom inherent in the solitary life."[77] Though bodily enclosed, the anchoress's mind "roams at random," while her tongue "runs all day through towns and villages, market-place and square."[78] In the passage cited earlier, Aelred's praise of St. Agnes for turning "a brothel into an oratory," may have been partly motivated by his fear of how easily an anchoress might turn her oratory into a brothel. "What was a cell has now become a brothel," he laments at the end of one salacious vignette.[79] As alarming to Aelred as the roving or the lascivious recluses are the holy entrepreneurs, who "shun every hint of impropriety" but "are yet so eager to make money or to increase the size of their flocks . . . that they could well be mistaken for châtelaines rather than anchoresses": "Finding pasture for their flocks and shepherds to tend them; demanding a statement of the numbers, weight and value of the flock's yearly produce; following the fluctuations of the market. Their money attracts money, it accumulates and gives them a thirst for wealth."[80] The enterprising anchoress disturbs Aelred

---

[75] Tolkien, 212; Salu, 184.

[76] Tolkien, 213; Salu, 185.

[77] Aelred of Rievaulx, *Treatises*, 45. For an extended discussion of Aelred's ambivalence toward his female readers, see Anne Clark Bartlett, *Male Authors, Female Readers: Representation and Subjectivity in Middle English Devotional Literature* (Ithaca: Cornell University Press, 1995), 34–55.

[78] Aelred of Rievaulx, *Treatises*, 46.

[79] Ibid., 47.

[80] Ibid.

not because she might indulge herself but because she might give her earn-
ings to others, thus enhancing her stature within the community. Aelred recoils
at the thought of the anchoress's cell "besieged by beggars . . . orphans and
widows crying for alms." He urges her to shun the "little old woman, perhaps,
mixed in with the poor, who brings her a pious token from some priest or
monk, whispering flattering words in her ear and . . . [kissing] her hand." [81]

The potential freedom that disturbs Aelred and the writer of the *Ancrene
Wisse* may have motivated some women to become anchoresses, especially
given the sharp curtailment of women's rights and liberties after the Conquest
in England. [82] Not all anchoresses, however, found either spiritual or material
satisfaction in their vocations. Some were lonely and disillusioned, their initial
enthusiasm worn down by the monotony of their daily routines, their financial
support dissipated as the interest of benefactors waned. [83] These women posed
special problems for clergymen charged with supervising the conduct of women
in religious life. Through rigorous investigations undertaken prior to enclosure, bishops tried to weed out applicants who were not psychologically suited
to endure decades of confinement or who lacked reliable financial support. [84]
Writers, for their part, sought to address the needs of dissatisfied or impover-
ished anchoresses whose plights were not anticipated in pre-enclosure investigations. The author of the *Ancrene Wisse*, for example, expects that his readership might include not only the three well-born sisters who form his immediate
audience but also those who are "ful ofte i derued mid wone & mid scheome . . .
& mid teone" (often afflicted with want, indignity, and vexation). If his work
comes into their hands, he hopes that "hit mei beon ham uroure" (it may be of
comfort to them). [85] Elsewhere he exhorts the anchoress to endure deprivation
without complaint, as if she were a martyr: "Ah ear þen þet biddunge areare
eani scandle, ear deie martir in hire meoseise" (But rather than that her asking
should cause any scandal, let her die like a martyr in her suffering). [86] The writers of the Katherine Group legends probably anticipated a similar audience,
composed both of zealous holy women and malcontents. Their dramatic accounts of feminine heroism may have been partially intended to boost the spirits of women whose disenchantment, if allowed to fester, might prove embar-
rassing, leading them to relax their habits or even to petition for a release from

[81] Ibid., 48.

[82] Robertson, *Early English Devotional Prose*, 13–31.

[83] Warren, *Anchorites*, 43–44, 123–24.

[84] On these procedures, see ibid., 53–91.

[85] This quotation is taken from MS Cotton Nero A.14, British Library. *The English Text of
the "Ancrene Riwle,"* ed. Mabel Day, EETS.OS 225 (London: Oxford University Press, 1952), 85;
Salu, 84.

[86] Tolkien, 57; Salu, 46.

their vocation.[87] By identifying with a St. Juliana or a St. Margaret, an anchoress could experience the autonomy that she did not actually have—and she might be dissuaded from exercising the choices she did have.

Encouraging anchoresses to identify with heroic female saints might backfire, however, for the martyrs' actions could easily inspire behavior that the early-thirteenth-century clergy vehemently discouraged.[88] Teaching, for example, figures prominently in *Seinte Katerine*, both in the saint's debate with the hundred philosophers and—perhaps even more suggestively—in her instruction of the emperor's wife and his best friend from within her prison cell. Moreover, as I mentioned earlier, women imagining themselves in the roles of the virgin martyrs might see their advisers not as stand-ins for Christ but as reincarnations of jealous fathers and suitors. Thus it is hardly surprising that we find a certain ambivalence toward feminine heroics within the legends. Lengthy prayers preserved from the Latin *passiones* remind readers that the saints are ultimately frail women who rely on God for both their physical and their spiritual preservation. Even the vituperative Juliana confesses, "Nam ich strong of na þing buten of þi strengðe, ant o þe i truste al, ant nawt o me seoluen" (25) (I am not strong except through your strength, and I trust you entirely, not myself). To these conventional admissions of weakness, the Middle English hagiographers frequently added their own references to the saint's vulnerability. For example, the writer of *Seinte Katerine* has his protagonist pause before confronting Maxentius to consider the magnitude of her task: "Þohte þah, as ha wes þuldi ant þolemod: se ʒung þing as ha wes, hwet hit mahte geinin þah heo hire ane were aʒein se kene keiser ant al his kineriche" (10) (She considered, though, since she was patient and thoughtful: as young as she was, what might she accomplish alone against the bold emperor and all his kingdom?). Scenes exalting the saint's triumph are often accompanied by comments qualifying her achievement. While Juliana thrashes the devil who attempts to deceive her, readers are reminded that God's strength resides in women who are meek, "as maidens ought to be" ("ʒef ha milde ant meoke beon as meiden deh to beonne" [*Seinte Iuliene*, 45]). When Margaret scores a similar victory, the devil observes that she is no ordinary woman ("Ne nawt nart tu, wummon, oþre wummen ilich" [*Seinte Marherete*, 30]). Likewise, when Maxentius, in the

---

[87] As an example of such concerns, Warren cites Bishop Richard Swinfield of Hereford's 1315 approval of an anchoress's enclosure "provided however that concerning those things which will be necessary such as food and clothes will be adequately provided for her by her friends, lest, because they are lacking, because of a lack of nourishment, she will be forced to retreat from her laudable way of life and go out, contrary to her vow, to the peril of her soul and the scandal of many" (*Anchorites*, 43–44).

[88] For a general discussion of the complex negotiations between male writers and female readers, see Bartlett, *Male Authors, Female Readers*.

passage quoted earlier, berates his philosophers for being bested by a mere woman, one of his scholars protests, "Ah nis nawt lihtliche [te leoten] of þis meidenes mot, for, ʒef ich soð schal seggen, in hire ne moteð na mon; for nawt nis hit monlich mot þet ha mealeð, ne nawt nis heo þet haueð us a[t]ome[t], ah is an heouenlich gast in hire swa aʒein us þet we ne cunnen . . . warpen" (*Seinte Katerine,* 68, 70) (But you should not belittle this maiden's arguments, for, if I speak truly, no human speaks in her, for it is not human argument that she speaks, nor is it she who has subdued us, but it is a heavenly spirit within her against whom we cannot prevail). Such apparent contradictions are not confined to the virgin martyr legends of the Katherine Group. *Hali Meiðhad,* the most radical of the five Katherine Group texts, exhorts female readers to reject the roles assigned to them in secular society but concludes by insisting that a woman's greatest virtue is meekness and that "meiðhad wiðuten hit is eðelich ant unwurð" (22) (virginity without it is worthless and of little value).

Legends for the Laity?

The tensions within the Katherine Group legends are even more marked when we consider the broader audience that the Middle English hagiographers anticipated for their legends.[89] That audience is suggested when the writer of *Seinte Iuliene* directs his work to a general audience of "alle leawede men" (3) or when the writer of *Seinte Marherete* speaks to "widewen wið þa iweddede" (4).[90] These references, among other things, have led Bella Millett to argue that the Margaret and Juliana legends, at least, were originally written to be recited in church to a lay congregation and that religious women formed a secondary audience.[91] As further evidence that the Middle English hagiographers were targeting a lay audience, Millett cites references to listeners within the legends, and she contends that the narratives' style seems "designed to please the ear and make comprehension easier for a listening audience."[92]

Though I share Millett's view that the Katherine Group legends were "written with more than a single group of users in mind,"[93] I do not find her claim that the legends were intended *primarily* for a lay audience convincing. The

[89] The most comprehensive discussion of the legends' possible lay audience is Millett, "Audience."

[90] I should point out that the reference to widows and married people is in some versions of Margaret's passio; however, the liberties that the Middle English hagiographer takes with his original throughout his narration suggest that he would have omitted the reference had he deemed it irrelevant.

[91] Millett, "Audience," 147–48.

[92] Ibid., 134.

[93] Ibid., 142.

isolated references to a general audience in *Seinte Marherete* and *Seinte Iuliene* are insufficient evidence for such a claim, nor can we read too much into addresses to listeners, which were a common *topos* in vernacular literature of the period. The stylistic indications of oral delivery are also inconclusive, because the legends of the Katherine Group grew out of a tradition of hagiography that was created to be read aloud—during the Divine Office, at mealtimes, or when the monks or nuns were engaged in manual labor. Moreover, even when saints' lives were read privately during the early and high Middle Ages, they were recited.[94] We would thus expect Middle English hagiographers composing for anchoresses to preserve and augment the qualities that made their sources pleasing to hear. The manuscripts containing the Katherine Group legends, moreover, do not appear to have been produced for lay readers or for their pastors. It seems most likely that the hagiographers wrote primarily for anchoresses, while anticipating a secondary audience of laypeople.

Of the two legends that actually refer to a lay public, *Seinte Iuliene* develops themes that would have been most immediately relevant to laypeople. Gayle Margherita has persuasively argued that the hagiographer's association of the saint's persecutor with French culture was designed to engage the political sympathies of an Anglo-Saxon aristocracy that had been disenfranchised by the Norman ruling elite.[95] *Seinte Iuliene*'s treatment of family conflict would also have absorbed the attention of a lay audience, though the message of that conflict is problematic. As I observed earlier, Juliana's quarrel with her father centers not so much on religion as on status, influence, property, and a woman's freedom to choose her mate—all key factors in thirteenth-century marriage brokering. The issue of choice in marriage, as Jocelyn Wogan-Browne has pointed out, was especially topical at the time *Seinte Iuliene* was written.[96] For well over a century, the Church had been working to establish its jurisdiction over the institution of marriage by dictating the criteria of a binding union.[97] Pope Alexander III (1159–81) had declared the consent of the prospective bride

---

[94] Leclercq, *Love of Learning*, 72–73. Paul Saenger has pointed out that silent reading was not "pervasive" until the fourteenth and fifteenth centuries, in "Silent Reading: Its Impact on Late Medieval Script and Society," *Viator* 13 (1982): 367–414. The author of the *Ancrene Wisse* specifically distinguishes prayers that are to be said silently from the bulk of devotions he recommends to his readers (Tolkien, 19; Salu, 19).

[95] Gayle Margherita, "Body and Metaphor: The Middle English *Juliana*," in *The Romance of Origins: Language and Sexual Difference in Middle English Literature* (Philadelphia: University of Pennsylvania Press, 1994), 43–61.

[96] Wogan-Browne, "Saints' Lives and the Female Reader," esp. 315–23.

[97] Discussions of this process include James A. Brundage, *Law, Sex, and Christian Society in Medieval Europe* (Chicago: University of Chicago Press, 1987), and John T. Noonan, Jr., "Power to Choose," *Viator* 4 (1973): 419–34.

and groom essential. What is more, the Church asserted that a man and a woman could contract a binding marriage simply by exchanging vows — even if those vows were unwitnessed and even if their families disapproved.

The Church's emphasis on consent by no means ended arranged marriages. There were, of course, ways of obtaining consent, and some thirteenth-century parents would not have considered Africanus's methods — threats, cajolery, beating — unreasonable. Christina of Markyate's parents used similar means of persuasion. On one occasion, Christina's mother "took her out from a banquet and . . . pulled her hair out and beat her until she was weary of it. Then she brought her back, lacerated as she was, into the presence of the revellers as an object of derision, leaving on her back such weals from the blows as could never be removed as long as she lived" (*Christina of Markyate,* 75). Such harsh measures are also attested in records of late medieval marriage litigation; these documents cite evidence of parents whipping their daughters and of fathers or suitors threatening to throttle an unwilling bride or to break her neck.[98]

Juliana, for her part, behaves much as a thirteenth-century daughter might. Engaged to a man she wants nothing to do with, she uses her wits to buy time (*Seinte Iuliene,* 7). When conflict becomes inevitable, she announces that she cannot marry Eleusius because she already has a husband: Christ. Speaking very deliberately, she tells her father, "Ich chulle þet he wite hit ful wel, ant tu eke mid al, ich am to an iweddet þet ich chulle treowliche to halden ant wiðute leas luuien" (13) (I want him [Eleusius] to know plainly — and you too — that I am married to one to whom I shall be faithful and love truly). By literalizing the *sponsa Christi* metaphor, the Middle English hagiographer creates a heroine who would have disturbed, irritated, and perhaps even alienated many people in a lay audience, parents especially.[99] Juliana is not only vetoing her father's se-lection of a husband but also asserting her right to choose a mate. Her father's response — "Hwet is he, þes were þet tu art to iweddet, þet tu hauest wiðute me se forð þi luue ilenet?" (13) (Who is this man you've married, whom you've presumed to love without [consulting] me?) — might have been uttered by any Herefordshire gentleman under similar circumstances.

Wogan-Browne has proposed that *Seinte Iuliene* conveys a radical social message to early-thirteenth-century women: "Defy authority if it elides you, do not be accommodating and other-determined, do not be socialised only as

---

[98] R. H. Helmholz, *Marriage Litigation in Medieval England* (Cambridge: Cambridge University Press, 1974), 90.

[99] Christina of Markyate also used the *sponsa Christi* motif in a surprisingly literal and legal-istic sense, as Thomas Head shows in "The Marriages of Christina of Markyate," *Viator* 21 (1990): 75–101.

object of desire and never subject: you do not have to marry, and there is a legitimate career of consecrated virginity available to you with its own emotional and ethical satisfactions."[100] But why would a hagiographer writing with a lay audience in mind produce a text that could impart such an extreme message? After all, there is no other evidence that the thirteenth-century English Church had any intention of radicalizing the daughters of the gentry. Though the Church upheld the crucial role of consent in marriage contracts, it deplored clandestine marriages, and in practice, clergymen often sided with parents trying to control their wayward children.[101] Summarizing the views of late medieval writers on canon law, R. H. Helmholz writes: "The headstrong girl marrying for love alone, against the desires of her family, did not win the approval of the canonists for upholding the ideal of free consent in marriage. She was within her rights, and she should incur no penalty or punishment, but she was acting against a legitimate authority."[102] Far from inciting young women to flee the embraces of suitors for the arms of Christ, clergymen of the early thirteenth century were propounding the dignity and value of marriage.[103] This stance, as Dyan Elliott has argued, was part of the clergy's larger strategy of self-

[100] Wogan-Browne, "Saints' Lives and the Female Reader," 323. Wogan-Browne similarly interprets the Katherine Group legends as showing a woman "how tough she will have to be if she wants to become a career virgin," in "The Virgin's Tale," in *Feminist Readings in Middle English Literature: The Wife of Bath and All Her Sect*, ed. Ruth Evans and Lesley Johnson (London: Routledge, 1994), 172–80 (quote on 180).

[101] See, for example, the discussion between Christina of Markyate, her parents, and the prior Fredebert concerning Christina's marriage with Burthred. Christina's parents admit that they "forced her against her will into this marriage," but they ask the prior to take their part: "If she resists our authority and rejects it, we shall be the laughing-stock of our neighbors. . . . Wherefore, I beseech you, plead with her to have pity on us" (*Christina of Markyate*, 59). In his subsequent interview with Christina, Fredebert establishes his *right* to overrule her parents, on the grounds that "the bond of marriage is so much more important than the authority of parents" (61). He then insists that because her parents are only ordering her to do what is right, she must obey them. Three centuries later, a very similar scenario follows Margery Paston's clandestine marriage with Richard Calle. Upon hearing that the Pastons have sequestered Margery and are attempting to bully her into denying the marriage, the bishop insists on questioning Margery and making a ruling. But when Margery is duly brought before him, he urges her to follow her parents' wishes. As Margaret Paston reports to her son John Paston II in a 1469 letter, "Þe Bysschop seyd to here ryth pleynly, and put here in rememberawns how sche was born, wat kyn and frenddys þat sche had, and xuld haue mo yf sche were rulyd and gydyd aftyre them; and yf sche ded not, wat rebuke and schame and los yt xuld be to here yf sche were not gydyd be them." *Paston Letters and Papers of the Fifteenth Century*, 2 vols., ed. Norman Davis (Oxford: Clarendon, 1971), 1:342. Clearly English prelates were more concerned with establishing their authority to overrule parents in disputes involving matrimony than with actually exercising that authority.

[102] Helmholz, *Marriage Litigation in Medieval England*, 91.

[103] For a comprehensive discussion of the Church's attitudes toward marriage and lay celibacy, see Dyan Elliott, *Spiritual Marriage: Sexual Abstinence in Medieval Wedlock* (Princeton: Princeton University Press, 1993).

promotion, for "from the standpoint of societal structure, a clerical celibate elite requires a copulating laity." [104] Laywomen who spurned marriage or who evaded the "conjugal debt" were transgressing on the holy ground reserved for the celibate clergy. Juliana's behavior is especially subversive, for in repudiating a marriage contract she entered into, albeit unwillingly, she is doing exactly what made Christina of Markyate so disturbing to many religious men. When the hermit Roger—a man of unimpeachable piety—was first asked to shelter the runaway Christina, he replied "angrily" with "glaring eyes": "Have you come here to show me how to dissolve marriages? Get out of here quickly and think yourself lucky if you get away safe and sound: you deserve a whipping" (*Christina of Markyate*, 83).

Of course, "the Church" did not write *Seinte Iuliene*. The narrative could have been composed by a liberal clergyman, like Christina's mentor Sueno, who did not mind stirring up trouble in the process of brokering marriages for Christ. Alternatively, the writer may have assumed that laypeople would take Juliana as a model of faith, disregarding those portions of her story that were obviously unsuitable for imitation.[105] The introduction to *Seinte Marherete* provides a telling indication of how the hagiographer may have regarded the laity as a potential public. After exhorting the members of his audience—married people, widows, and virgins—to pay attention, he explains at length how Margaret's story should inspire virgins, but he says nothing of what the saint's passion means for the "widewen wið þa iweddede." Though the legend is *addressed* to everybody, its message is clearly for "meidnes nomeliche" (4) (virgins especially). If, as the *Seinte Marherete* writer's remarks suggest, hagiographers were only casually aware of their possible lay audience, the writer of *Seinte Iuliene* may have considered only that "alle leawede men" would benefit from knowing more about the saint, without giving much thought to how they might act on his tale of filial defiance.

Seinte Marherete also raises the sensitive issue of marital choice, and its treatment of that issue recalls *Seinte Iuliene* in certain respects. Margaret chose ("ches") Christ as her lover ("to luue & to lefmon" [4]), and she cements the union in terms that literalize the traditional *sponsa Christi* metaphor. The hagiographer explains that, upon pledging herself to Christ, Margaret "bitahte in his hond þe meske of hire meiðhad, hire wil & hire werc, & al þet heo eauer i þe world i wald hahte, to witen & to welden wið al hire seoluen" (4; emphasis

---

[104] Ibid., 141.

[105] Elliott has proposed that the clergy produced a related genre of hagiography, exempla of chaste marriages, with an equally conservative expectation, namely, "that the hierarchy of merit (i.e., chastity over marriage) would be reinforced, and nothing more" (ibid., 177).

mine) (put into his hands the honor of her virginity, her will and her deeds, *and all the livestock in her possession* to keep and manage, along with herself.[106] She later rejects Olibrius on the grounds that she has already given her love and faith to another (8, 10).

What distinguishes *Seinte Marherete* from *Seinte Iuliene* is that Margaret's actions do not challenge parental authority. Indeed, the Middle English hagiographer omits indications that Margaret's faith antagonizes her father, Theodosius: the passio on which he draws points out that Theodosius placed all his hope in his only child and that he eventually grew to hate her.[107] The Middle English hagiographer preserves only one oblique reference to animosity between father and daughter. That reference occurs in the course of a long prayer, in which the beleaguered Margaret begs God to act as her father, for "min ahne flesliche feader dude & draf me awei, his an-lepi dohter" (18) (my own fleshly father drove me away, his only child). Incorporated into a lengthy request for divine aid, Margaret's allusion to her father's hostility demonstrates her dependence on God without suggesting that she has done anything to incur a father's wrath. Unlike *Seinte Iuliene*, which initially portrays Eleusius as a debonair suitor, *Seinte Marherete* immediately demonizes the wealthy "schireue," representing him quite literally as the suitor from Hell ("þe ueondes an foster" [6]). A medieval parent would have to be greedy indeed to be disturbed by Margaret's rejection of such a lover.

While the Middle English hagiographer omits traditional allusions to the hostility between Margaret and her father, he preserves—and sometimes embellishes—references to her close relationship with her foster-mother, portraying the saint as a beloved and obedient daughter to the woman who raised her. He comments, for example, on how dearly Margaret's foster-mother loves her (4) and emphasizes how the foster-mother tends Margaret in prison (20).[108] Though Margaret's father rejected her, the saint's body was ultimately restored to her family in Antioch and interred "i graue-stan in hire grandame

---

[106] Interestingly, MS Royal 17 A.XXVII omits the phrase that would have made Margaret's commitment to Christ sound most like an actual marriage contract, namely, "hire wil & hire werc, & al þet heo eauer i þe world i wald hahte" (*Seinte Marherete,* 4).

[107] The Latin hagiographer says that Margaret's father "had one child born of him, in whom he placed his hope"; shortly afterward, he writes that Margaret "was hated by her father and she was loved by the Lord Jesus Christ" (Hic habebat unam filiam de se natam, in quam spem suam ponebat. . . . Odiosa erat suo patri, et dilecta erat Domino Iesu Christo [*Seinte Marherete,* 128]).

[108] The Middle English hagiographer's account of how Margaret's nurse succors her, which I quoted earlier, expands the passio's terse comment that "Theotimus [Margaret's future biographer] . . . was in prison as was her nurse, giving her bread and water" (Theotimus autem erat in carcere et nutrix eius, ministrantes ei panem et aquam [133]). The Middle English hagiographer, in fact, spotlights Margaret's foster-mother by removing the reference to Theotimus.

hus, þe wes icleopet Clete" (52) (in a tomb in the house of her grandmother, Clete).

Intentionally or not, the writer of *Seinte Marherete* produced a legend that would reinforce a professional virgin's pride in her vocation without undermining family values. He emphasized that Margaret chooses her husband but dissociated the issue of choice from that of parental authority. He lauded virginity without denigrating motherhood. In fact, Margaret's dying request to become the patron saint of women in childbirth shows that the virgin martyr has no scorn for "þa iweddede" (4). The thirteenth-century mother could thus take comfort in the saint's appreciation of her vocation, while the anchoress who spent long hours contemplating *Hali Meiðhad* might detect in Margaret's prayer a certain pity for her less fortunate fellow martyrs.

When we consider the Katherine Group legends' possible lay audience, we are left with perplexing questions. With their eminently "human" heroines, did these legends inspire young women to dream of becoming Brides of Christ? Did they encourage others of a less religious inclination to choose their own spouses or to refuse the mates chosen for them? It would be tempting to speculate that thirteenth-century daughters (and perhaps even sons) interpreted *Seinte Iuliene* and *Seinte Marherete* in ways that were just as radical as was Christina of Markyate's reading of the Cecilia legend. One might further speculate that socially disruptive readings prompted a subsequent generation of hagiographers to change their representation of the saints. Such a colorful sequence of events is improbable, though; regardless of their intended public, few people other than religious women appear to have read the legends. It is not improbable, however, that as this next generation of hagiographers addressed themselves to an increasingly lay audience, they began to worry about the examples that rebel saints might set for the laity. As I will discuss in the next chapter, late-thirteenth-century hagiographers began systematically blocking those avenues of identification that might have made it easy for a devout Huntingdon teenager to imagine herself as St. Cecilia's spiritual sister.

2

Unruly Virgins and the Laity, 1250–1400

The sweeping program of lay religious instruction instituted by the Fourth Lateran Council in 1215 resulted in a proliferation of religious literature directed specifically at laypeople. In addition to spurring the production of a wide range of didactic works—penitential manuals, instructions for parish priests, treatises on the vices and virtues—the Church's commitment to lay education promoted the development of portable collections of saints' lives and, with them, new varieties of sacred biography.[1] The lavish and often massive legendaries that had for centuries been produced in monasteries were obviously unsuitable for preachers and parish priests. If pastors were to have ready access to information about the saints, a different method of assembling and imparting that information had to be devised.

To this end, the Dominican friar Jean de Mailly produced a new kind of legendary in about 1245.[2] The introduction to his work, the *Abbreviatio in gestis et miraculis sanctorum*, provides a clear statement of his motivations and methods: "Since many pastors do not have access to the passions and lives of the saints that they must know and preach in order to carry out their charge of exciting the devotion of the faithful toward the blessed, we will assemble these lives in an abridged form, especially those of the saints whose names appear in the calendar. The brevity of this little work will not risk engendering boredom, and a lack of books will no longer excuse these pastors."[3] Other clerics, with similar motives, followed Jean de Mailly in compiling collections of saints' lives in abridged forms.[4] The most successful of these *abbreviationes* or *legendae no-*

---

[1] W. A. Pantin provides an overview of the religious literature written in England for both clerical and lay readers in *The English Church in the Fourteenth Century* (1955; reprint, Toronto: University of Toronto Press, 1980), 189–243. See also M. Dominica Legge, *Anglo-Norman Literature and Its Background* (Oxford: Clarendon, 1963), 208–42.

[2] The most comprehensive discussion of Jean's achievement is Antoine Dondaine's "Le dominicain français Jean de Mailly et la *Légende dorée*," *Archives d'histoire dominicaine* 1 (1946): 53–102.

[3] Because Jean's *Abbreviatio* has not been edited, in preparing my own translation, I have used Antoine Dondaine's French translation, *Abrégé des gestes et miracles des saints* (Paris: Cerf, 1947), 23.

[4] Guy Philippart surveys these collections in *Les légendiers latins et autres manuscrits hagiographiques* (Turnhout, Belgium, 1977), 45–48.

vae was Jacobus de Voragine's *Legenda aurea*, written during the second half of the thirteenth century. The clergy's concern with lay religious instruction also stimulated the translation of saints' legends. Indeed, at roughly the same time that Jean de Mailly and Jacobus de Voragine were completing their abbreviationes in Latin, translators were beginning to adapt saints' lives and to assemble vernacular legendaries. In thirteenth- and fourteenth-century England, their efforts resulted in two large collections—the *South English Legendary* and the *North English Legendary*—as well as numerous freestanding narratives.[5] By the end of the fourteenth century, lay writers, too, were retelling saints' lives. Curiously enough, the only two saints' legends that are known to be written by laymen are virgin martyr legends: Geoffrey Chaucer's Cecilia legend and William Paris's legend of Christine.

We might expect that the widespread production of abbreviationes and vernacular adaptations simply made traditional models of sainthood more readily accessible to the general public. Yet when we compare these texts with the traditional passiones from which they derived, we find that this was not the case. In condensing elaborate Latin passiones, hagiographers formulated a different paradigm of sainthood. Whereas earlier writers emphasized the virgin's devotion, later adapters in the thirteenth and fourteenth centuries celebrated the exploits of a charismatic heroine who defies society and humiliates her adversary. Writers of the unabridged passiones represented the virgin martyr as a humble supplicant, as one of the faithful, but later writers accentuated the differences between the saint and ordinary people, presenting her as a powerful intermediary with God, to be admired rather than imitated. In fact, many later hagiographers portrayed her as a fractious virago presiding over a world turned upside down.

The representation of virgin martyrs as powerful, often disorderly women may be seen in a variety of late medieval sources, including Jacobus de Voragine's widely circulated *Legenda aurea*, which was a model for many English hagiographers; the two major collections of Middle English legends, the *South English Legendary* and the *North English Legendary*; the legends of the two known lay hagiographers, Chaucer and Paris; and renditions of virgin martyrs and their legends in the visual arts. These saints were so popular because they lent themselves to diverse interpretations and uses—many of which were not intended by their creators. The clerical writers who were largely responsible for producing and disseminating virgin martyr legends probably meant the saints, as Brides of Christ, to represent the authority and power of the institutional Bride of Christ, the Church. Yet the narratives could also be read in ways which subverted the authority of the clergy over the laity and which challenged other

---

[5] For a summary of this material, see Charlotte D'Evelyn, "Saints' Legends," in *A Manual of the Writings in Middle English, 1050–1500*, vol. 2 (Hamden, Conn.: Archon, 1970), 413–39, 556–635 (catalogue).

traditional relationships of dominion and subordination—for example, the authority of husbands over wives or of masters over servants. The virgin martyr legends told in late-thirteenth- and fourteenth-century England, which simultaneously celebrate and punish the saints' unruliness, register both the anxieties and the fantasies that were rife in a society undergoing rapid and profound social and economic change. They formed, indeed, part of the environment that produced this change.

Jacobus de Voragine and the *Legenda aurea*

Some of the earliest and most striking examples of unruly female saints in late medieval hagiography occur in the *Legenda aurea* of Jacobus de Voragine. Jacobus's methods for condensing the earlier and longer virgin martyr legends of monastic legendaries are fairly straightforward: he relates the basic events of the martyrdom but reduces or omits the prayers, doctrinal exposition, and teachings that had accompanied and explained those events.[6] Though he prefaces most of his legends with an etymological analysis of the virtues implicit in the saint's name, the narratives themselves are brisk accounts of ultimatums, tortures, and miracles. The virgin's repeated refusals to marry or sacrifice to the gods dominate the dialogue, shifting the orientation of Jacobus's abridgments from the saint's affirmation of faith to her rejection of the world.

Unlike the heroines of the traditional *passiones*, Jacobus's saints show few traces of weakness. His virgin martyrs never call themselves sinners, nor do they flinch before horrifying ordeals. In contrast to the behavior described in the *passiones*, Jacobus's Margaret does not tremble at the sight of a dragon in her prison cell, and his Justina does not hesitate before stepping into a cauldron of boiling pitch. Gone from Jacobus's legends are the many assurances that God understands human frailty. Instead of coaxing unbelievers into the fold with promises of Christ's love, his heroines decry error and dazzle wrongdoers with miracles.

In all his virgin martyr legends, Jacobus displays more interest in affirming the saint's authority than in celebrating God's power. In fact, God's overt presence is notably reduced in the *Legenda aurea*. The following passage from the legend of Christine, for example, describes a succession of miracles, including a resurrection, without once mentioning God:

> Julianus . . . had a furnace stoked and fired, and ordered Christina to be thrown into it. There for five days she walked about, singing with angels, and was un-

---

[6] All quotations and page references given in the text are from Jacobus de Voragine, *The Golden Legend: Readings on the Saints*, 2 vols., trans. William Granger Ryan (Princeton: Princeton University Press, 1993).

harmed. Being informed of this, Julianus ascribed it to magical arts, and had two asps, two vipers, and two cobras put in with her; but the vipers licked her feet, the asps clung to her breasts without hurting her, and the cobras wrapped themselves around her neck and licked her sweat. Julian called to the court conjurer: "You're a magician too, aren't you? Stir those beasts up!" The conjurer did as ordered, and the serpents came at him and killed him in a thrice. Then Christina commanded the reptiles to hie themselves to a place in the desert, and brought the dead man back to life. Next, Julianus had Christina's breasts cut off, and milk flowed from them instead of blood. Lastly, he had her tongue cut out, but she, never losing the power of speech, took the severed tongue and threw it in Julianus's face, hitting him in the eye and blinding him. (1:387)

The only allusions to heaven are the angels who keep Christine company in the furnace. Accounts, such as this one, that relate miracles with little or no reference to God make Jacobus's saints seem bolder and more autonomous than most of the protagonists of earlier Latin legends.

More concerned with the saint's efficacy than with her faith, Jacobus dramatizes those incidents that show how easily a "tender maiden" overcomes her formidable adversaries. His preoccupation with the saint's victories is especially obvious in his retelling of the Justina legend. Whereas the unabridged *Passio S. Justinae* consists of a long sequence of episodes celebrating the saint's devotion and showing how her faith leads to the growth of the Christian community as a whole, Jacobus focuses on a single event: the magician Cyprian's unsuccessful attempt to seduce the virgin.[7] In his adaptation, he tells how Cyprian employs the aid of ever more powerful devils to bring Justina to his bed. Each demon boasts that the task is trivial: "I was able to throw man out of paradise; I induced Cain to kill his brother; I caused the Jews to put Christ to death; I have brought every kind of disorder among men! How could I not be able to let you have one mere girl and do what you please with her?" (2:193). Armed with the sign of the cross, however, the saint foils all their stratagems, and Cyprian exclaims in disgust, "What kind of power do you have, you wretch, that you can't overcome a simple girl or have any control over her?" (2:194). When the prince of devils is finally forced to admit that Justina's God is greater than all the demons in Hell put together, Cyprian converts to Christianity.

Although the incidents Jacobus describes also occur in the passio, his emphasis is different. The passio's version of Cyprian's assault on Justina centers on the virgin's faith, relating her long supplications after each temptation and only briefly summarizing Cyprian's repeated interviews with the demons. Jacobus, by contrast, focuses on the lively dialogues and futile scheming of Cyprian and

---

[7] For the *Passio S. Justinae*, see Boninus Mombritius, *Sanctuarium, seu Vitae Sanctorum,* 2 vols. (Hildesheim: Georg Olms Verlag, 1978), 2:75–76, or *Acta Sanctorum* (Brussels [etc.], 1643–), Sept., 7:195–262.

his cohorts, reducing Justina's long supplications to a terse "she devoutly com-
mended herself to God" (2:193), accompanied by a sign of the cross. Even
Cyprian's conversion has more to do with self-interest than with faith. The
magician had thought that the devil was the source of all power. Once he
discovers his mistake, he promptly transfers his allegiance to Justina's God:
"The Crucified is greater than you? . . . I too should become a friend of the
Crucified" (2:195).

In a similar manner, Jacobus trims the *Passio S. Julianae* so that his retelling
consists almost exclusively of a showdown between Juliana and the devil.[8] The
devil, Jacobus relates, appears in Juliana's prison cell disguised as an angel, hoping to confound the saint with bad advice. Juliana, however, quickly exposes
the impostor and thrashes him soundly. Adding insult to injury, she hauls him
along on a chain when she appears in the forum before the prefect Eleusius.
When the wretched fiend begs for mercy ("Lady Juliana, stop making a fool of
me"), she pitches him into a latrine. Still unwilling to concede defeat, the devil
shows up at Juliana's execution in the guise of a young man, but one dirty look
from the saint sends him skittering off, wailing, "Woe is me! I think she still
wants to catch me and tie me up!" The saint's confrontation with the prefect
likewise highlights her strength and her enemy's impotence, for, like the devil,
Eleusius is powerless against Juliana. Unable to intimidate or even to injure the
saint, he orders her execution, cursing his gods, "who were unable to punish a
mere girl" (1:161). Having no moral exposition or doctrinal debate whatsoever,
this action-packed legend illustrates the extent to which might has replaced
faith as the central concern of Jacobus's legends.

Although Jacobus deletes or summarizes most of the long debates that had
been common in his sources, he invariably retains discourse pertaining to
power. For example, the only passage of any didactic substance in his legend of
Juliana deals with the competing claims of temporal and spiritual authority.
When Juliana's suitor explains that he cannot convert to Christianity for fear of
imperial wrath, the saint demands, "If you are so afraid of a mortal emperor,
how can you expect me not to fear an immortal one?" (1:160). Agatha's debate
with Quintianus also centers on power. When Quintianus tells her that she will
be sorry if she does not renounce her faith, she replies that no torment he can
devise can possibly bother her. When he beats her, she boasts that he is merely
contributing to her future glory, and when he has her breasts torn off, she assures him that her spiritual breasts remain untouched. The apostle Peter summarizes the theme of Jacobus's Agatha legend (and of all Jacobus's virgin martyr legends) when he visits the saint in prison and assures her, "Though this

8 For the *Passio S. Julianae*, see Mombritius, *Sanctuarium*, 2:77–80.

mad consul has inflicted torments on you, the way you have answered him has tormented him even more" (1:155). The most resounding affirmations of the virgin martyrs' power, however, come from the mouths of their adversaries, for while Jacobus removes the virgins' declarations of vulnerability, he carefully preserves those of their persecutors: "O blessed Margaret, I'm beaten! If I'd been beaten by a young man I wouldn't mind, but by a tender girl . . . ," the devil complains after Margaret wrestles and tramples him (1:369).

At first sight, Jacobus's presentation of the virgin martyrs might seem curious, for the headstrong heroines of his legends certainly do not exhibit the kind of behavior that the clergy was promoting for the laity during the thirteenth century. It might seem especially surprising that he removed so many references to penance—a theme that figured prominently in the Church's pastoral objectives and, correspondingly, in the religious literature of the late Middle Ages. Jacobus, however, was apparently less interested in providing examples for ordinary Christians than in celebrating the power and authority vested in God's representatives on earth.[9] Vigorous, aggressive, and indomitable, Jacobus's heroines were indeed commanding symbols of ecclesiastical prerogative. Through their triumphs, Jacobus celebrated the exposure and humiliating defeat of error, whether it took the form of the devil, the state, or the pagan gods.

As Sherry Reames has observed, in his sermons, as well as in his narratives, Jacobus rarely attempts to show how the experiences of the saints are relevant to the lives of individual Christians but instead emphasizes elements of the legends that separate the saints from the rest of humanity, such as miracles or other extraordinary deeds.[10] For example, he explains that Katherine of Alexandria's merit derives from the fact that she converted queens and princes rather than common people, philosophers rather than illiterates. The strengths and virtues that Jacobus celebrates in the virgin martyrs are traits he repeatedly denies to women in general. In another Katherine sermon, he declares that beauty ruins most women, that youth causes licentiousness, that wealth brings about extravagance, and that liberty and security are perilous; Katherine was a rare exception. He begins one of his sermons on Agatha with the assertion that although strength in women is exceedingly praiseworthy, it is also exceedingly rare. Similarly, in a sermon on Agnes he explains that the saint overcame those obstacles which would cause most women to forsake their chastity—namely, youth, beauty, gifts, noble lovers, and fear of punishment.

---

[9] On this point, see Sherry L. Reames, *The "Legenda aurea": A Reexamination of Its Paradoxical History* (Madison: University of Wisconsin Press, 1985), 197–209; and Alain Boureau, *La "Légende dorée": Le système narratif de Jacques de Voragine* (Paris: Cerf, 1984), 140–41.

[10] Reames, *"Legenda aurea": A Reexamination,* 107–13. Reames quotes or paraphrases the passages on women I refer to in this paragraph.

Scholars generally agree that Jacobus produced the *Legenda aurea* for the use of preachers and parish priests rather than for lay readers.[11] Nonetheless, in the centuries after its composition, his collection was read by people of a wide variety of backgrounds and professions. Indeed, within decades of its appearance, translators and adapters throughout Europe were beginning to make Jacobus's work available to the growing number of devout lay readers who were not proficient in Latin.[12] More than any other work, the *Legenda aurea* shaped late medieval readers' conception of the conventions of hagiographical genres, including the virgin martyr legend.

Jacobus's influence seems to have been as considerable in England as it was elsewhere. "In Britain," Manfred Görlach points out, "there appears not to be a single compilation of saints' legends that was copied as frequently" as the *Legenda aurea*.[13] English laypeople who claimed to own a *Legenda aurea* in the fourteenth and fifteenth centuries include John de Cantebrigge, a London fishmonger; Eleanor, Duchess of Gloucester; Walter, Lord Hungerford; and John Burton, a mercer.[14] Two major English translations of Jacobus's work were produced during the fifteenth century—the 1438 *Gilte Legende* and William Caxton's 1483 edition—and the legendary also circulated among English readers in French translation.[15] Adapters of Jacobus's legends include Nicholas Bozon, Geoffrey Chaucer, Osbern Bokenham, and John Lydgate, as well as the anonymous revisers of the *South English Legendary*.[16] Jacobus's influence was by no means restricted to writers; according to Ernest W. Tristram, the *Legenda*

---

[11] For a discussion of the intended and actual audiences of the *Legenda aurea,* see ibid., 85–87.

[12] See Robert Francis Seybolt, "Fifteenth-Century Editions of the *Legenda aurea,*" *Speculum* 21 (1946): 327–38; and Reames, *"Legenda aurea": A Reexamination,* 4–5. By Seybolt's calculations, there were more editions of the *Legenda aurea* in the fifteenth century than of the Bible. See his "The *Legenda aurea,* Bible, and *Historia scholastica,*" *Speculum* 21 (1946): 339–42.

[13] Manfred Görlach, "The *Legenda aurea* and the Early History of *The South English Legendary,*" in *"Legenda aurea": Sept siècles de diffusion,* ed. Brenda Dunn-Lardeau (Montreal: Bellarmin, 1986), 302.

[14] For John de Cantebrigge and Walter, Lord Hungerford, see Susan Hagen Cavanaugh, "A Study of Books Privately Owned in England: 1300–1450," Ph.D. diss., University of Pennsylvania, 1980, 163 and 452; for Eleanor of Gloucester, see Margaret Deanesly, "Vernacular Books in England in the Fourteenth and Fifteenth Centuries," *Modern Language Review* 15 (1920): 351; and for John Burton, see M. B. Parkes, "The Literacy of the Laity," in *The Medieval World,* ed. David Daiches and Anthony Thorlby (London: Aldus, 1973), 568. We know from manuscript evidence that John Burton's *Legenda aurea* was a copy of the 1438 *Gilte Legende* (MS Douce 372, Bodleian Library). References to the *Legenda aurea* in wills and other written sources must, however, be viewed with some caution, for "legenda aurea" appears to have been applied as a general term for legendaries. For example, a colophon in one manuscript of the *South English Legendary* (MS Lambeth Palace 223) refers to that work as a "Legenda aurea."

[15] Charlotte D'Evelyn, "Saints' Legends," in *Manual of the Writings in Middle English,* 2:430–39, 559–61 (catalogue). A selection of only eight items, known as the *Vernon Golden Legend,* appeared in the late fourteenth century.

[16] For a discussion of the *Legenda aurea*'s impact on revisions of the *South English Legendary,* see Görlach, "The *Legenda aurea* and the Early History of *The South English Legendary.*"

aurea "was the painter's main source of inspiration, even though he may often, if not usually, have obtained his knowledge of it at second hand." [17]

The extent of Jacobus's influence on English representations of virgin martyrs is a matter of continuing debate. Nevertheless, one thing is clear: the same dauntless, aggressive heroines who dominate his virgin martyr legends pervade the hagiography of late-thirteenth- and fourteenth-century England. We encounter them in the narratives of both the *South English Legendary* and the *North English Legendary*. They are celebrated in anonymous legends, such as those of Margaret and Katherine preserved in the Auchinleck manuscript, and in the saints' lives written by known authors, both clerical and lay. They adorn the walls and windows of parish churches, and they decorate the pages of late medieval books.

The *South English Legendary*

The collection now known as the *South English Legendary* was assembled in the southwest Midlands during the second half of the thirteenth century, then revised and supplemented around 1380–90; versions of it proliferated through much of southwestern and northeastern England.[18] More than fifty manuscripts of the legendary survive, making it one of the best-represented works in Middle English. Indeed, only the *Prick of Conscience*, the *Canterbury Tales*, and *Piers Plowman* exist in more copies.[19] Despite its apparent popularity, however, virtually nothing is known about the *Legendary*'s authors, its purpose, or its public. Scholars have assigned the collection to almost every major group of clerics: friars, Benedictines, Cistercians, Augustinian canons, and the secular clergy; yet objections have been raised to all these attributions, and no conclusive evidence has been garnered from the manuscripts.[20]

The intended use of the legendary is also a mystery. Scholars generally agree

[17] Ernest W. Tristram, *English Medieval Wall Painting: The Thirteenth Century*, 2 vols. (Oxford: Oxford University Press, 1950), 1:51.

[18] For a thorough study of the complicated textual history of the *South English Legendary*, see Manfred Görlach, *The Textual Tradition of the "South English Legendary"* (Leeds: University of Leeds, 1974). Görlach provides a map of the geographical distribution of major manuscripts of the collection on page 305 of his study. Page/line references are to the following editions: *The Early South-English Legendary*, ed. Carl Horstmann, EETS.OS 87 [henceforth cited as ESEL] (1887; reprint, Millwood, N.Y.: Kraus, 1987); and *The South English Legendary*, ed. Charlotte D'Evelyn and Anna J. Mill, EETS.OS 235, 236 [henceforth cited as SEL] (London: Oxford University Press, 1956).

[19] Charlotte D'Evelyn, "Saints' Legends," in *Manual of the Writings in Middle English*, ed. J. Burke Severs, 2:413.

[20] Görlach provides a convenient summary of the arguments for and against different groups of clerics as originators of the legendary in *Textual Tradition*, 45–50. For a more recent argument in favor of Franciscan authorship, see Karen Bjelland, "Franciscan versus Dominican Responses to the Knight as a Societal Model: The Case of the *South English Legendary*," *Franciscan Studies* 48 (1988): 11–27.

that the work was composed for a lay audience, but they disagree over what kinds of people made up this audience and under what circumstances they encountered the legends. Certain features of the narratives suggest that the collection was a handbook used by pastors or preachers to instruct a broad lay audience. These features include the narratives' relative brevity, their vivid descriptions, dramatic accounts of action, simple characterization, and straightforward sentence structure.[21] Yet there are also indications that the legendary was owned by middle-class townspeople or by members of the country gentry.[22] Two surviving manuscripts of the *South English Legendary* were bound with romances during the fourteenth century: MS Laud 108, Bodleian Library, includes *Havelok* and *King Horn*, and MS 13, King's College, Cambridge, contains *William of Palerne*. A colophon to MS Lambeth Palace 223, London (circa 1400) provides further evidence that the legendary was circulating among lay readers by the late fourteenth century: "Her endeþ legenda aurea writen by R. P. of þis toun / To a gode mon of þe same is cleped Thomas of Wottoun."[23]

Thomas of Wottoun was probably not the only layperson to possess a copy of the *South English Legendary*. At the time that Lambeth Palace 223 was commissioned, there was a substantial audience for legendaries among the middle classes and the aristocracy. Collections of saints' lives occur with relative frequency in the wills of laypeople from the mid–fourteenth century onward.[24] Lay testators owning legendaries in the second half of the fourteenth century include William Walleworth, Lord Mayor of London; Thomas de Roos, knight of Ingmanthorp; Thomas Carleton, an alderman of Cripplegate Ward and member of Parliament for London; John de Worstede, a London mercer; and Elizabeth de Burgh, Lady of Clare. In the early fifteenth century, Thomas,

[21] Scholars who have argued that the legendary was read aloud to an unsophisticated audience of laypeople include Laurel Braswell, "The *South English Legendary* Collection: A Study in Middle English Religious Literature of the Thirteenth and Fourteenth Centuries," Ph.D. diss., University of Toronto, 1964, 268; Manfred Görlach, *An East Midland Revision of the "South English Legendary"* (Heidelberg: Carl Winter, 1976), 8; and Klaus P. Jankofsky, "*Legenda aurea* Materials in the *South English Legendary*: Translation, Transformation, Acculturation," in *"Legenda aurea": Sept siècles de diffusion*, ed. Dunn-Lardeau, 320. See also Thomas J. Heffernan, *Sacred Biography: Saints and Their Biographers in the Middle Ages* (New York: Oxford University Press, 1988), 261–65; Bella Millett, "The Audience of the Saints' Lives of the Katherine Group," *Reading Medieval Studies* 16 (1990): 143–45; and Gregory M. Sadlek, "The Image of the Devil's Five Fingers in the *South English Legendary*'s 'St. Michael' and in Chaucer's 'Parson's Tale,'" in *The "South English Legendary": A Critical Assessment*, ed. Klaus P. Jankofsky (Tübingen: Francke Verlag, 1992), 49–64.

[22] Annie Samson examines those indications in "The *South English Legendary*: Constructing a Context," in *Thirteenth-Century England I*, Proceedings of the Newcastle upon Tyne Conference, 1985, ed. P. R. Coss and D. S. Lloyd (Wolfeboro, N.H.: Boydell, 1986), 185–95.

[23] Quoted by Görlach in *Textual Tradition*, 83.

[24] I have obtained the information in this paragraph from Cavanaugh, "Books Privately Owned in England."

Lord Berkeley, and William Stourton, a lawyer and knight of the shire for Somerset, both mention English legendaries in their wills. Among the other owners of legendaries at that time are John Clifford, a mason of Southwark, London; Elizabeth de Juliers, Countess of Kent; and William Burton, a London esquire. Though medieval wills offer no more than fragmentary evidence of book ownership, they do indicate that the clergy was by no means the only audience for legendaries during the years in which the *South English Legendary* was popular. It is, of course, impossible to identify particular works on the basis of such vague designations as "legenda sanctorum" or "magna legenda," but because the *South English Legendary* was the principal legendary in Middle English up until the mid–fifteenth century, it may well have circulated among such readers.[25]

One of the distinguishing features of the *South English Legendary* is its graphic description of violence, which by far exceeds what we find in both the *Legenda aurea* and in most contemporary vernacular legends. Typical of the lurid detail we encounter in the collection is this passage from the legend of Juliana:

> A weol of ire swuþe strang : byuore hure hy caste
> Al were þe uelien aboute : wiþ rasours ystiked uaste
> þat weol hi turnde al aboute : þe maide þerbi hi sette
> Dupe wode in hure naked fleiss : þe rasors kene iwette
> Þat þo hure uless was al to torne : so deope wode & gnowe
> Þat þe bones hy to slitte : and þe marrou out drowe
> Þat marrou sprang out alaboute.
>
> (SEL 1:67/141–47)

One might conclude that violent passages such as this one are designed to evoke readers' compassion for the saint's pain.[26] This interpretation is too simple, however, for descriptions of grisly tortures are almost invariably accompanied by assurances that the saint feels nothing. Quintianus's mutilation of Agatha might have made readers of the *South English Legendary* squirm — but not the saint. Instead of writhing in pain, she calls her adversary an "vnwreste bouk" (SEL 1:56/61) and scolds him for his audacity. On the rare occasions when the hagiographer does mention that his protagonist suffered, he hastens to add that the damage was not permanent. In Juliana's case, angels fly down from

---

[25] For a discussion of the increasingly broad use of the term "legenda" beginning in the second half of the thirteenth century, see Paul Strohm, "*Passioun, Lyf, Miracle, Legende*: Some Generic Terms in Middle English Hagiographical Narrative," *Chaucer Review* 10 (1974/75): 72.

[26] See, for example, Klaus P. Jankofsky, "Entertainment, Edification, and Popular Education in the *South English Legendary*," *Journal of Popular Culture* 11 (1977/78): 710–11.

heaven to end the saint's ordeal, and the saint emerged "al hol as hure noþing nere" (SEL 1:67/155). Repeatedly, the saints make it clear to those around them that they neither need nor welcome pity. Margaret calls weeping bystanders "wikkede conseillers," and Cecilia orders mourners to be quiet.[27] Though grisly mutilation scenes may have initally elicited compassion for the saints' ordeals, as listeners or readers realized that the virgins were not actually suffering (or that their suffering was only temporary), sympathy must have given way to wonder and delight at the impotence of evil. Ultimately, the saints' extraordinary imperviousness to pain may have *discouraged* many people from identifying with them. In fact, given the highly subversive actions of virgin martyrs in these legends, it seems likely that one reason that Middle English hagiographers emphasized the saints' resilience was to distance readers from their heroines and in so doing to make it less likely that they would imitate their unruliness.

The *Legendary* writers often record their protagonists' prayers, but unlike the long devotions of the passiones or of the Katherine Group, these prayers tend to be terse requests for aid—which are promptly answered. Far from suggesting vulnerability, they establish the saint's authority by implying that divine power is hers to invoke. Sometimes the saint's requests explicitly establish her role as a mediator between God and his creatures, as when Katherine entreats God to take special care of her devotees and God explicitly promises to do so (SEL 2:542/289–92).[28] In other instances, the virgin's prayers establish her power over her own life and death, as, for example, when Christine prays:

> Louerd . . . þench on me : myne limes akeþ sore
> Me þingþ it is time nou : þat þou sende after me
> Mi bodi is weri inou : mi soule wilneþ to þe
> 3if ich am iwasse clene inou : let me to þe wende
> Þis maide sede hure preere : and bro3te hure lif to ende
> (SEL 1:327/354–58)

Significantly, she makes this request only after three judges have tried and failed to kill her and their henchmen have given up and gone away (327/351–53). Similarly, Agatha prays for death—but only after an insurrection has forced her persecutor to flee in disgrace: "Let me Louerd to reste wende : for her me þencheþ longe / Time it is to endy mi lif : mi soule þou auonge / Mid þis word biuore þat folk : he[o] bigan to dei3e" (SEL 1:58/105–107). The saint's efficacious prayers for death confirm her triumph over her adversary, demonstrating

[27] SEL 1:296/135; ESEL 495/225.
[28] See also Margaret's request, which is one of the longest prayers in the *Legendary*, in SEL 1:301/269–88.

that for all his power and for all his threats, she, not he, will determine the hour of her demise.

Like Jacobus, the writers of the *South English Legendary* devote more attention to the saint's exploits than to her faith. Their narratives describe how feisty heroines humiliate the "luþer men" who take them for "fol wenches." They vividly capture the anger, frustration, and despair of tyrants who learn that not only are they unable to intimidate their prisoners but they also cannot hurt them, and—worse still—they cannot get rid of them. After thirty days without food or drink, Katherine of Alexandria appears before Maxentius "swiþe fat and round" (ESEL 98/199). Having failed to burn or drown Margaret, Olibrius exclaims with more hope than confidence, "Certes . . . in som manere we ssolleþ hure to deþe bringe" (SEL 1:300/246). At the end of the Christine legend, Julian concedes defeat as he orders his thugs to kill the saint, if they can, "for i ne can do namore" (SEL 1:327/350).

Through dialogue, hagiographers further affirm their heroines' superiority. In fact, the writers of the *South English Legendary* produced some of the most vituperative saints of Middle English hagiography. "Luþer hound," "foule hond," "wrecche bouk": with such language the virgin martyrs of this collection taunt their hapless persecutors. In a typical outburst, Christine rails against Julian for reproaching her about her faith:

> Beo stille . . . berkinge hound beo stille
> Go li and ne berk namore : so muche aȝen my wille
> To berke þoru þin hondes mouþ : mi swete Louerdes name
> Þer of my mouþ isoilled is : go li God ȝeue þe ssame.
> (SEL 1:324/277–80)

When Almachius asks Cecilia what family she comes from, the saint retorts, "Of betere kunne . . . þan þou euere were" (ESEL 494/186), and when he reproaches her for her foolishness, or "gydihede," she turns his own words against him:

> Þou seist þat ich gydi am . . .
> Ac þou art gydi, ȝ ek blind, i-sene is on þi rede.
> Scholde I honure þine [godes] ymad of ston ȝ tre?
> I nelle it do, for-soþe, for þou ne myȝt nat I-se.
> Bote þou myȝth i-se þat art blynd, þat þis þing soþ is;
> ȝif þou sixt ȝ ne leuest it naut, gydi þou art, I-wys,
> for gydi he is þat nelle I-leue þat he seþ myd his eye;
> Gydi ȝ blind þou schalt deye, in helle pyne deye.
> (ESEL 495/209–16)

Such sparring, with saints and persecutors battling for the last word, is characteristic of the virgin martyr legends in the *South English Legendary*.

As in Jacobus's legends, passages expressing the virgin's contempt for traditional figures of authority, such as fathers, well-placed suitors, and magistrates,
assume a prominent place in the virgin martyr legends of the *South English
Legendary*.[29] Moreover, by consistently emphasizing that the voices of authority
against which the virgin struggles are male voices, the Middle English hagiographers present their stories as gender conflicts. Frequently, the virgin martyrs
assert that the actions of their persecutors are crimes against womankind. For
example, when the prefect orders Agnes stripped, paraded through town, and
installed in a brothel, she admonishes him: "Ertou noȝt assamed in þi þoȝt / bi
eny womman þus do / Wanne þou of womman ert icome" (SEL 1:20/45–46).
In similar language, Agatha berates Quintianus for commanding that her breasts
be torn off (SEL 1:56/61–63). When the prefect strips, shaves, and tortures
Christine, all the women of the town cry out in rage:

> Iustice hi seide þou art : an vnwreste man
> Þat þou so ssenfolliche : defoulest a womman
> In ssennesse of alle oþere : boþe nou and er
> Alas þat eny womman : so luþer mon ber.
>
> (SEL 1:323/243–46)

The comments of the saint's persecutors eloquently confirm that her victory is
woman's triumph. Maxentius, for example, scoffs at the very thought that a
mere woman might discredit the wisdom of "alle men":

> Maide seide þemperour : if þat þis soþ were
> Al þe men of þe wordle were in gydihede : & þu one hem scholdest lere
> & me schal leoue alle men : & more hit wole beo note
> Þan a fol womman as þu ert : ȝoure bolt is sone ischote.
>
> (SEL 2:535/51–54)

The emperor's philosophers share his skepticism, bristling with indignation
when he commands them to debate against "a ȝung wenche" (SEL 2:536/78).
Their confidence, of course, makes the inevitable moment when they must
acknowledge her "maistrie" (SEL 2:537/130) only the more degrading. Such examples of masculine wrath in the face of feminine mastery abound. When a

---

[29] As in my discussion of the *Legenda aurea*, my point is not that earlier Latin *passiones* did not
contain many of the same or similar passages but rather that Middle English hagiographers consistently retain or augment passages of this sort and that in these shorter legends themes of social and
gender conflict assume a more central position.

fire meant to destroy Juliana instead kills her persecutor's followers, the tyrant bawls, "Ssel a womman wiþ hure wicchinge us alle ouercome?" (SEL 1:68/182). Dismayed by Justina's indifference to the succession of devils he has sent to tempt her, Cyprian challenges the master of all devils: "Schal a wenche us ouercome nolle ȝe non oþer rede?"[30] In the Juliana legend, as in the Justina legend, even the devil is forced to acknowledge the power of women, complaining: "Wy ertou so strang maidenot : þat þou nemiȝt ouercome be[o] / Alas maidenot alas : wi woltou wiþ us fiȝte / Maidens ichelle euere eft drede : inabbe aȝen hom no miȝte" (SEL 1:66/118–20).

The authority, strength, and desires of men are invariably the objects of contempt in the *Legendary*'s virgin martyr legends. As in the *Legenda aurea*, the Justina legend centers on the mishaps of Cyprian and the (male) devils he employs to help him seduce Justina. It, too, lampoons the pompous demons who see no reason why they should have trouble delivering to Cyprian the "wenche" of his choice. Perhaps the best example of the degradation of powerful men, however, occurs in the legend of Anastasia, which revolves around the ways in which the saint manages to evade the embraces of various powerful captors. In the most colorful episode, a prince goes to a kitchen where he has imprisoned Anastasia and her three female companions, intending to rape them.[31] Fortunately for the women, God distorts his vision, and he embraces some dirty pots and pans, mistaking them for the maidens. Having spent a few hours frolicking in the cauldrons, the prince departs, but as soon as he appears in public, caked with food, he becomes the laughingstock of the town. The people revile him, spit on him, thrash him, and stone him. His own followers take part in the public mockery, showering him with blows and repudiating his authority:

> Anon so is men him iseie : so grislich and amad
> Hi wende it were þe deuel of helle : & sore hi were adrad
> Wiþ staues & stones hi leide him on : þat he gan nei þat lyf lete
> Wy uare ȝe so quaþ þis wrecche : wolle ȝe ȝoure louerd bete
> Þo were hi wroþer þanne hi were er : hi smite on him duntes grete
> He nuste weþer him betere was : faire speke oþer þrete
> Oure louerd hi sede neuere þou nere : þi miȝte þe is bynome
> Þe were betere atom in helle : þanne amang us habbe icome

[30] The Justina legend has not been edited. I am quoting from MS Egerton 1993, fol. 204r, British Library.

[31] The *North English Legendary* also offers a dramatic rendition of this legend. Although the kitchen episode is a central event in the narratives of both these Middle English collections, it is only a minor incident in the *Passio S. Anastasiae*. See Hippolyte Delehaye, *Étude sur le légendier romain: Les saints de Novembre et Décembre*, Subsidia hagiographica 23 (Brussels: Société des Bollandistes, 1936), 230–31. To my knowledge, the only early Latin text to focus on this issue and to exploit its inherent humor is Hrotsvitha of Gandersheim's play *Dulcitius*.

Þe wrecche nuste non oþer red : bote atorn attelaste
And hi leide him on as he atorn : mid stones wel faste.

(SEL 2:587/41–50)

This episode of the Anastasia legend, with its festive mockery of a man by women, of a lord by his retainers, epitomizes the sort of carnivalesque reversal that is characteristic not only of virgin martyr legends in the *South English Legendary* but also of almost all late-thirteenth- and fourteenth-century virgin martyr legends.

The *North English Legendary*

The second major collection of English saints' lives is the *Tractus de legenda sanctorum*, or *North English Legendary*, associated with the *Northern Homily Cycle*. This legendary was produced at the end of the fourteenth century and contains the legends of six virgin martyrs: Lucy, Anastasia, Agatha, Christine, Cecilia, and Katherine.[32] Unlike the *South English Legendary*, which reveals little about its purpose or intended audience, this collection explicitly presents itself as a work designed to be read privately by laypeople ("laud men" [NEL 3/6]): "Here may men luke, who likes to lere, / Of liues and dedis of saintes sere" (NEL 3/1–2). That the collection was indeed read rather than preached is suggested by the fact that both manuscripts containing the legendary are religious miscellanies that appear to have been designed for private study. Besides the *Northern Homily Cycle* and the legendary, MS Harley 4196, British Library, contains the *Gospel of Nicodemus* and the *Prick of Conscience*. Cotton MS Tiberius E VII, British Library, includes a paraphrase of chapters 1–4 of Richard Rolle's *Form of Living*, the *Gast of Gy*, and several other religious pieces.[33]

The *North English Legendary* features the same cast of unruly maidens and blustering villains that we encounter in the *South English Legendary*. The *North English Legendary* does, however, differ from the *South English Legendary* in several important respects. To begin with, it contains less violence, and its heroines are somewhat less vociferous than those of the earlier Middle English collection. Two of its legends, those of Anastasia and Cecilia, play up the saints' resourcefulness rather than their outright defiance of male authority. Forced to marry against their will, Anastasia and Cecilia at first appear to be pawns of

---

[32] All page/line references are to Carl Horstmann's edition in *Altenglische Legenden: Neue Folge* [henceforth cited as NEL] (Heilbronn: Henninger, 1881), 3–173.

[33] For a thorough description of these manuscripts, see Saara Nevanlinna, introduction to *The Northern Homily Cycle*, 3 vols. (Helsinki, 1972), 1:5–17.

their relatives: "Cisill durst none oþer do / Bot als hir frendes tald hir to" (NEL 159/29–30); similarly, Anastasia's "frendes ware myghty men of mode, / Þai marid hir with mekyl gude / Vnto a man, hight Pupillus" (NEL 25/13–15). It soon becomes obvious, however, that the saints are not as helpless as they seem. Pretending to have contracted an illness, Anastasia "feyned hir to be so bysted / Þat scho might cum to no mans bed" (NEL 25/19–20). Having thwarted the designs of her powerful relatives, she further deceives her husband by stealing out late at night and distributing his goods among the poor. The writer of the Anastasia legend accentuates his heroine's sneakiness in the early portion of the narrative by using "preuely" to describe virtually everything the saint does (see 25–26/12, 21, 46). Cecilia, too, becomes a more devious character in the *North English Legendary*'s rendition of her legend. When, in earlier versions of the legend (both vernacular and Latin), she tells her bridegroom that an angel is guarding her virginity, there is no hint of subterfuge. The writer of the *Legendary*, however, puts Cecilia's famous nuptual catechism in a new light by providing a glimpse into her mind: "With hir husband scho went to bed, / Als þe law wald, for scho was wed. / Bot in hert ful wele scho thoght / To kepe hir clene, if þat scho moght" (NEL 160/53–56). Prefaced in this manner, Cecilia's story about the angel might be read as a last-minute ploy to keep Valerian at arm's length. As I will discuss shortly, the hagiographer concludes his Cecilia legend by showing how the saint outmaneuvers the pagan magistrate, Almachius; he omits the famous trial scene in which Cecilia humiliates her judge in his own courtroom.

At times, the writer of the *North English Legendary* introduces details that make the saints seem more like ordinary people. He occasionally reveals them in moments of vulnerability, as when Maxentius coaxes Katherine into his palace "sum-dele ogaines hir will" (166/150) or when, in the passage cited above, Cecilia dares not oppose the plans for her marriage. In describing St. Peter's visit to Agatha's prison cell, the hagiographer portrays an anxious, even fearful, saint. As soon as she sees the old man, she suspects the worst: "Saint Agace þan wele trowed and wend / Þat he for syn war þeder send; / Þarfore in hert scho was affraid" (47/173–75). Though a saint, Agatha is clearly not omniscient. Indeed, at the end of the encounter, she is as baffled by Peter's disappearance as anyone might be: "Þan was he went, scho wist noght how" (47/208).

In addition to making the saints more vulnerable than their counterparts in the *South English Legendary*, the hagiographer occasionally uses them to illustrate exemplary habits and conduct. For example, he calls attention to Anastasia's modest clothing, and he commends the diligence with which the newly converted saint studies the Christian faith (25/32, 9–12). In the same vein, he praises Cecilia for her piety, her knowledge of Christian doctrine, and her indifference to finery (159/12–16, 32–36).[34] Indeed, the introduction to that legend implicitly invites readers to imitate the saint, for it uses Cecilia's example to make the general assertion that God works through women as well as men and especially through maidens who "will be boun to his biding" (159/8).

The recurring references to money, property, and other possessions constitute the hagiographer's most intriguing effort to make his legends relevant to a middle-class audience. Indeed, the *North English Legendary* almost always portrays the saints' struggles in economic as well as sexual terms. Property plays a key role in bringing about persecution in five of the six virgin martyr legends: those of Agatha, Lucy, Cecilia, Anastasia, and Christine. In three of these five legends, the villain's desire for financial gain is closely associated with sexual desire. Agatha is hounded by a man whom the Middle English hagiographer condemns for covetousness as well as for lechery: "He was lothly and litcherous / And of ryches ful couaytous" (45/11–12). Similarly, Lucy is indicted when her betrothed realizes that she plans to keep both her body and her goods from him: "He þat suld haue wed hir, vnderstode / How þat scho gaf oway hir gude / And how scho hight to kepe hir clene" (17/71–73). Anastasia's troubles begin when her husband discovers that, while she claims to be too ill for sex, she is healthy enough to undertake nocturnal almsgiving missions (25–26/37–44). After his timely death leaves her a wealthy widow, she is plagued by men who are attracted to her "grete reches" as well as to her beauty (27–28/158, 179–208). The saints, however, are not merely the passive victims of greedy men, for they repeatedly use material possessions to rebel against social convention: Christine defies her father by breaking his bejeweled gods into small pieces and distributing them among the poor; Lucy escapes marriage by spending her dowry; Anastasia flouts her husband's authority by giving away his money, and she later mortifies her captors by keeping her riches out of their hands (28/213–14).

The Cecilia legend offers the most extreme example of how the conventional battle between the sexes is played out in economic terms. In the *Legenda aurea*, the *South English Legendary*, and Chaucer's "Second Nun's Tale," Cecilia comes to the attention of the pagan authorities when she buries the bodies of her husband, Valerian, and his fellow martyrs in defiance of the law. By contrast, the writer of the *North English Legendary* presents the saint's conflict with "Almachius, þat wikked king" (163/377), as a struggle over her husband's estate. Having executed Valerian and his cohorts, Almachius immediately orders his men to confiscate the martyrs' property:

---

[34] For a detailed discussion of Cecilia's "exemplary" qualities, see Sherry L. Reames, "Artistry, Decorum, and Purpose in Three Middle English Retellings of the Cecilia Legend," in *The Endless Knot*, ed. M. Teresa Tavormina and R. F. Yeager (Cambridge: D. S. Brewer, 1995), 178–85.

> Þarfore he thinkes in his mode
> At geder to him al þaire gude.
> To Valiriane hows first þai haste,
> For he was man of reches maste.
> Þai come unto Ciscill, his wife,
> Stoutly and with ful grete strife
> And bad hir lay furth þe reches
> Þat war hir maysters, more & les,
> "For als traitur to dede he ȝode
> And (þe) king sall haue all his gude."
>
> (163–64/381–90)

Cecilia, however, thwarts Almachius's efforts by converting his lackeys and giving her husband's goods to the needy. In all Middle English legends as well as in the *Legenda aurea*, Cecilia and Almachius quarrel over religion, yet in the *North English Legendary*, Almachius cares nothing about Cecilia's faith. Instead of a prolonged trial scene, the writer reports this brief interview:

> Bot first he frained with eger mode,
> Whare was all Valirian gude.
> And scho said þat scho gan it take
> Vnto pouer men for goddes sake.
> At þa wordes was he full tene
> And bad all suld be brint bidene
> Hows and catell, more and min,
> And als hir-self he bad þam brin.
>
> (164/405–12)

In no other legend have the spiritual issues at stake in a martyrdom been so thoroughly eclipsed as in this brief tale of greed and vengeance.

Although references to property and to the saints' charity are hardly unique to the *North English Legendary*, the density of those references is striking. At first glance, one might interpret them as part of the hagiographer's concerted effort to portray the virgin martyrs as exemplary figures for middle-class readers — and perhaps specifically for middle-class women. Sharon Farmer has pointed out that a number of late medieval clerics actually did encourage wives to be active agents of charity, even if it meant going behind the backs of tightfisted spouses.[35] In his *Manual for Confessors*, written circa 1215, Thomas of Cobham

---

[35] Sharon Farmer, "Persuasive Voices: Clerical Images of Medieval Wives," *Speculum* 61 (1986): 517–43.

advised that if the husband will not yield to persuasion, his wife "should se-
cretly give alms from their common property, supplying the alms that he omits.
For it is permissible for a woman to expend much of her husband's property,
without his knowing, in ways beneficial to him and for pious causes."[36] Like
the writings that Farmer discusses, the virgin martyr legends of the *North English Legendary* extol women who play an aggressive role in almsgiving; indeed,
they go so far as to present unilateral acts of charity as heroic. Yet the virgin
martyrs do not share Cobham's concern for the spiritual well-being of the men
they defy. Far from abetting the salvation of their adversaries, the heroines of
the *North English Legendary* use wealth to assert economic, sexual, and religious freedom and to score yet another victory in the ongoing gender wars that
dominate the saints' legends of the thirteenth and fourteenth centuries. The
legendary's celebration of saintly beneficence thus *conflicts* with the exemplary
impulses that I discussed earlier. The saints' often discreetly subversive behavior, combined with their exemplary qualities, may have made readers especially
uneasy, for it suggests that even the most mild-mannered women may be sur-
reptitiously destabilizing the household and the state.

Lay Hagiographers

Powerful, autonomous virgin martyrs were introduced into Middle English
hagiography and popularized by the thirteenth-century clergy. But some of the
best examples of these masterful heroines were produced by laymen Geoffrey
Chaucer and William Paris at the end of the fourteenth century.

Although critics frequently assert that Chaucer broke with the popular tradition of the *South English Legendary* by transforming the saint's legend into a
"literary" genre, his adaptation of the Cecilia legend has much in common
with the so-called popular legends discussed above. Chaucer's concise rendering of the Cecilia legend centers on those moments in which the saint's tran-
scendent perspective comes into conflict with the ordinary points of view of
the men around her—her bridegroom, Valerian; her brother-in-law, Tiburtius; and finally her judge, Almachius.[37] In each encounter, the predictable responses of average people become ludicrous: Valerian's surprise when his bride
tells him that a jealous angel will prevent him from consummating his mar-

---

[36] Translated by Farmer, "Persuasive Voices," 517.

[37] For an extensive discussion of the devaluation of human perceptions and experience in the
"Second Nun's Tale," see Sherry L. Reames, "The Cecilia Legend as Chaucer Inherited It and Retold
It: The Disappearance of an Augustinian Ideal," *Speculum* 55 (1980): 38–57. In light of her discovery of Chaucer's probable source, Reames modifies some of her conclusions in "A Recent Discovery concerning the Sources of Chaucer's 'Second Nun's Tale,'" *Modern Philology* 87 (1990): 337–61.

riage; Tiburtius's dismay when he discovers that becoming a Christian may actually be dangerous; Almachius's disbelief that a young widow should scoff at his power over life and death. In keeping with her reputation for "bisynesse," Cecilia diligently exposes the folly of worldly assumptions, persuading her converts to renounce this world for a "bettre lif in oother place" (323).[38] Having convinced Tiburtius and Valerian that, as Valerian puts it, "in dremes . . . han we be / Unto this tyme" (262–63), she incites them to martyrdom as "Cristes owene knyghtes" (383), then uses her own trial to launch a vociferous attack on secular authority, spurning the law just as she had previously spurned marriage. In one of the most dramatic trial scenes in Middle English hagiography, Cecilia dubs Almachius a "lewed officer and a veyn justise" (497), while claiming that his "princes erren" (449), that his judgment is "wood" (450), and that his power is no more than "a bladdre ful of wynd" (439). Having stunned him with her impudence, she mocks his confusion: "Lo, he dissymuleth heere in audience; / He stareth, and woodeth in his advertence!" (466–67). His esteem for stone gods, Cecilia predicts, will soon make him the laughingstock of his people (498–511).

Chaucer's narrative is more rhetorically polished than any of the virgin martyr legends examined thus far, but nothing about its message is new. Like the virgin martyr legends of the *South English Legendary*, the *North English Legendary*, and the *Legenda aurea*, it celebrates an ideal of sainthood based on the saint's unconditional rejection of the world and her aggressiveness in challenging those around her to discard their human modes of perception. An indefatigable soldier of Christ, Cecilia is in command of every situation and always in action: teaching, organizing baptisms, rallying converts, and reducing her persecutor to a babbling fool. Through her steadfast refusal to acknowledge the authority or validity of temporal institutions, she transforms circumstances over which she has no control: marriage provides a context for virginity, and execution becomes martyrdom.

An even more dramatic story of feminine mastery than Chaucer's "Second Nun's Tale" is the legend of Christine composed by William Paris, Chaucer's contemporary.[39] In an epilogue to this legend, Paris identifies himself as the squire of Thomas Beauchamp, Earl of Warwick, whom Richard II exiled to the Isle of Man in 1397.[40] By his own account, Paris was the only man to remain

---

[38] For all line references and quotations from Chaucer, I have used *The Riverside Chaucer*, 3d ed., ed. Larry D. Benson (Boston: Houghton Mifflin, 1987).

[39] William Paris, "Cristine," in *Sammlung Altenglischer Legenden*, ed. Horstmann (Heilbronn: Henninger, 1878), 183–90. References in the text are to lines given in this volume.

[40] For a more detailed consideration of the political circumstances surrounding Paris's exile, see Gordon Hall Gerould, "The Legend of St. Christina by William Paris," *Modern Language Notes* 29 (1914): 129–33.

faithful to Beauchamp despite the Earl's political misfortunes, writing the Christine legend to lighten the boredom of incarceration:

> In prisone site þer lorde alone,
> Ofe his mene he hath no moo—
> Bute Willam Parys, be seint Johne!
> That withe his wille wolle noȝt hime fro.
> He made this lyfe in ynglische soo,
> As he satte in prisone of stone,
> Euer as he myghte tent þerto
> Whane he had his lordes seruice done.
>
> (513–20)

His loyalty was evidently appreciated, for Beauchamp granted him the Worcestershire manor of Great Comberton "for the rent of a rose at Midsummer"—a gift that was confirmed annually during the lifetime of the earl's son Richard, in whose service Paris achieved the comfortable status of gentleman.[41]

Paris's version of the Christine legend consists of a series of lively encounters in which a "merye maye" mocks the pretensions of her powerful captors, adding injury to insult by flinging newly flayed slices of herself at them. Though Christine had always been a pugnacious saint, the details and comments Paris provides augment her bellicosity. For example, after blinding her third judge with her severed tongue, Christine actually pauses to admire her marksmanship: "For she hyme hite, softely smylide she" (469). Repeatedly, Paris punctuates grisly descriptions of torture with Christine's scathing invective. Urban's men beat the saint until they are about to collapse from exhaustion, yet Christine is as fresh as ever (157–68). Likewise, after her next judge has boiled her in a vat of pitch, the saint dares him to carry on, predicting that he and her father "togedire shalle wone / In dyrnesse grete & sorow vnesoughte, / Ande bothe togedir to drynke of a towne" (342–44). Paris obviously delights in relating how God and the saint foil the designs of her adversaries. When Christine's father brags that she will be put to death in the morning "ife I be lyuand mane" (296), Paris gloats:

> Yit ife he saide alle in play,
> Yite saide he sothe, þat cursyd wighte:
> For he was dede, or it was daie,

[41] Mary-Ann Stouck, "A Poet in the Household of the Beauchamp Earls of Warwick, c. 1393–1427," *Warwickshire History* 9 (1994): 114. For other discussions of Paris's family and career, see Elizabeth Salter, *Fourteenth-Century English Poetry: Contexts and Readings* (Oxford: Clarendon, 1983), 64–65; and Gerould, "Legend of St. Christina."

Ande Cristyne lyuede, þat maydene brighte.
Thus he thrette hire ouer nyghte
Thate she shulde one þe morne alway;
Yit was he dede for alle his myghte,
Ande Cristyne lyuede a merye maye.

(297–304)

In no other Middle English legend does the saint's wit and energy make the gruesome tortures she endures seem so trivial. More than any other hagiographer, Paris transforms his heroine's passion into a gleeful recitation of the mishaps and indignities that she heaps on her persecutors.

As we have seen, Chaucer and Paris produced the same kind of conflict-oriented virgin martyr legends that their clerical counterparts had been writing for over a century. If anything, these lay writers only enhanced the themes of discord and rebellion that were already so pronounced in earlier Middle English legends as well as in the *Legenda aurea*. In writing his "Second Nun's Tale," for example, Chaucer combined Jacobus de Voragine's version of the Cecilia legend with an anonymous abridgment from a Franciscan breviary to produce an even more animated encounter between Cecilia and Almachius than Jacobus had supplied.[42] Though the source or sources of Paris's legend are unknown, the zest with which he described Christine's triumphs suggests that he truly relished his heroine's aggressiveness. If Chaucer and Paris are at all representative of the tastes of fourteenth-century laypeople, it would seem that tales of "disorderly" virgin martyrs became so widespread not only because these were the tales that clerical writers chose to disseminate to their lay public but also because laypeople themselves formed an enthusiastic audience for such tales.

Unruly Virgins in the Visual Arts

Any study of how medieval men and women experienced virgin martyr legends requires a consideration of how the saints and their stories were represented in the visual arts, because sculptures, wall paintings, stained-glass windows, and illustrated manuscripts were among the most important sources of religious information, particularly for laypeople. As the anonymous writer of the prose dialogue *Dives and Pauper* (circa 1405) explains:

þey [images] been ordeynyd to steryn manys mende to thynkyn of Cristys incarnacioun and of his passioun and of holye seyntys lyuys. Also þey been ordeynyd to steryn mannys affeccioun and his herte to deuocioun, for often man is more

---

[42] On Chaucer's combination of sources, see Reames, "A Recent Discovery," and Reames, "Retellings of the Cecilia Legend," 189–99.

steryd be syghte þan be heryng or redyngge. Also þey been ordeynyd to been a tokene and a book to þe lewyd peple, þat þey moun redyn in ymagerye and peyn-
ture þat clerkys redyn in boke.[43]

Images of the saints surely influenced the ways in which people understood the
legends they read or heard, just as written texts must in turn have shaped viewers' interpretations of the images. Because thirteenth- and fourteenth-century
laypeople played an active role both in producing and in commissioning religious images, the visual arts provide especially useful evidence of lay "readings" of saints' legends.[44]

When we examine the so-called books of "lewyd peple," we encounter many
of the same themes that characterize contemporary written legends. For example, scenes depicting the torture and mutilation of virgin martyrs figure as
prominently in the visual arts as they did in the narratives of the *South English
Legendary*. The miniatures introducing virgin martyr legends in MS HM 3027,
Huntington Library, a thirteenth-century *Legenda aurea* of French provenance
that was owned in England, exemplify an iconographic program found in many
illustrated legendaries of the late Middle Ages.[45] In most of the fifteen scenes
from virgin martyr legends, sneering henchmen toil over the bodies of their
victims, while monarchs watch the performance. Small details suggest that the
thugs savor their tasks. In one case, torturers on either side of Agatha step on
the saint's feet while they tug at her breasts with ropes (figure 9). The miniature
accompanying Lucy's passion shows an executioner yanking the saint's hair as
he runs her through with his sword (figure 10). With similar touches, many English miniatures and wall paintings capture their villains' enthusiasm. For example, the earliest English wall painting depicting Katherine of Alexandria's
execution, at Winchester Cathedral (circa 1230), portrays a grinning executioner beside the saint's headless corpse, wiping his sword on his cloak.[46] Likewise, images from the twenty-seven–scene cycle of the Katherine legend in the
Church of Sporle, Norfolk, show Maxentius and his councilors tittering as the
saint is being tortured and tormenters jeering and sticking their tongues out
at Katherine.[47] In the *Queen Mary's Psalter*, two men dance about Juliana as she

[43] *Dives and Pauper*, ed. Priscilla Heath Barnum, EETS.OS 275 (London: Oxford University
Press, 1976), 82.

[44] For a discussion of lay involvement in the arts, see Alan Caiger-Smith, *English Medieval Mural
Paintings* (Oxford: Clarendon, 1963), 76–101.

[45] For a description and discussion of the provenance of this manuscript, see C. W. Dutschke,
Guide to Medieval and Renaissance Manuscripts in the Huntington Library, 2 vols. (San Marino,
Calif.: Huntington Library and Art Gallery, 1989), 2:590–94.

[46] Reproduced in Ethel Carleton Williams, "Mural Paintings of St. Catherine in England," *British
Archaeological Association Journal*, 3d ser., 19 (1956): plate VII.1.

[47] Reproduced in ibid., plate X.

9. Torture of St. Agatha, Jacobus de Voragine, *Legenda aurea*, MS HM 3027, fol. 33r, by permission of the Huntington Library, San Marino, Calif.

hangs from a tree by her hair.[48] As this depiction of Juliana illustrates, artists, too, were often concerned with such "feminine" parts of the saints' bodies as their long hair or breasts. Some scenes have specifically sexual overtones. For example, in the Sporle Katherine cycle, a guard's sword suggestively penetrates the folds of the saint's skirt. In HM 3027, a leering executioner thrusts his sword into Euphemia's abdomen in a gesture strongly suggestive of rape (figure 11), and the illustrator of the *Queen Mary's Psalter* portrays Christine's execution in a similar manner (figure 12). This rendering of Christine's martyrdom is especially striking because in all written versions of the Christine legend that I know of, Julian's men dispatch the saint by shooting her full of arrows.

Despite their graphic representation of torture and dismemberment, how-

[48] *Queen Mary's Psalter: Miniatures and Drawings by an English Artist of the Fourteenth Century Reproduced from Royal MS.2B.VII in the British Museum* (London: Oxford University Press, 1912), 247.

10. Torture of St. Lucy, Jacobus de Voragine, *Legenda aurea,* MS HM 3027, fol. 4v, by permission of the Huntington Library, San Marino, Calif.

ever, late medieval artists rarely suggest that the saints suffer.[49] In this respect, the iconography of martyrdom differs from the iconography of the Passion, which was so profoundly concerned with Christ's agony. The long section in *Dives and Pauper* explaining how people should "read" sacred images points up this contrast. Whereas Pauper explains that the crucifix should move people to reflect on Christ's suffering, he indicates that images of the martyrs with their emblems demonstrate how the saints' faith enabled them to *escape* suffering.[50] For example, he interprets the popular representations of Katherine of Alexandria in this manner: "Seynt Katerine is peyntyd wyt a qheel in þe to hond in tokene of þe horrible qheelys qheche þe tyraunt Maxence ordeynyd to rendyn here lyth fro lyth. But þe aungel distroyid hem and slow manye thowsandys of þe hethene peple, *and so þey dedyn here noon harm.*"[51] Similarly,

[49] Hilary Maddocks comments on this phenomenon in "Illumination in Jean de Vignay's *Légende dorée,*" in *Legenda aurea: Sept siècles de diffusion,* ed. Dunn-Lardeau, 157–58.

[50] For the discussion of the crucifixion, see *Dives and Pauper,* ed. Barnum, 83–85.

[51] Ibid., 92, emphasis mine.

11. Execution of St. Eupheńnia, Jacobus de Voragine, *Legenda aurea*, MS HM 3027, fol. 128r, by permission of the Huntington Library, San Marino, Calif.

he maintains that portrayals of Margaret "wyt a dragoun vnder here feet and wyt a cros in here hond" are intended to remind people that by making the sign of the cross, Margaret burst the dragon that was trying to devour her and "cam out of hym heyl and hool." [52]

As these comments indicate, though there was a strong impulse in late medieval iconography to represent the virgin martyrs as the objects of men's cruelty and desire, there was an equally strong tendency to celebrate their triumph. One of the most frequently portrayed scenes from a virgin martyr legend—both individually and as part of pictorial cycles—is the destruction of the great spiked wheels in the Katherine of Alexandria legend. An early-thirteenth-century version of the incident in stained glass depicts an angel shielding the saint as fragments of the shattered wheel fall onto the surrounding crowd. [53] In

[52] Ibid., 93.

[53] Reproduced in John Baker, *English Stained Glass* (New York: Harry N. Abrams, 1960), 59, plate 10.

12. Execution of St. Christine, *Queen Mary's Psalter*, MS Royal 2.B.VII, fol. 257, by permission of the British Library, London.

an even more emphatic testimony to the saint's victory, a wall painting from a parish church at Burton Latimer, Northamptonshire, shows an angel breaking the wheel with a sword while the corpses of spectators litter the ground. Standing nearby, the half-naked saint gazes on the carnage with a faint smile.[54] An analogous scene in the Sporle cycle shows Maxentius on the sidelines, blood streaming down his face, while in yet another version, at the parish church in Little Missenden, Buckinghamshire, the emperor recoils from the destruction, his tongue thrust out in surprise or, possibly, frustration.[55] We find a somewhat different interpretation of the same theme in one of the historiated initials of the *Salvin Hours*. There the triumphant saint sits aloft on one intact wheel; below her, the emperor gestures toward the ground, where the other wheel (also intact) rolls over the heads of the bystanders.[56]

Nonnarrative portrayals of the virgin martyrs—of which there are many—also proclaim the saints' victories and celebrate their power. Margaret towers above the dragon she conquered, often holding a book in one hand and piercing the beast with a sword or staff (figure 13). Beginning in the thirteenth century, Katherine of Alexandria appears in an analogous pose, trampling Maxentius (figure 14). We encounter this image everywhere: in stained-glass windows, wall paintings, and sculpture and in the margins and miniatures of

[54] Ernest W. Tristram, *English Wall Painting of the Fourteenth Century* (London: Routledge and Kegan Paul, 1955), plate 47.

[55] See Tristram, *English Medieval Wall Painting: The Thirteenth Century*, vol. 2, plate 199.

[56] Reproduced in Peter Brieger, *English Art, 1216–1307* (Oxford: Clarendon, 1957), plate 82a.

13. Margaret tramples the dragon, Brewes-Norwich Commentary on the *Liber Sextus*, MS 4A, vol. 2, fol. 37, by permission of the Master and Fellows of St. John's College, Cambridge.

14. Katherine tramples Maxentius, Brewes-Norwich Commentary on the *Liber Sextus*, MS 4A, vol. 4, fol. 36, by permission of the Master and Fellows of St. John's College, Cambridge.

manuscripts.[57] In some instances, the saint simply stands on the emperor; in others, she runs a sword through his head or throat. Such images, in which the saint stabs her persecutor with the instrument of her own death, display the same stunning reversal of roles we find in so many contemporary narratives. Another variation on the Katherine-Maxentius theme has the prostrate emperor stabbing himself in a gesture conveying not only the futility but also the self-destructiveness of evil.[58]

Although some artists focused on the majesty of the triumphant saints, others portrayed the virgin martyrs in homey, almost lighthearted terms. For example, in the *Luttrell Psalter*, Katherine totes a tiny spiked wheel on a pole over her shoulder, and Apollonia dangles a necklace made of teeth (for Apollonia, see figure 15).[59] There is no hint of the violence of martyrdom as the saints mingle with the grotesques and scenes from secular life that also adorn the margins of this manuscript. In an equally light tone, some wall paintings and stained-glass windows depict Katherine merrily balancing a tiny spiked wheel in one hand or running a finger along the once horrifying instrument of torture.[60]

Cycles narrating the lives of virgin martyrs offer many images of women teaching, preaching, leading, and rebelling. One of the most eloquent celebrations of feminine authority occurs in the fourteen-scene cycle of Margaret's passion in the *Queen Mary's Psalter*.[61] Here, scenes of the placid martyr being beaten and boiled alternate with scenes of her gesturing furiously at Olibrius

[57] For an early example, see the pair of wall paintings depicting Margaret on the dragon and Katherine standing on Maxentius reproduced in Tristram, *English Medieval Wall Painting: The Thirteenth Century*, vol. 2, plate 112. The numerous images of Katherine trampling Maxentius in the Princeton Index of Christian Art and in the photoarchives of the Warburg Institute attest to this image's popularity both in England and throughout late medieval Europe. For a later example of this motif, see figure 30, this volume.

[58] Francis Cheetham lists four English alabaster carvings on this theme—at Tromsø, Norway; Daroca, Spain; Lisbon; and the church of St. Pierre de Pont-Audemer, Normandy—in *English Medieval Alabasters* (Oxford: Phaidon, 1984), 84. Christopher Woodforde describes several examples in fifteenth-century stained-glass windows in his *Stained Glass in Somerset, 1250–1830* (London: Oxford University Press, 1946), 179. See also Francis Bond, *Dedications and Patron Saints of English Churches: Ecclesiastical Symbolism, Saints, and Their Emblems* (London: Oxford University Press, 1914), 24 n. 2, 163.

[59] For Katherine, see *The Luttrell Psalter: Two Plates in Colour and One Hundred and Eighty-Three in Monochrome from Additional Manuscript 42130 in the British Museum* (London: British Museum, 1932), plate 2, figure 2d (fol. 30b).

[60] See, for example, the west window, south aisle, at Priory Church, Deerhurst, Gloucestershire, reproduced in Baker, *English Stained Glass*, 95, plate 12, or the wall painting at Cold Overton Church, Leicester, reproduced in Tristram, *English Medieval Wall Painting: The Thirteenth Century*, vol. 2, plate 113a.

[61] *Queen Mary's Psalter*, 307–14.

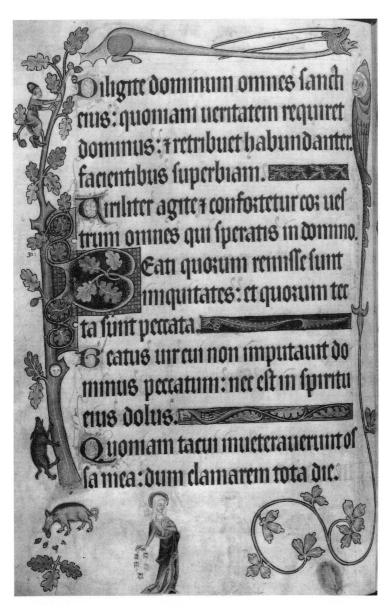

Diligite dominum omnes sancti eius: quoniam ueritatem requiret dominus: ꞇ retribuet habundanter facientibus superbiam.

Uiriliter agite ꞇ confortetur cor uestrum omnes qui speratis in domino.

Beati quorum remisse sunt iniquitates: et quorum tecta sunt peccata.

Beatus uir cui non imputauit dominus peccatum: nec est in spiritu eius dolus.

Quoniam tacui inueterauerunt ossa mea: dum clamarem tota die.

15. St. Apollonia, *Luttrell Psalter*, MS Add. 42130, fol. 59v, by permission of the British Library, London.

16. Margaret and Olibrius: first interrogation, *Queen Mary's Psalter*, MS Royal 2.B.VII, fol. 308, by permission of the British Library, London.

(figures 16 through 19). In one drawing, Margaret continues to scold him even as a guard drags her off to prison (see figure 17). Although the saint gestures with equal authority in all the scenes depicting her interviews with the prefect, Olibrius's posture changes significantly. In the first encounter, he is seated on his throne, scepter in hand and arm raised, as he admonishes the saint (figure 16). The next two interviews find him slightly slumped on his throne, without his scepter, gesturing limply toward the saint (figures 17 and 18). At last, he sits vexedly, one hand on his knee and the other in his lap, as the saint continues to denounce him (figure 19). A similar progression occurs in the *Psalter*'s eight-scene Katherine cycle.[62] By the third interview between the saint and her foe, a subdued Maxentius cups his chin in his hand while Katherine points at him angrily. Throughout the cycle, Katherine is engaged in actions that convey her confidence and authority—denouncing the emperor, preaching to Porphirius and the empress, presiding over the destruction of the Katherine wheel. Her poise and the serenity of her face in the three scenes of her torture and death (one of which is the breaking of the Katherine wheel) mock the emperor's naïveté in supposing that he can harm her.

We find subtler allusions to feminine insubordination in many illustrations of Margaret's first meeting with Olibrius. These scenes typically show the saint sitting on a grassy mound, busy with her distaff and surrounded by grazing

[62] Ibid., 274–78.

17. Margaret and Olibrius: second interrogation, *Queen Mary's Psalter*, MS Royal 2.B.VII, fol. 309, by permission of the British Library, London.

18. Margaret and Olibrius: third interrogation, *Queen Mary's Psalter*, MS Royal 2.B.VII, fol. 310v, by permission of the British Library, London.

sheep, as Olibrius and his men ride toward her (figure 20). Though modern viewers might consider these charming portrayals of rustic life, whose tranquility is marred only by the approaching prefect, I suspect that the response of medieval viewers was far more ambivalent. By the late Middle Ages, the distaff had become a highly charged symbol. On the one hand, it could be used as

19. Margaret and Olibrius: final interrogation, *Queen Mary's Psalter,* MS Royal 2.B.VII, fol. 311v, by permission of the British Library, London.

shorthand to indicate behavior deemed appropriate for women, a meaning implicit when one of Margery Kempe's critics admonished her to "forsake þis lyfe þat þu hast, & go spynne & carde as oþer women don."[63] On the other hand, the "woman's scepter," often associated with workingwomen and shrewish wives who lorded it over their husbands and households, had become an emblem of disorder and misrule.[64] Eve and Noah's wife are two of the best-known examples of the aggressive, distaff-wielding women of medieval popular culture. Wives carved in misericords use their weapons to batter their cowering husbands, while within the topsy-turvy world depicted in the margins of medieval manuscripts, women brandish distaffs as they flaunt their power over men.[65]

[63] *The Book of Margery Kempe,* ed. Sanford Brown Meech, EETS.OS 212 (Oxford: Oxford University Press, 1940), 129.

[64] Philippe Verdier, "Woman in the Marginalia of Gothic Manuscripts and Related Works," in *The Role of Woman in the Middle Ages,* ed. Rosmarie Thee Morewedge (Albany: State University of New York Press, 1975), 134. For a discussion of the association of spinning with feminine virtue and vice, see Frances M. Biscoglio, "'Unspun' Heroes: Iconography of the Spinning Woman in the Middle Ages," *Journal of Medieval and Renaissance Studies* 25 (1995): 163–76. Biscoglio does not, however, consider the intriguingly ambiguous use of the spinning wheel or distaff in portrayals of the virgin martyrs and in some portrayals of the Virgin Mary.

[65] Lilian M. C. Randall cites instances of women with distaffs beating, scolding, and chasing men. Some sketches show women with distaffs on horses charging unarmed knights. See Randall, *Images in the Margins of Gothic Manuscripts* (Berkeley: University of California Press, 1966), 157, for a list of occurrences, and see also figures 708 and 709. Verdier provides a useful discussion of this motif in "Woman in the Marginalia," 134–38. For a discussion of the images on misericords, see Christa Grössinger, "Misericords" in *Age of Chivalry: Art in Plantagenet England, 1200–1400,* ed. Jonathan Alexander and Paul Binski (London: Weidenfeld and Nicolson, 1987), 122–24.

20. Olibrius courts Margaret, *Queen Mary's Psalter*, MS Royal 2.B.VII, fol. 307v, by permission of the British Library, London.

The disorderliness of such "armed" women was enacted in mystery plays and in the festive battles of the sexes that marked St. Distaff's Day in towns and villages on January 7.[66] For some medieval viewers, at least, the instrument in Margaret's hand probably conveyed a sly insinuation about which character turns out to be the legend's real victim.[67]

As the miniatures accompanying the legends of Margaret and Agatha discussed in Chapter 1 demonstrate, there are many ways in which artists might have chosen to represent the virgin martyrs as exemplary—or at least less disruptive—figures. Had they wished, they might have conveyed such reactions as fear, hesitancy, or anguish. They might also have portrayed their heroines in the act of praying. Yet the scenes depicting the saints' devotion that figured so prominently in monastic *libelli* are notably absent from English art of the thirteenth and fourteenth centuries. Also absent are images that might suggest anxiety or suffering of any kind. Because few English paintings or carvings of virgin martyrs survive from before the thirteenth century, it is impossible to

[66] For a discussion of St. Distaff's Day, see Gail McMurray Gibson, *The Theater of Devotion: East Anglian Drama and Society in the Late Middle Ages* (Chicago: University of Chicago Press, 1989), 43.

[67] In the *Queen Mary's Psalter*, the only other women with distaffs are clearly disorderly: Eve and Rebecca (in a scene in which she is urging Jacob to obtain his brother's birthright), depicted on plates 7 and 24. Virgin martyrs are also associated with distaffs indirectly. Katherine of Alexandria appears in the margin with a distaff-bearing monster in the *Luttrell Psalter* (page 2, fol. 30v), and on the page facing Apollonia is a drawing of a woman beating a man with her distaff (pages 14–15, fols. 59v–60).

say whether the popularity of unruly virgins represents a change in English art, as it certainly does in literature. Yet the images I have just discussed correlate closely with contemporary trends in hagiography. Moreover, the representation of the saints as disorderly virgins abates at about the same time in both literary texts and in the visual arts.

The Implications of Disorder

As the examples I have given might suggest, the universe of late-thirteenth- and fourteenth-century virgin martyr legends is a world turned upside down: maidens batter devils; girls reduce princes to buffoons; wives and daughters outmaneuver husbands, fathers, and magistrates. Needless to say, the heroines of these texts hardly exemplify the behavior endorsed for women in late medieval England. In defying husbands, fathers, and civil authorities, these women stood society on its head. Their heroism consisted in their fearless confrontation of their adversaries, their undisguised scorn for the world, and their unequivocal rejection of social values. Middle English hagiographers not only neglected the "exemplary" aspects of the virgin's character that earlier hagiographers had emphasized, such as her piety, devotion, penance, and humility, but they also celebrated behavior deemed inappropriate in laypeople, especially in women. For example, though canon law rigorously upheld the conjugal rights of spouses, saints who were married against their wills, such as Cecilia and Anastasia, seemed willing to try any ploy to avoid fulfilling their sexual obligations.[68] Similarly, the numerous portrayals of women preaching and disputing gainsaid the conventional wisdom that women have no business teaching men.[69] While writers of late medieval conduct books agreed that women should be gracious, humble, obedient, and soft-spoken, virgin martyrs tended to be abrasive, defiant, shrewish, and sharp-tongued.[70] As the devil complains to Juliana in the *South English Legendary*:

[68] For discussions of the Church's attitude toward marital sex, see Elizabeth M. Makowski, "The Conjugal Debt and Medieval Canon Law," *Journal of Medieval History* 3 (1977): 99–114; James A. Brundage, *Law, Sex, and Christian Society in Medieval Europe* (Chicago: University of Chicago Press, 1987), 325–550; and Dyan Elliott, *Spiritual Marriage: Sexual Abstinence in Medieval Wedlock* (Princeton: Princeton University Press, 1993).

[69] Alcuin Blamires considers how examples of such preaching saints as Katherine of Alexandria could prove troublesome for the orthodox clergy; see his "Women and Preaching in Medieval Orthodoxy, Heresy, and Saints' Lives," *Viator* 26 (1995): 135–52.

[70] For a discussion of the qualities emphasized in conduct books, see Diane Bornstein's *The Lady in the Tower: Medieval Courtesy Literature for Women* (Hamden, Conn.: Archon, 1983); and Kathleen M. Ashley, "Medieval Courtesy Literature and Dramatic Mirrors of Female Conduct," in *The Ideology of Conduct: Essays in Literature and the History of Sexuality*, ed. Nancy Armstrong and Leonard Tennenhouse (New York: Methuen, 1987), 25–38.

Leoue leuedy . . . þin ore : yssend ich am inou
Ne make namo men [gawe] on me : nertou corteis & hende
Þench þat maidens ssolde milde be[o] : & bring me of þis bende
War is þe kunde of þi maidenot : þat ssolde be[o] milde & stille
& þou ert aȝen me so sterne : hou miȝtou habbe þe wille.

(SEL 1:66/124–28)

Such commentary suggests that medieval hagiographers were well aware that, in their manner as well as their actions, virgin martyrs were everything that actual women were not supposed to be.[71] Although writers sometimes showed their heroines acting in ways considered more feminine by contemporary standards, such portrayals were rarely sustained.[72] Indeed, as I suggested in my discussion of the *North English Legendary*, even such "exemplary" behavior as charity has subversive implications.

Energetic, resourceful, and desirable, the saints bear a certain resemblance to the protagonists of fabliaux. The emphasis that Middle English hagiographers place on the saint's invective—accompanied in some legends by physical abuse—heightens her affinity with the infamous unruly woman.[73] That affinity is further enhanced by the legends' plots. As Paul Strohm has observed, Cecilia's story about the jealous angel might have reminded Chaucer's readers of such stories as the "Miller's Tale," involving "the use of pious pretense for adulterous deception."[74] Similarly, Anastasia's craftiness in the *North English Legendary* transforms her legend into a sort of sacred fabliau that demonstrates

---

[71] Compare that outburst with the devil's gender-neutral exclamation in the Katherine Group's legend of Juliana: "Ne beoð *cristene men,* ȝef hit is soð þet me seið, merciable ant milȝfule?" (*Þe Liflade ant te Passiun of Seinte Iuliene,* ed. S.R.T.O. d'Ardenne, EETS.OS 248 [London: Oxford University Press, 1961], 47; emphasis mine) (Aren't Christians—if I've been told correctly—meek and mild?). As I noted in the last chapter, the devil of *Seinte Iuliene* actually confirms that Juliana conforms to appropriate feminine behavior when he declares in an aside to God: "To wel þu witest ham þe treowliche habbeð hire in heorte ihalden, ȝef ha milde ant meoke beon as meiden deh to beonne" (45) (You know well those who have you truly in their hearts, if they are meek and mild as maidens ought to be).

[72] For example, the writer of the *South English Legendary* explains that Cecilia stays at home, as a good wife should, while Tiburtius and Valerian win converts for Christianity: "Cecilie, for ȝe wyfman was, at hom ȝe moste a-byde; / Ak þese breþeren, þat men were, a-boute wenten wyde" (ESEL 493/133–34). However, Cecilia's domestic inclinations evaporate when she appears before the prefect and makes her husband and brother-in-law look tame by comparison. Here, as in most other virgin martyr legends of the period, the saint's apparent docility makes her subsequent metamorphosis in court all the more astonishing. The sole example I have found of a consistently meek virgin martyr in a late-thirteenth- or fourteenth-century text is the Virgin of Antioch, whose martyrdom is recounted in the *Vernon Golden Legend* (circa 1385).

[73] As R. Howard Bloch has pointed out, women's speech appears to have bothered misogynists more than anything else. See *Medieval Misogyny and the Invention of Western Romantic Love* (Chicago: University of Chicago Press, 1991), 13–35.

[74] Strohm, *"Passioun, Lyf, Miracle, Legende,"* 167.

the Wife of Bath's boast that "half so boldely kan ther no man / Swere and lyen, as a womman kan" ("Wife of Bath's Prologue," 227–28). The saint's behavior— flouting her husband while he lives and rejoicing when he dies—recalls the observation of Noah's wife in the Towneley Cycle that many women would rather be widows than wives:

> So wold mo, no frese that I se on this sole
> of wifis that ar here,
> ffor the life that thay leyd,
> Wold thare husbandis were dede.[75]

Stocked with heroines like Anastasia, Middle English virgin martyr legends have more in common with the "legendes and lyves" of "wikked wyves" ("Wife of Bath's Prologue," 685–86) that Janekyn inflicts on Alison than one might have imagined.

How, one wonders, did the assertive, often destructive heroines of Middle English hagiography speak to the experience of medieval men and women? To be sure, many women probably found the examples of feminine mastery in virgin martyr legends rather attractive. Yet there is little evidence that the male authors of virgin martyr legends were writing specifically for women or that they anticipated a predominantly female audience.[76] Indeed, if they were tailoring their narratives to women, it is hard to see why they would exaggerate behavior that they would surely not want their readers to emulate. On the other hand, it is certainly not obvious how the self-confident heroines who best all the men they meet could have appealed either to the clerics who composed saints' lives or to the men who must have constituted a substantial segment of their audience.[77] In fact, many women must have been disturbed

---

[75] *The Towneley Plays*, ed. George England, EETS.ES 71 (1897; reprint, Millwood, N.Y.: Kraus, 1966), 34–35, lines 391–94.

[76] Klaus P. Jankofsky cites lines from the Edmund of Canterbury, Lucy, and Ursula legends in the *South English Legendary* (SEL 2:496/100, 570/133–36, 444/256–58) to support his claim that the collection's original audience "seems to have consisted at one time of unlettered listeners, probably women." But only the line from Edmund directly addresses women ("Wele whar eni of 30u couþe such an hosebonde fynde"). See his "National Characteristics in the Portrayal of English Saints in the *South English Legendary*," in *Images of Sainthood in Medieval Europe*, ed. Renate Blumenfeld-Kosinski and Timea Szell (Ithaca: Cornell University Press, 1991), 83. In a possible allusion to his own audience, the anonymous writer of the Margaret legend preserved in the Auchinleck manuscript asserts that the saint's passion "mirþe is of to here to maiden and to wiif" (Horstmann, *Altenglische Legenden: Neue Folge*, 235/408). The evidence that Middle English hagiographers were especially attuned to the tastes of women in their audience is sparse and ambiguous, at best.

[77] For a different treatment of these issues, see Heffernan, *Sacred Biography*, 231–99. Heffernan's provocative analysis of the ideological complexity of virgin martyr legends is flawed, however, by his erroneous assumption that most Middle English saints' lives were composed for peasant audiences (261–65).

by the saints' flagrant disregard for social proprieties and parental authority.

The most obvious explanation for the emergence and apparent success of legends featuring aggressive, sharp-tongued martyrs is that the clergymen who produced and popularized so many of these texts saw the saints as embodiments of *clerical* rather than *feminine* authority. In the wake of Lateran IV, the clergy had the formidable task of educating laypeople while preserving its own authority over them. There was, after all, the risk that highly committed and informed lay Christians would negotiate relationships with Christ on their own terms or, worse still, that they would invest their enthusiasm in heresy. The virgin martyr legends examined in this chapter were in many respects admirably suited to the needs of clerical educators. While bringing the deeds of long-dead heroines to life for many late medieval English people, these dramas of Christian valor affirmed the superiority of clerical values, such as celibacy, over lay values, such as marriage.[78] Such images of sacred might as Katherine of Alexandria trampling the crowned emperor Maxentius provided powerful reminders of the authority of the Church over the secular state, reminders that clergymen who were engaged in disputes over jurisdiction with secular leaders surely found useful. And although the saints themselves may not have illustrated exemplary conduct for women, the fates of their suitors provided pastors concerned with enforcing sexual morality with excellent lessons on the dangers of lasciviousness.[79]

Chaucer's attribution of the Cecilia legend to a professional virgin and a member of the Church might lead us to believe that the clergy succeeded in presenting virgin martyrs as emblems of clerical authority and in discouraging the laity from identifying with them. This conclusion is reinforced by the "Wife of Bath's Prologue," which emphatically identifies the hagiographical tradition to which the Cecilia legend belongs with clerical authority:

[78] Heffernan has similarly proposed that "the conventions of piety and the anti-marital invective depicted in vernacular sacred biographies from the twelfth century seek as part of their dialectic to constrain the growth of the laity as an autonomous class with the capacity for some degree of self-determinism" (ibid., 253). I should point out that Middle English legends of male saints reveal much the same hostility toward secular life as the virgin martyr legends. For a general discussion of how the clergy used vernacular saints' legends to reinforce its own authority, see Susan Crane, *Insular Romance: Politics, Faith, and Culture in Anglo-Norman and Middle English Literature* (Berkeley: University of California Press, 1986), 92–104, 130–33.

[79] I do not wish to imply that all clergymen were comfortable with the approach to the virgin martyr legend discussed in this chapter. Indeed, Sherry Reames's study of abridgments of the Cecilia legend in late medieval breviaries indicates that many adapters were disturbed by the saint's role as a teacher as well as with the combativeness she displays during her trial. See "*Mouvance* and Interpretation in Late-Medieval Latin: The Legend of St. Cecilia in British Breviaries," in *Medieval Literature: Texts and Interpretation*, ed. Tim William Machan (Binghamton, N.Y.: Medieval and Renaissance Texts and Studies, 1991), 159–89. My point is that the popularization of "unruly" virgin martyrs in texts that were most directly accessible to the laity could not have been accomplished without fairly widespread clerical support.

❀ Virgin Martyrs ❀

For trusteth wel, it is an impossible
That any clerk wol speke good of wyves,
But if it be of hooly seintes lyves,
Ne of noon oother womman never the mo.

(688–91)

The Wife's dismissive tone suggests that "hooly seintes lyves" are of little rele-
vance to women like herself, who "nyl envye no virginitee" (142). At the same
time, however, Chaucer emphatically associates the "Second Nun's Tale" with
female—one might say even "feminist"—interests. The Second Nun's heroine, who finesses her bridegroom and mocks her tormentor, contrasts strik-
ingly with the long-suffering, chaste "martyrs" celebrated by Chaucer's male
pilgrims: the Man of Law's Constance, the Clerk's Griselda, and the Physi-
cian's Virginia.[80] What is more, the "Second Nun's Tale" reprises the theme of
women's conjugal sovereignty introduced in the "Wife of Bath's Prologue" and
"Tale." The account of how Cecilia negotiates marriage on her own terms,
transforming her bridegroom from a "fiers leoun" into a "meke . . . lomb"
(198–99), is strangely similar to that in the "Wife of Bath's Tale." The Wife's tale
also features a wedding-night "conversion" prompted by a bride's unexpected
catechism—though in this case an *unwilling* bridegroom is transformed into
a congenial bedmate. Such parallels suggest that Chaucer knew very well that
the differences in outlook separating a nun from a wife were not as profound as
the Wife's prologue implies.

Felicity Riddy's study of patterns of women's book ownership in the fourteenth and fifteenth centuries, in fact, indicates that the literary tastes, interests,
and reading practices of nuns and laywomen were "more or less indistinguish-
able."[81] We might thus expect that late medieval wives could appreciate stories
about virgin saints as well as could their cloistered sisters. The *Book of Margery
Kempe* indeed testifies that there was at least one wife among Chaucer's contemporaries who enjoyed legends of virgin martyrs and appropriated those
saints as role models. Admittedly, Margery Kempe is not a representative laywoman, and her references to the saints often mention their enviable virginity.
Yet Kempe appears to have admired the martyrs as teachers and public figures,
too. In her account of her activities during the early 1400s, she not only presents herself as a "belated St. Cecilia," enlisting divine protection to keep her
importunate husband at bay, but also as a bourgeois St. Katherine, disputing

[80] Karen A. Winstead, "Saints, Wives, and Other 'Hooly Thynges': Pious Laywomen in Middle
English Romance," *Chaucer Yearbook* 2 (1995): 137–54.
[81] Felicity Riddy, "'Women Talking about the Things of God': A Late Medieval Sub-culture," in
Women and Literature in Britain, 1150–1500, ed. Carol M. Meale (Cambridge: Cambridge University Press, 1993), 110.

with lawyers and priests, just as Katherine debated philosophers, and rebuking mayors, as Katherine chastised the Roman emperor.[82] Kempe's resemblance to Katherine is especially striking in this description of her encounter with lawyers in Lincoln:

> Sche cam to Lyncolne, & þer sufferd sche many scornys & many noyful wordys, answeryng a-ȝen in Goddys cawse wyth-owtyn any lettyng, wysly & discretly þat many men merueyled of hir cunnyng. Þer wer men of lawe seyd vn-to hir, "We han gon to scole many ȝerys, & ȝet arn we not sufficient to answeryn as þu dost. Of whom hast þu þis cunnyng?" & sche seyd, "Of þe Holy Gost."[83]

This scene replicates the conclusion of Katherine of Alexandria's debate with the philosophers, as it is reported in the *South English Legendary*:

> Þo þe maistres ihurde hire speke : of so gret clergie
> Necouþe hi answerie noȝt o word : ac ȝyue hire þe maistrie
> Certes sire quaþ þis maistres : so gret cler[c] non þer nis
> Þat to hire reisouns hire scholde answerie : for hi beoþ soþe iwis
> We seoþ þat þe Holi Gost is mid hire : & in hire mouþe
> We ne conne answerie hire noȝt : ne we neþore þeȝ we couþe
> Þerfore bote oure lawe.
>
> (SEL 2:537/129–35)

Kempe explicitly invokes St. Katherine in describing her confrontation with the mayor of Leicester, who, angered by her public speaking, accuses her of being a counterfeit saint. Summoning her into his presence, he "askyd hir of what cuntre sche was & whos dowtyr sche was"—the same question Maxentius asked Katherine. When Kempe replies, he charges: "Seynt Kateryn telde what kynred sche cam of & ȝet ar ȝe not lyche, for þu art a fals strumpet, a fals loller, & a fals deceyuer of þe pepyl, & þerfor I xal haue þe in preson."[84] If, as David Aers has proposed, the *Book of Margery Kempe* expresses the broader "frustrations and aspirations" of women in Kempe's community, one wonders whether other wives also found the virgin martyrs attractive—not just the "many wifys"

---

[82] David Aers discusses Kempe as a "belated St. Cecilia" in "The Making of Margery Kempe," in *Community, Gender, and Individual Identity: English Writing, 1360–1430* (New York: Routledge, 1988), 93–95. For other interpretations of Kempe's appropriation of St. Katherine, see Gayle Margherita, *The Romance of Origins: Language and Sexual Difference in Middle English Literature* (Philadelphia: University of Pennsylvania Press, 1994), 34–36; and Ruth Shklar, "Cobham's Daughter: *The Book of Margery Kempe* and the Power of Heterodox Thinking," *Modern Language Quarterly* 56 (1995): 294.

[83] *Book of Margery Kempe*, 135.

[84] Ibid., 111–12.

who yearn to live "frely fro her husbondys" but also wives who, like the fictional Alison, "nyl envye no virginitee."[85]

Chaucer's attribution of his Cecilia legend to a nun conceals not only the potential appeal of virgin martyr legends for laywomen but also their demonstrable appeal for laymen. We must bear in mind, after all, that the "Second Nun's Tale" was originally a *man's* story—Chaucer's own; even relocated within the *Canterbury Tales,* the voice of "I, unworthy sone of Eve" (62), breaks through, reminding us of the tale's origin. We might well wonder what prompted Chaucer—and William Paris, for that matter—to adapt virgin martyr legends. Both writers explicitly praise the saints as efficacious intercessors. Yet there were many powerful saints these men could have chosen to honor: why write about virgin martyrs?

Given what we know about Chaucer and Paris, we cannot dismiss the possibility that they actually identified with the saints. William Paris's epilogue to "Christine" suggests that he was attracted to the saint as a fellow political prisoner. By concluding his work with an account of his own experience as a captive, Paris implicitly invites readers to compare him to the woman whose heroism "in depe prisone" (170) he has just narrated. Paris, the dedicated servant of Thomas Beauchamp, is not unlike Christine, "Goddes owne seruaunte" (16). A mere squire might seem as unlikely a hero as a maiden, and Paris touts his willingness to risk everything, standing by his lord when so many others (among them knights, his social superiors) have fled:

> Where are his knyghtes þat withe hyme yede
> Whane he was in prosperite?
> Where are the squiers now at nede,
> That sumtyme thoughte þei wolde note flee?
> Of yomene hade he grete plente,
> Thate he was wonte to clothe & feede:
> Nowe is þer none of þe mene
> Thate ous dare se, þer lorde, fore drede.
>
> (505–12)

Like Christine, the captive squire will not be silenced. Indeed, I suspect that "as he satte in prisone of stone" (518), rehearsing all the ways in which the seem-

---

[85] Aers, "The Making of Margery Kempe," 98; *Book of Margery Kempe,* 212. Julian of Norwich, who may have been a laywoman at the time of her visions, was equally adept at transforming the virgin martyr into a model suited to her own needs. St. Cecilia's death by three blows to the neck inspired Julian to pray that God "wolde grawnte me thre wonndys in my lyfe tyme, that es to saye the wonnd(e) of contricyoun, the wonnde of compassyoun and the wonnde of wylfulle langgynge to god." See *A Book of Showings to the Anchoress Julian of Norwich,* ed. Edmund Colledge and James Walsh (Toronto: Pontifical Institute of Mediaeval Studies, 1978), 204–6.

ingly helpless virgin martyr outwitted and humiliated her powerful captors, he "softly smylide" (469) a little himself, for through his writing, he could lob a metaphorical tongue at his own enemies. Chaucer's relation to Cecilia is less obvious; however, it seems likely he admired the virgin martyr's role as a social critic, much as Margery Kempe appears to have done. Given his recurring criticism of the worldliness of the institutional Church, he may have viewed Cecilia's eloquent indictment of political and religious institutions as an inspiring model and a vehicle for his own more cautious project of dissent.[86] Cecilia was, after all, a laywoman, and her legend might easily be read as an example of lay heroism or of lay authority. Indeed, John Wyclif used St. Cecilia to argue that laypeople are empowered to consecrate.[87]

We must not, however, overestimate identification as a factor in explaining the popularity of legends featuring disorderly virgin martyrs. It is surely no coincidence that these narratives flourished at a time when traditionally sanctioned social relations were being contested and renegotiated. Stories of disorderly virgins captured the varied tensions that attended changes in the socioeconomic fabric of late medieval England.

To take the most obvious example, Middle English virgin martyr legends spoke simultaneously to the gender-based fears and aspirations of late medieval men and women at a time when women's economic activities threatened to undermine traditional definitions of a woman's place. With the growth of a market economy during the later thirteenth century, women's opportunity to gain some measure of economic autonomy expanded. Records from many cities indicate that women participated in a wide variety of crafts and professions. In London, for example, Kay E. Lacey found references to women as bakers, brewers, merchants, brokers, armorers, artists, and jewelers.[88] In Shrewsbury, a few women could be found even in such elite professions as weaving.[89] Some of these women were single; in his study of pre-plague Halesowen, R. H. Hilton found a "remarkable" number of "women whose activity was on their own behalf rather than simply reflecting their association with father or

---

[86] For a discussion of how Chaucer expresses his dissatisfaction with the contemporary Church within the "Second Nun's Tale" itself, see Lynn Staley Johnson, "Chaucer's Tale of the Second Nun and the Strategies of Dissent," *Studies in Philology* 89 (1992): 314–33. On this point, see also Reames, "Retellings of the Cecilia Legend," 198–99.

[87] John Wyclif, *Trialogus cum supplemento trialogi*, ed. G. V. Lechler (Oxford: Clarendon, 1869), 280–81. Margaret Aston discusses this example in *Lollards and Reformers: Images and Literacy in Late Medieval Religion* (London: Hambledon, 1984), 67.

[88] Kay E. Lacey, "Women and Work in Fourteenth and Fifteenth Century London," in *Women and Work in Pre-Industrial England*, ed. Lindsey Charles and Lorna Duffin (London: Croom Helm, 1985), 24–82.

[89] Diane Hutton, "Women in Fourteenth Century Shrewsbury," in *Women and Work*, ed. Charles and Duffin, 83–99.

husband." [90] However, many towns and cities allowed wives engaged in business to claim the status of *femme sole*, enabling them to buy, sell, make contracts, sue, and possess property independently of their husbands. [91] Though a wife's economic success normally benefited her husband, it undermined the patriarchal structure of the household, insofar as "work that required the institution of feme sole or similar legal privileges removed control over economic resources from the household and its head." [92]

To be sure, the late thirteenth and fourteenth centuries were no golden age for women. From all indications, their social and economic gains were modest; for the most part, they worked in low-skill, low-status, and low-paid occupations. [93] The institution of *femme sole* may in practice have benefited men more than women, for it shielded a husband from his wife's debts. [94] Nevertheless, as Paul Strohm has commented, "even small economic successes could . . . affect the distribution of power within the household." [95] John Kempe discovered that his wife, Margery, despite the failure of her business ventures, had learned to drive a hard bargain. That a woman could redeem—or could *think* of redeeming—her conjugal debt in cash must have frightened many men—and, for that matter, many women—even if no women of their acquaintance were inclined to attempt anything that radical. Likewise, the relative freedom of the *femme sole* might have generated friction even within traditional households by making the *femme covert* resent her husband's nearly absolute control.

[90] R. H. Hilton, "Small Town Society in England before the Black Death," *Past and Present* 105 (1984): 53–78 (quote on 68). Halesowen borough records both indicate that "women heads of household were not unusual" and suggest that these women were "quite self-assertive, a reflection of their importance in retail trade" (Hilton, "Small Town Society," 72, 71). P. J. P. Goldberg discusses the relatively high proportion of female-headed households in late-fourteenth-century York in *Women, Work, and Life Cycle in a Medieval Economy: Women in York and Yorkshire, c. 1300–1520* (Oxford: Clarendon, 1992), esp. 309–18.

[91] Lacey, "Women and Work," 42.

[92] Martha C. Howell, *Women, Production, and Patriarchy in Late Medieval Cities* (Chicago: University of Chicago Press, 1986), 20.

[93] See, for example, Judith M. Bennett, "Medieval Women, Modern Women: Across the Great Divide," in *Culture and History, 1350–1600: Essays on English Communities, Identities, and Writing*, ed. David Aers (Detroit: Wayne State University Press, 1992), 147–75, and Bennett, *Women in the Medieval English Countryside: Gender and Household in Brigstock before the Plague* (New York: Oxford University Press, 1987), esp. 177–98; Helena Graham, "'A Woman's Work . . .': Labour and Gender in the Late Medieval Countryside," in *Woman Is a Worthy Wight: Women in English Society, c. 1200–1500*, ed. P. J. P. Goldberg (Wolfeboro Falls, N.H.: Alan Sutton, 1992), 126–48; Maryanne Kowaleski, "Women's Work in a Market Town: Exeter in the Late Thirteenth Century," in *Women and Work in Preindustrial Europe*, ed. Barbara A. Hanawalt (Bloomington: Indiana University Press, 1986), 145–64; and Hutton, "Women in Fourteenth Century Shrewsbury," 83–99.

[94] Bennett, "Medieval Women, Modern Women," 155.

[95] Paul Strohm, "Treason in the Household," in *Hochon's Arrow: The Social Imagination of Fourteenth-Century Texts* (Princeton: Princeton University Press, 1992), 126.

The economic opportunities in postplague England offered tempting alter-natives to early marriage.[96] During the fourteenth century, there was a marked increase in adolescents migrating from the countryside to towns in search of often short-term employment.[97] "Leaving home in early adolescence," Riddy has reasonably postulated, may well have "encouraged independence and self-assertiveness."[98] In any case, civic ordinances and court records repeatedly associate female migrants with social disruption. These women were accused of trading without license, for example, or of otherwise violating a town's "fraunchyse."[99] Charges of drunkenness and slander abound, and laws were enacted to regulate the living arrangements of women who might gravitate to cheap lodgings of questionable repute.[100] As P. J. P. Goldberg has pointed out, the female migrant's "high profile within the borough court would only serve to strengthen the prejudice that the 'ungoverned' woman was a trouble-maker."[101]

Fears of autonomous women manifested themselves in sermons, misoga-mous tracts, fabliaux, and romances, as well as in the often venomous stereo-typing of predominantly female occupations, such as small-scale retailing, brewing, and spinning.[102] Virgin martyr legends complement the antifeminist messages of these popular texts, for they demonstrate that *all* women, even chaste saints, are aggressive and destructive. It is, I suspect, no coincidence that as the virgin martyr became more domineering in the late thirteenth century, the tortures inflicted on her became more brutal (or at least the descriptions of her ordeals became more graphic). To be sure, hagiographers also detailed the torture of male martyrs, and the violence of these legends must to some degree reflect a broad taste for blood and gore among medieval English writers, artists, and audiences. Yet the sexual nature of the tortures that the saint endures and the loathing that the virgin martyr's persecutors express toward her not just as a Christian but as a woman have no equivalent in the passions of male martyrs.

[96] See especially Goldberg, *Women, Work, and Life Cycle*; and Richard M. Smith, "Geographical Diversity in the Resort to Marriage in Late Medieval Europe: Work, Reputation, and Unmarried Females in the Household Formation Systems of Northern and Southern Europe," in *Woman Is a Worthy Wight*, ed. Goldberg, 16–59. For a qualified view of the actual opportunities for single women in postplague England, see Ruth Mazo Karras, *Common Women: Prostitution and Sexuality in Medieval England* (New York: Oxford University Press, 1996), 50–53.

[97] For different perspectives on this phenomenon, see Hilton, "Small Town Society"; and Gold-berg, *Women, Work, and Life Cycle*, 280–304.

[98] Felicity Riddy, "Mother Knows Best: Reading Social Change in a Courtesy Text," *Speculum* 71 (1996): 76.

[99] Hilton, "Small Town Society," 65–66.

[100] Ibid., 64, 71–72.

[101] Goldberg, *Women, Work, and Life Cycle,* 288. On the association of single women with disor-der, see also Karras, *Common Women.*

[102] Judith M. Bennett, "Misogyny, Popular Culture, and Women's Work," *History Workshop* 31 (1991): 166–88.

Hagiographers themselves betray a certain ambivalence toward their protagonists; in fact, some seem to defy readers to sympathize with their villains. Maxentius, for example, is more pathetic than contemptible as he mourns the loss of his friend, Porphirius, who has deserted him for Katherine and her alien faith:

> Allas . . . I lif ouer-lang
> To suffer all þir stowres strang!
> Al erthly wele wendes o-way
> Þat me suld confort night or day!
> Lo here mi nobil knight, allas,
> Þat mi keper and confort was,
> Mi sekerest help in ilka nede
> And mi solace in ilkadede—
> Now es he most man me to noy
> & has liking oure lawes to stroy
> & grantes him anely forto ken
> & serue þe god of cristen men.
> (NEL 172/653–64)

Similarly, William Paris's Urban decries the behavior of his daughter Christine in terms that many fourteenth-century parents might have found reasonable: "She saide my doughter was she noghte . . . / She braste my goddes so richely wrouthe: / What wondur ife I were wrothe þane?" (205–8). By the end of the Christine legend, readers of the *North English Legendary* probably understood why Julian's men "thoght scho lifed ouer-lang" (NEL 96/282).[103]

It is important to bear in mind, however, that even as virgin martyr legends participated in misogynistic discourse, they also undermined that discourse. By associating "dangerous" traits with indisputably "good" women, these texts called into question traditional formulations about gender. For example, virgin martyr legends belie the long-standing association of women's speech with sexual and moral depravity, and they might well seem to authorize dissent from patriarchal definitions of acceptable conduct for women. Virgin martyr legends also subvert fantasies of women as sexual objects. On the one hand, hagiographers explicitly portray the saints as the objects of men's desire. Their enemies frequently allude to them as potential bedfellows, as when Olibrius tells Mar-

---

[103] I should note that virgin martyr legends were not the only lives of female saints to contain misogynistic elements. In the *South English Legendary,* for example, Mary of Egypt is represented as a workingwoman who entices men to sin for the sheer fun of it; Mary did not need to charge for her services, the narrator explains, for "mid spinnynge & mid souwinge hure lif lode heo wan" (SEL 1:137/18) (she earned her living by spinning and sewing).

garet that "such hendi body as þou berst bicome bet in boure / In min armes
ligge iclupt þanne a false god honure" (SEL 1:294/81–82) or when Paschasius
commands his men to haul Lucy off to a brothel, where she would be forced to
endure the embraces of "alle þat wolde bi such a fair womman do eni folie"
(SEL 2:569/100). Hagiographers themselves often betray a candid fascination
with their protagonists' bodies. William Paris, for example, virtually leers at his
heroine's nakedness: "Hire paps were als rounde ywy(s)e / As an appille, thate
growes in felde" ("Cristine," 441–42). The same fascination is obvious in the
visual arts, which often feature the saints as naked, voluptuous young
women.[104] Yet the saint invariably evades masculine appropriation. In pictorial
cycles and narratives alike, assaults on her virginity end with the humiliation of
her persecutor, as we so clearly see in the kitchen episode of the Anastasia legend and in the Margaret cycle of the *Queen Mary's Psalter*. Ultimately, the virgin thwarts the designs of her tormentor and realizes her own goals—autonomy on earth and glory in heaven.

Virgin martyr legends did not simply embody tensions about changing
gender roles and relations, however. As I discussed earlier, secondary conflicts
within the legends often show the disintegration of other traditional power relations: in the Anastasia legend, for example, servants thrash their lord, while
in the Katherine of Alexandria legend, a lord repudiates his emperor. Non-
gendered conflicts of this sort are, moreover, symbolically represented in the
conflicts between the saints and their persecutors. Medieval social theorists frequently described the well-functioning society as a system of interlocking and
closely analogous hierarchies. As the writer of *Dives and Pauper* put it: "Þe
offys of teching & chastysyng longyth . . . to euery gouernour aftir his name &
his degre, to þe pore man gouernynge his pore houshold, to þe riche man
gouernynge his mene, to þe housebond gouernynge his wif, to þe fadir & þe
moodir gouernynge her childryn, to þe iustice gouernynge his contre, to þe
kyng gouernynge his peple."[105] Because hierarchies were commonly related
to one another in this fashion, the virgin martyr's disruption of the gender
hierarchy could stand for a spectrum of activities that threatened traditional

---

[104] V. A. Kolve considers the erotic dimensions of Cecilia iconography in "Chaucer's *Second Nun's
Tale* and the Iconography of Saint Cecilia," in *New Perspectives in Chaucer Criticism,* ed. Donald M.
Rose (Norman, Okla.: Pilgrim Books, 1981), 137–58.

[105] *Dives and Pauper*, 328. As Paul Strohm points out, such analogical relations of domination
and subordination were enacted into law with the 1352 Statute of Treason, which extended the
definition of treason to include not only crimes against the king but also cases "when a servant kills
his master, a woman kills her husband . . . when a secular man or man in religious orders kills his
prelate, to whom he owes faith and obedience" ("Treason," 124). For a historical survey of the analogy between household and state, see Constance Jordan, "The Household and the State: Transformations in the Representation of an Analogy from Aristotle to James I," *Modern Language Quarterly* 54 (1993): 307–26.

relations of dominion and subordination, particularly in the years following the Black Death—activities ranging from workers' defiance of labor statutes to the social strivings of civil servants and bureaucrats such as Chaucer. Virgin martyr legends, with their simultaneous celebration and punishment of the socially disruptive saints, could play to the divergent, and perhaps ambivalent, views that readers would have harbored toward the socioeconomic changes that were occurring in late medieval England. For example, though middle-class professionals such as Chaucer certainly benefited from the increased fluidity of social categories, they looked askance at the mobility of peasants and may even have resented the ambitions of members of their own rank.[106] Chaucer, indeed, deftly brings out the various inconsistencies that colored the attitudes and assumptions of members of the rising middle classes. Harry Bailly is a case in point: though content to govern knights and squires on the trip to Canterbury, the Host has little patience with other enterprising pilgrims, such as the Franklin, who are eager to establish a place for themselves among the elite.

In her now classic study of the "woman on top," Natalie Zemon Davis argues that the image of the disorderly woman performed a variety of ideological functions during the later Middle Ages and Renaissance:

> It was a multivalent image that could operate, first, to widen behavioral options for women within and even outside marriage, and, second, to sanction riot and political disobedience for both men and women in a society that allowed the lower orders few formal means of protest. Play with the unruly woman is partly a chance for temporary release from the traditional and stable hierarchy; but it is also part of the conflict over efforts to change the basic distribution of power within society.[107]

Because their rebellious heroines were also saints, virgin martyr legends could easily be interpreted as sanctioning social disruptiveness. Hence, they may have been especially likely to "prompt new ways of thinking about the system and reacting to it."[108] We have, unfortunately, little evidence of how late medieval people actually interpreted or applied virgin martyr legends. Yet I would suppose that their influence extended far beyond the direct imitation of the saints or the conscious appropriation of their legends to political or social ends. The

---

[106] As Lee Patterson put it, "The crucial ideological opposition is not between the seigneurial nobility and the urban merchant class but between both of these elements of the exploiting class and the increasingly independent and self-sufficient productive classes in the country"; see his "The Miller's Tale and the Politics of Laughter," in Chaucer and the Subject of History (Madison: University of Wisconsin Press, 1991), 253.

[107] Natalie Zemon Davis, "Women on Top," in Society and Culture in Early Modern France (Stanford: Stanford University Press, 1975), 131.

[108] Ibid., 143.

texts studied in this chapter were the products of an increasingly restless society, yet they also were part of the environment fostering that restlessness. That is, such heroines as William Paris's Christine or the *North English Legendary*'s Anastasia helped *create* a milieu in which wives were prone to argue about theology; workers, to defy labor statutes; and haberdashers, to flout sumptuary laws. Those people need not have been *consciously* influenced by hagiography; indeed, if pressed to offer an opinion about saints' legends, they might have echoed Alison of Bath's complaint that such pious tales had little to do with their experience. Fascinating as it is to analyze the ways in which Margery Kempe self-consciously transforms herself into a second Katherine of Alexandria in order to authorize her role as a teacher and public figure, it is perhaps more intriguing still to contemplate how saints' legends might have shaped the disorderliness of the pair of Lollards lambasted in Henry Knighton's *Chronicon* for burning a statue of St. Katherine to cook their dinner.[109]

---

[109] Henry Knighton, *Knighton's Chronicle, 1337–1396*, ed. and trans. G. H. Martin (Oxford: Clarendon, 1995), 296–99. For discussions of this incident, see Aston, *Lollards and Reformers*, 167–70; and Nicholas Watson, "The Composition of Julian of Norwich's *Revelation of Love*," *Speculum* 68 (1993): 662.

3

Decorous Lives: Saints and Consumers, 1400–1450

Toward the end of Thomas Hoccleve's facetious "Letter of Cupid" (circa 1402), the God of Love delivers a passionate tribute to St. Margaret, acclaiming her suffering, admiring her steadfastness, and commending her for converting "many a wyght . . . Vnto the feith of God." We hardly expect a god whose business is promoting sex to sing the praises of a professional virgin. Indeed, as if realizing that his encomium might sound foolish, Cupid hastens to explain that he is in no way commending Margaret's virginity—"trusteth ryght wel it cam neuer in my thoght, / for euer werre y ayein chastyte, / and ever shal"— but rather her constancy and devotion. This tribute is startling not only because it is uttered by Cupid but also because Margaret has so little in common with the typical heroines of late-fourteenth-century hagiography. In lieu of the Christian champion who scourges the devil with her chains and binds him with her wimple, we find a decorous lady who overcomes the fiend through steadfastness. The virago who taunts her suitor and dies to escape marriage has become a "preciouse gemme" whose virginity is incidental and whose most commendable qualities—"hir louyng hert and constant to hir lay"—are (as Cupid's enthusiasm implies) readily transferable to other areas of human experience.[1]

Cupid is hardly a serious hagiographer, yet, as the fifteenth century progressed, many producers of legends appear to have shared his view of what makes a virgin martyr admirable. Beginning in the early 1400s, numerous Middle English hagiographers were focusing less on the saints' hostility toward men than on their suffering. For example, in retelling Jacobus's legend of Margaret, John Mirk eliminated the saint's altercations with Olibrius and directed his audience's attention to "what scho suffyrde for Godys loue."[2] Similarly, the anonymous writer of the *Speculum Sacerdotale* produced a Katherine

---

[1] *Hoccleve's Works: The Minor Poems*, ed. Frederick J. Furnivall and Sir I. Gollancz, EETS.ES 61, 73 (London: Oxford University Press, 1892, 1925), rev. Jerome Mitchell and A. I. Doyle and reprinted as one volume (London: Oxford University Press, 1970), 89, lines 421–34.

[2] *Mirk's Festial*, ed. Theodor Erbe, EETS.ES 96 (1905; reprint, Millwood, N.Y.: Kraus, 1987), 199.

legend that dwells on the saint's suffering and teaching, without even alluding to her spirited defiance of Maxentius.[3] Like Cupid, many fifteenth-century hagiographers were eager to emphasize "transferable" qualities—courtesy, patience, diligence, humility, piety, charity—which would make the saints suitable models for laywomen as well as for consecrated virgins.[4] A striking example of this shift in the values embodied in virgin martyr legends occurs in a prose legend of Ursula composed around 1450. After reporting the traditional story of the slaughter of Ursula, her bridegroom (the king of England), and ten thousand companions by pagans, the Middle English writer concludes, "And so she was wedded that day to the kyng of Englond full gloriously byfore the kyng of heven."[5] This is an astonishing variation on the usual theme of the martyr's union with Christ, her heavenly bridegroom. Cupid would have approved.

In much the same spirit, contemporary artists tended to represent the virgin martyrs as refined gentlewomen rather than triumphant viragos.[6] When depicting torture scenes, they adapted the iconography of Christ's passion to convey an impression of vulnerability that is rare in earlier images. In one fifteenth-century alabaster, for example, two ruffians prod and kick the blindfolded St. Katherine toward the block on which she is to be executed (figure 21). Katherine's abjection is made all the more apparent by the majestic presence of Maxentius, who gazes disdainfully on his vanquished adversary. Like many other artists of the period, this sculptor affirms the saint's faith without undermining the power of the secular state, which is so obviously able to inflict anguish and humiliation on its enemies. In written legends as well as in the visual arts, topoi that once demonstrated the impotence of temporal power

[3] *Speculum Sacerdotale*, ed. Edward H. Weatherly, EETS.OS 200 (1936; reprint, Millwood, N.Y.: Kraus, 1971), 243–44.

[4] In "Attitudes toward the Cult of the Saints in the Late Middle Ages: The Light Shed by English Breviary Manuscripts," a paper presented at the eleventh meeting of the Illinois Medieval Association, Loyola University, Chicago, February 18–19, 1994. Sherry L. Reames notes a similar phenomenon in secular breviaries produced in late medieval England: "There is a strongly marked tendency, beginning in the fourteenth century and accelerating in the fifteenth, for the breviaries to abridge and rewrite the legends of many saints so as to bring their conduct into better conformity with late-medieval rules and expectations." Although "not confined to female saints," this rewriting is "especially clear" in virgin martyr legends. I thank Professor Reames for sending me a copy of her paper and allowing me to quote from it. I should point out that in vernacular hagiography the tendency to fashion more "exemplary" saints is not confined to virgin martyrs either. I discuss an analogous tendency in the lives of male martyrs in "Lydgate's Lives of Saints Edmund and Alban: Martyrdom and *Prudent Pollicie*," *Mediaevalia* 17 (1994): 221–41.

[5] "A Middle-English Prose Life of St. Ursula," ed. G. N. Garmonsway and R. R. Raymo, *Review of English Studies*, n.s., 9 (1958): 359.

[6] For some excellent examples of virgin martyrs depicted as fashionable gentlewomen on the fifteenth-century screens of parish churches, see Eamon Duffy, *The Stripping of the Altars: Traditional Religion in England, c. 1400–1580* (New Haven: Yale University Press, 1992), plates 59–60, 68.

21. The execution of St. Catherine, A119B–1946. © The Board of Trustees of the
Victoria and Albert Museum, London.

22. St. Agatha, *South English Legendary*,
MS Tanner 17, fol. 19r, by permission of
the Bodleian Library, Oxford.

were reworked or abandoned: where, in fourteenth-century legends, torturers
wore themselves out beating saints who only mocked their efforts, the exhaustion of the "beteris" in John Capgrave's life of Katherine conveys the saint's
"bitter peyne."[7]

Writers and artists were not only refashioning the virgin martyrs but also
reframing old texts so as to invite new interpretations. For example, the illustrations that were added during the fifteenth century to the *South English Legendary*, MS Tanner 17, Bodleian Library, portray Agnes and Agatha as graceful
women rapt in prayer, whose serene otherworldliness contrasts with the pugnacity of their literary counterparts (for Agatha, see figure 22). The demon-
thrashing Juliana has been transformed into a pious reader glancing up from

[7] John Capgrave, *The Life of St. Katharine of Alexandria*, ed. Carl Horstmann, EETS.OS 100 (1893;
reprint, Millwood, N.Y.: Kraus, 1987), 5.638–39.

23. St. Juliana, *South English Legendary*, MS Tanner 17, fol. 22r, by permission of the Bodleian Library, Oxford.

her book, her thumb marking her place on the page (figure 23). Because readers would see these pictures before reading the texts, the illustrations serve as introductions of sorts, mitigating the emphasis on social disorder within the narratives proper by predisposing readers toward dramas of steadfastness rather than of confrontation. A similar effect is achieved in the introductions to the anonymous prose adaptations of Jacobus's lives of Margaret and Katherine that are preserved in an early-sixteenth-century miscellany (MS Harley 4012, British Library), which both call attention to the saints' imitable qualities. The translator commends St. Katherine for constantly meditating on Christ's passion and urges readers to follow her example: "This muste euery creaturee remember as did this holy maiden and virgen; for she rememberde this daily and howrely and printid hit in hir mynde, and thoght on his passion and payne and rewardid hym with hir consiens and good herte to hir power."[8] He introduces Margaret as a "maiden . . . araide with instans of the drede of god, abiding in religion, presonable in honeste, singular in paciens." In an apparent attempt to present the saint as a model for all good Christians, not just beautiful virgins, he writes that Margaret "was faire in face and full of beute but she was fairer in bewte of ffaithe. She was not only a maiden of hir body but alsoo in mynde."[9]

Nonhagiographical works that were written or translated for fifteenth-century laypeople likewise represented the saints as exemplary laywomen. A case in point is the *Book of the Knight of La Tour-Landry*, an early-fifteenth-century translation of a French conduct book written in the 1370s by Geoffroy de la Tour-Landry for his daughters.[10] Intermittently throughout his book, Geoffroy uses virgin martyrs as examples of proper behavior. Anastasia, for example, is a paragon of charity and compassion to prisoners: "Assone as she wost where there was any pore prisonere that was yprisoned for ani necessite of wronge, of enmyte, or be any deseite, she wolde goo releue hem, and yeue hem of her goodes, and helpe hem vnto her deliueraunce."[11] There is no hint of impropriety: the captives she aids were wrongly imprisoned, and Geoffroy does not indicate (as do other sources) that her charity infuriated her husband by depleting his assets. The knight notes that God rewarded Anastasia's goodness to captives by releasing her from prison, without revealing that her husband put her there for insubordination and that she was released through widowhood. Geoffroy likewise commends Saints Lucy and Cecilia "and mani other ladyes" for their charity: "They gauen the most parte of thayre good vnto pore peple that were in necessite and mischeef, as it is expressed and shewed in thaire legende."[12] From this synopsis, the casual reader would never think of the many more subversive deeds and qualities that are also "expressed and shewed" in the legends of these saints. Geoffroy even cites Saints Katherine, Margaret, Lucy, and Ursula in admonishing his daughters to avoid "lechery"; the saints preferred to die rather than to commit that sin, he observes, as he exhorts his daughters to "drede God and youre husbonde."[13]

---

[8] Jacqueline Jenkins discusses the contemplative character of this introduction in "An English Life of St. Catherine and the Fifteenth Century Female Audience," paper delivered at the International Medieval Congress, University of Leeds, 4–7 July 1994. I thank Ms. Jenkins for allowing me to quote from her transcription.

[9] MS Harley 4012, 124r, British Library.

[10] Geoffrey de la Tour-Landry, *The Book of the Knight of La Tour-Landry*, ed. Thomas Wright, EETS.OS 33 (1906; reprint, New York: Greenwood, 1969).

[11] Ibid., 113.

[12] Ibid., 152.

[13] Ibid., 83.

Readers of Nicholas Love's "best-selling" *Myrrour of the Blessed Lyf of Jesu Christ*, an early-fifteenth-century translation of Pseudo-Bonaventure's *Meditationes Vitae Christi*, were similarly encouraged to follow the example of a virgin martyr, St. Cecilia:

> Amonge oþer vertuese commendynges of þe holy virgine Cecile it is writen þat she bare alwey þe gospel of criste hidde in her breste, þat may be undirstand þat of þe blessed lif of oure lord Jesu criste writen in þe gospele, she chace certayne parties most deuoute. In þe which she set her meditacion & her þouht niȝt & day with a clene & hole herte. And when she hade so fully alle þe manere of his life ouer gon, she began aȝayne. And so with a likyng & swete taste gostly chewyng in þat manere þe gospell of crist, she set & bare it euer in þe priuyte of her breste. *In þe same manere I conseil þat þou do.*[14]

The passage proceeds to explain how meditation gave Cecilia the fortitude to live surrounded by the "vanytees of þe worlde" without being corrupted by them—a message that Love's well-to-do readers would certainly have found apposite.[15] Even Cecilia's passion is made directly relevant to the experience of a late medieval reader, for the *Myrrour* explains that martyrs endured hideous torments not through miraculous powers but through contemplation: "For what tyme þe Martire stant with alle þe body to rent, & neuer þe lesse he is ioiful & glade in alle his peyne, where trowest is þan his soule & his herte? soþely in þe wondes of Jesu." By meditating on Christ's life and passion, "not onlich Martires" but all pious Christians will be able to bear tribulations with patience, even joy.[16]

In this chapter, I examine the changes in the representation of virgin martyrs that took place during the first half of the fifteenth century as they are illustrated in the works of two popular East Anglian hagiographers, John Lydgate and Osbern Bokenham.[17] Though both Suffolk writers—Lydgate was a monk of the Benedictine Abbey of Bury St. Edmunds, and Bokenham was an Austin friar from Stoke-Clare, some ten miles southwest of Bury—these hagiographers had somewhat different audiences. Taken together, their readers provide a representative sample of the growing audience for saints' legends among the bourgeoisie and gentry, whose tastes were coming to have a major impact on

---

[14] Nicholas Love, *Mirror of the Blessed Life of Jesus Christ*, ed. Michael G. Sargent (New York: Garland, 1992), 11; emphasis mine.

[15] Ibid., 12.

[16] Ibid.

[17] References will be to lines in the following editions: *The Minor Poems of John Lydgate*, vol. 1, ed. Henry Noble MacCracken, EETS.ES 107 (London: Oxford University Press, 1911), 154–59 (Petronilla), and 173–92 (Margaret); and Osbern Bokenham, *Legendys of Hooly Wummen*, ed. Mary S. Serjeantson, EETS.OS 206 (1938; reprint, Millwood, N.Y.: Kraus, 1988).

religious literature. A writer famous in his own lifetime, whose audience encompassed kings, courtiers, provincial gentlepeople, and London guildsmen, Lydgate composed two virgin martyr legends: a life of Margaret, written between 1415 and 1426 at the request of Ann Mortimer, Lady March; and a life of Petronilla, written for the lepers' hospital at Bury, perhaps around 1434.[18] Unlike Lydgate, who explicitly envisioned that his Margaret legend, at least, would transcend class lines and circulate among a broad audience of "noble princesses and ladyes of estate," "gentilwomen lower of degre," and "alle wymmen" (519–23), Bokenham wrote for a more circumscribed public of local aristocrats, landowners, and members of religious houses.[19] His patrons formed part of an East Anglian network of avid readers and book collectors, who were, as Samuel Moore established, "closely connected by ties of kinship, neighborhood, marriage, or interest."[20] Whereas Lydgate's legend of Margaret was widely anthologized, Bokenham's legends survive in a single manuscript.[21] Composed for particular readers during the 1440s, Bokenham's narratives were perhaps circulated in ephemeral "pious booklets,"[22] in much the same way that Symon Wynter urged that his life of St. Jerome be passed along, when he wrote to his patron Margaret Beaufort: "I said that . . . y wold write his lyf and myraclis in ynglyshe . . . that not only ye shuld knowe hit the more clerely to your gostely profecte, but also hit shuld mow abyde and turne to edificacion of othir that wold rede hit and do to copy hitt, for youre selffe, and sithe to lat other to rede

[18] On the probable dates of these legends, see Walter F. Schirmer, *John Lydgate: A Study in the Culture of the Fifteenth Century,* trans. Ann E. Keep (Westport, Conn.: Greenwood, 1961), 154 n. 11, and 158.

[19] Discussions of Bokenham's cultural context and patrons include A. S. G. Edwards, "The Transmission and Audience of Osbern Bokenham's *Legendys of Hooly Wummen,*" in *Late-Medieval Religious Texts and Their Transmission: Essays in Honour of A. I. Doyle,* ed. A. J. Minnis (Cambridge: D. S. Brewer, 1994), 157–67; Sheila Delany, introduction to *A Legend of Holy Women: A Translation of Osbern Bokenham's "Legends of Holy Women"* (Notre Dame: University of Notre Dame Press, 1992), ix–xxxiii; Gail McMurray Gibson, "Saint Anne and the Religion of Childbed: Some East Anglian Texts and Talismans," in *Interpreting Cultural Symbols: Saint Anne in Late Medieval Society,* ed. Kathleen M. Ashley and Pamela Sheingorn (Athens: University of Georgia Press, 1990), 95–110; and Karen K. Jambeck, "Patterns of Women's Literary Patronage: England, 1200–ca. 1475," in *The Cultural Patronage of Medieval Women,* ed. June Hall McCash (Athens: University of Georgia Press, 1996), 228–65.

[20] Samuel Moore, "Patrons of Letters in Norfolk and Suffolk, c. 1450," pt. 2, *PMLA* 28 (1913): 102. The most definitive study of East Anglian culture circa 1450 is now Gail McMurray Gibson's *The Theater of Devotion: East Anglian Drama and Society in the Late Middle Ages* (Chicago: University of Chicago Press, 1989). See also Richard Beadle, "Prolegomena to a Literary Geography of Later Medieval Norfolk," in *Regionalism in Late Medieval Texts: Essays Celebrating the Publication of "A Linguistic Atlas of Late Mediaeval English,"* ed. Felicity Riddy (Cambridge: D. S. Brewer, 1991), 89–108.

[21] MS Addit. 36983, British Library, a mid-fifteenth-century miscellany, however, does contain a fragment of Bokenham's Dorothy legend (Edwards, "Transmission," 162–63).

[22] Edwards, "Transmission," 162.

hit and copy hit, who so will. For ther is ther-in nedfull to be had and know and had in mynd of all ffolke."[23] In 1447, Bokenham's friend Thomas Burgh had the various legends assembled into a collection, which, according to the manuscript's colophon, he gave to a "holy place of nunnys that þei shulde haue mynd on hym & of hys systyr Dame Betrice Burgh."[24]

We would expect the legends of Bokenham and Lydgate to be quite similar to the legends examined in Chapter 2, for both hagiographers based their works on the *Legenda aurea* and were enthusiastic admirers of Chaucer.[25] In fact, the legends have little in common with their acknowledged source, the *Legenda aurea*; with Chaucer's "Second Nun's Tale"; or with other Middle English legends of the late thirteenth and fourteenth centuries. Bokenham and Lydgate extol vulnerable, suffering saints, whose heroism consists in patience, humility, and devotion. They explore the saints' emotions and provide models of secular conduct as well as of religious faith. Their works, moreover, are more indebted to early Latin *passiones* than any vernacular virgin martyr legends since those of the Katherine Group. With their emphasis on prayer and instruction as well as with their increased respect for temporal concerns, they counter the subversive impulses of the Middle English legends that were so popular a generation earlier and that, indeed, continued to be copied well into the fifteenth century.

Fifteenth-century saints' lives were shaped by their authors' consciousness that they were addressing a sophisticated audience that included laypeople with a lively interest in moral and theological issues. One representative of this new breed of confident, spiritually informed lay reader appears in the prologue to Capgrave's *Life of St. Augustine* (circa 1450):

> A noble creatur, a gentill woman, desired of me with ful grete instauns to write onto hir, þat is to sey, to translate hir treuly oute of Latyn, þe lif of Seynt Augustyn, grete doctour of þe cherch. Sche desired þis þing of me rather þan of a-noþer man be-cause þat I am of his profession, for sche supposed veryly þat I wold do it with þe bettir wil. Sche desired eke þis lif of þis Seynt more þan of ony oþir for sche was browt forth in-to þis world in his solempne feste. Than wil I, in þe name

[23] Symon Wynter, "S. Hieronymus," in "Prosalegenden," ed. Carl Horstmann, *Anglia* 3 (1880): 328–29.

[24] Bokenham, *Legendys*, 289. For another interpretation of the collection's genesis, see Delany's introduction to *Legend of Holy Women*, xvii–xxvii. Delany contends that Bokenham was originally responsible for organizing his legends into "the first all-female hagiography in any language" (xxvii), which he modeled on Chaucer's *Legend of Good Women*.

[25] Eileen S. Jankowski discusses evidence of Bokenham's familiarity with Chaucer's Cecilia legend in "Reception of Chaucer's *Second Nun's Tale*: Osbern Bokenham's *Lyf of S. Cycyle*," *Chaucer Review* 30 (1996): 306–18.

of our Lord Ihesu, beginne þis werk, to þe worchip of þis glorious doctour, and to þe plesauns and consolation of þis gentil woman þat hath so willed me with sundry [r]etribucione[s] þat I coude not disobeye hir desir.[26]

Writing for laypeople who knew, as Capgrave's "noble creatur" did, that they could choose among providers of religious literature must have made hagiographers more inclined to please their clientele by composing legends that were, insofar as possible, compatible with secular values and interests. That inclination was doubtless augmented by the fact that religious authors had more in common with their lay readers than they had had a century ago: on the one hand, the laity had become increasingly studious and more attracted to traditionally monastic religious practices; on the other hand, monks and friars such as Lydgate and Capgrave were leading increasingly active lives.[27] Given the well-documented conservatism of fifteenth-century readers and writers, it is hardly surprising that hagiographers toned down the subversive themes that had characterized saints' lives a century before. Nor is it surprising that they emphasized the saints' refined manners and wise speech. Indeed, the genteel martyrs of Lydgate, Bokenham, and their contemporaries were perfectly suited to a middle- and upper-class readership whose preoccupation with good breeding affected nearly all genres of fifteenth-century literature.[28]

The emergence of exemplary saints' lives is not solely attributable, however, to a greater rapport between religious writers and their lay public. These legends grew out of a climate that was also marked by a suspicion of lay literacy. Throughout the century, Lollardy was closely associated with vernacular books and lay learning; through that association, reading was linked with social disruptiveness, even to the point of treason.[29] Widespread anxieties about unorthodox lay scholars, particularly during the first decades of the

[26] John Capgrave, *Lives of St. Augustine and St. Gilbert of Sempringham, and a Sermon*, ed. J. J. Munro, EETS.OS 140 (1910; reprint, Millwood, N.Y.: Kraus, 1987), 1.

[27] For a discussion of the convergences between monastic and lay values and practices during the late Middle Ages, with reference to Lydgate and Bury St. Edmunds, see Gibson, *Theater of Devotion*, 107–35.

[28] For an excellent discussion of the obsession with manners in fifteenth-century literature, see Seth Lerer, *Chaucer and His Readers: Imagining the Author in Late-Medieval England* (Princeton: Princeton University Press, 1993), 57–84. Jonathan Nicholls examines courtesy as a central value in religious as well as secular institutions in *The Matter of Courtesy: Medieval Courtesy Books and the Gawain-Poet* (Woodbridge, Suffolk: D. S. Brewer, 1985), 22–44.

[29] Margaret Aston, *Lollards and Reformers: Images and Literacy in Late Medieval Religion* (London: Hambledon, 1984), 193–217; Anne Hudson, *Lollards and Their Books* (London: Hambledon, 1985); Janet Coleman, *Medieval Readers and Writers, 1350–1400* (New York: Columbia University Press, 1981), 204–31.

fifteenth century, probably made hagiographers such as Lydgate nervous about the potentially dangerous messages of saints' lives and eager to construct models of holiness that did not lend themselves to "misinterpretation."

Mapping the Soule Inward

One of the most conspicuous ways in which fifteenth-century saints' lives differ from the Middle English legends composed during the thirteenth and fourteenth centuries is in their didactic and devotional orientation. Though writers such as Bokenham and Lydgate often based their narratives on the *Legenda aurea*, they routinely embellished Jacobus's action-packed narratives with extended discussions of the saints' imitable virtues, with descriptions of their suffering and devotion, and with elaborate passages of prayer and exposition garnered from the *passiones*. In the process, they mitigated the antiworldly thrust that dominated previous Middle English legends, and they transformed the saints into benevolent figures whom lay and religious readers could not only admire but emulate as well.

The tendency of fifteenth-century hagiographers to place greater emphasis on exemplary virtues and on the saints' emotions is especially well illustrated in Lydgate's transformation of St. Margaret—one of the most pugnacious virgin martyrs in earlier Middle English hagiography—into a model of humility and piety. At first glance, Lydgate's rhetorically embellished life of St. Margaret seems much like Chaucer's Cecilia legend. As Lois Ebin has observed, Lydgate "follows the structural design of the *Second Nun's Tale* with a lengthy prologue, an extended interpretation of Margaret's name, a lofty invocation, a central narrative section, and an elaborate envoy."[30] Within this Chaucerian structure, however, he develops a model of sainthood very different from that of his predecessor. In the prologue to the "Second Nun's Tale," Chaucer emphasized Cecilia's virtuous activity—her "good werkynge," "charite," "good techynge," and general "bisynesse"—and developed these attributes of sainthood in the tale proper.[31] Given Jacobus's etymology, Lydgate might have cultivated similar themes, for Jacobus placed a great deal of emphasis on Margaret's deeds, including her victory over the devil and her teaching. Lydgate, however, omits all mention of Margaret's potentially disorderly role as a teacher, drawing attention to her "parfit holynesse" (16), "chaste lyf" (17), and "tendre Innocence" (17). Furthermore, he introduces new themes—her "delyte" in "Crystes feith" (22) and her suffering:

[30] Lois A. Ebin, *John Lydgate* (Boston: Twayne, 1985), 130.
[31] *The Riverside Chaucer*, ed. Larry D. Benson (Boston: Houghton Mifflin, 1987), 263, lines 116, 118, 93, 98.

> Hir martirdam wrought by grete duresse,—
> Ay vnmutable in hir stablenesse,
> Vn-to the dethe ay one in hir suffraunce,
> So was hir herte roted on constaunce.
>
> (18–21)

Only quickly mentioning Margaret's victory over the devil (47–48), he dwells on her sacrifice:

> . . . of hir flesshe she made a sacryfice
> Vnto the lorde, that starf vpon the rode,
> Whan he liste deye for oure redempcyoun;
> So this virgine, taquyte him, shad hir blode
> Ful benygnely in her passyoun.
>
> (49–53)

And though he has already devoted much attention in his prologue to Margaret's virtues, he quickly elaborates on them as he introduces the young saint tending her nurse's sheep:

> Devoyde of pride, of rancour and of Ire,
> She called was a mirrour of mekenesse,
> The Holy Gost hir herte so dede enspire
> That wille and thought were sette on parfitnesse,
> To thynke on Criste was holy hir gladnesse,
> And chere benygne to alle she dede shewe,
> Softe of hir speche, and but of wordys fewe.
> She gat hir love vpon euery syde,
> By cause she was so inly vertuous,—
> For God and grace with hir dide abide—
> Al thyng eschewyng that was vycious.
>
> (99–109)

These virtues are the source of Margaret's power, as the vanquished devil later attests: "Thou allone, thurgh thy virginite, / Thi chast[e] lyf, thy parfyt holynesse / Han me venquysshed and outrayed in distress" (341–43). Lydgate concludes his Margaret legend with a long encomium on the saint's virtues (499–518) that specifically establishes her as a model for others: "Hir blyssed lyf, hir conuersacioun / Were example of parfite pacience, / Of grounded clennesse and of religioun, / Of chastite founded on prudence" (505–8).

In contrast to the heroines of earlier Middle English legends, who are neither pained nor frightened during their horrendous ordeals, the heroines of fifteenth-century hagiography are vulnerable figures. In Bokenham's life of Margaret, for example, when Olibrius's men tell the saint of their master's love for her, she is alarmed: "And anoon al the blood owt of hyr faas / For sodeyn feer was styrt awey" (481–82). When the dragon appears in her cell, Bokenham's Margaret is "ful pale of cher / . . . for very fer trewly" (701–2). She has forgotten, Bokenham explains, that she had asked God for a chance to see her enemy, and she now fervently prays for deliverance (703–7). When Christ appears before Christine, the saint is overwhelmed: "Doun plat she fel up-on þe watyr clere, / For wyth grete feer astoynyd was she" (2572–73). The saints' vulnerability, moreover, is often directly linked to their holiness. For example, the excruciating pain that Lydgate's Petronilla endures during her prolonged illness demonstrates her "parfyte pacience" and her great love of God:

> Though she had of brennynge greate feruence
> Twene colde and hote, vexacion inportable,
> There was no grutchinge, but vertuous Innocence,
> Gaue thanke to God, of hert and thought most stable,
> From hir entent nat found variable,—
> So was she groundyd on parfyte charite,—
> Professyd to God to perseuere immutable,
> In her auough made vnto chastyte.
>
> (17–24)

Margaret's "grete duresse" (18) and "suffraunce" (20) likewise demonstrate for Lydgate her abiding love of God.

Like many fifteenth-century hagiographers, Bokenham and Lydgate distinguish their protagonists from the intrepid heroines of earlier legends by drawing on the unabridged Latin *passiones* to restore to their virgin martyr legends the material that Jacobus had systematically excised: the long passages of prayer and teaching. For example, Lydgate transforms Margaret into a demure and retiring figure by replacing the vitriolic arguments she advances in the *Legenda aurea* with reflections on God's power and Christ's passion (204–10, 218–24). In so doing, he constructs a legend focusing on the significance of the saint's martyrdom rather than on her heroic actions—just as "traditional" monastic hagiographers had done for centuries.[32]

Bokenham's legends offer particularly good examples of the varied uses of prayers and lessons garnered from the *passiones*. Prayers in his work typically express a range of emotions, including a very human fear of the trials to come.

---

[32] Theodor Wolpers comments on the liturgical quality of this work and its similarity to earlier Latin hagiography in his *Die englische Heiligenlegende des Mittelalters* (Tübingen: Niemeyer, 1964), 310.

During her trials, for example, Margaret beseeches: "Besegyd I am wyth wykkyd counsel, / And many doggys han enuyround me, / Wych ben ageyn me fers and cruel. / Wherfore me counfort, lord, I prey the" (638–41). Only a few lines later, she refers to her isolation, at the beginning of another long prayer: "Behold me, lord, wych am the only / Doughtyr of my fader, and he hath me / For the forsakyn" (673–75). By relating the virgin's constant supplications in this manner, Bokenham insists on her vulnerability as a human being while celebrating her victories as a saint. Never does he allow his readers to forget that the saint's power derives "thorgh grace of god entere" (716), a point Jacobus and earlier Middle English hagiographers often omitted.

Bokenham uses expository passages as well as prayers to humanize his protagonists. Cecilia comforts the sympathetic crowd lamenting her arrest with the following practical lesson:

> But now of you I ask a questyoun:
> For ych peny [if] ye receyue shuld moun
> At a market or a feyr an hool shylyng,
> As many as þedyr ye dede bryng,
> Wolde ye not spedyn you þedyr hastly?
> I trowe ye wold! now, serys, treuly
> God of hys goodnesse hath up set
> In hys courht abouyn a bettyr market;
> For to euery thyng þat to hym ys soulde
> The reward ys ordeynyd an hundyr-foulde,
> And þer-to lyf þat neuere shal cees.
> Now thynke ye not þis a noble encrees,
> An hundyrd for oon, wyth hys addytament?
> Hou trou ye? seyith your entent.
>
> (8079–92)

This extract is typical of the way long passages of instruction portray the saint as a benevolent figure, one who is well aware of the limitations of human understanding and more eager to convince than to condemn. Bokenham's saints do not simply assert points of doctrine. They strive to persuade those around them of Christian truths by presenting them in the clearest manner, reinforcing their lessons with analogies drawn from everyday life and appeals to common sense. "[I]f my sentence / Ye not beleue, makyth experience," Margaret challenges her listeners (615–16).

The saint's teachings moderate the relentless rejection of human feelings and impulses that was common in virgin martyr legends of the previous century and a half. This use of exposition is illustrated in Christine's treatment of the women her father has employed as her companions. When Christine refuses to sacrifice to the gods, her attendants beg her to comply with her father's wishes so that they will not be punished for her intransigence. In the *South English Legendary*, the saint snaps, "ȝe conseilers . . . þat luþer beoþ be[o] stille / Þis maumes nabbeþ no power to helpe us worþ a uille."³³ Bokenham's Christine, by contrast, responds "benyngly" (2214) and "wyth a sad chere" (2213). She appeals to her companions' reason and explains her actions:

> Why sey ye þus, maydyns? wold ye þat I
> Schuld to þese ydols for socour craue,
> Wych as I wel know sensibylly
> Mow me nere other hurt nere saue?
> Not so, damysels, but þis hold I best,
> Hym to worschip & seruyn wych wyl & may
> Both body & soul makyn to rest
> Here and in joye þat lestyth ay,
> Wher neuer is nyht but euyr day
> A thousend-fowld bryhter þan ony is here.
> Hym wyl I worchip, þis is no nay,
> Euyr whyl I lyue wyth hert entere.
>
> (2215–26)

There is no condemnation in this passage, no hint that the maidens' fear for their safety is in any way reprehensible. Christine's explanation reveals human feelings—sympathy for her companions, love of God, and commitment to her faith—rather than indifference to the world and its weaker inhabitants. Bokenham treats in a similar manner Margaret's response to bystanders who beg her to spare herself by giving in to Olibrius. Jacobus's Margaret peremptorily tells the weeping spectators not to waste any sympathy on her: "Oh bad counselors, go away! begone! This torture of the flesh is the salvation of the soul!"³⁴ Likewise, the Margaret of the *South English Legendary* retorts, "ȝe wikkede conseillers : goþ fram me anon / Anoþer conseil ich habbe itake : ich forsake ȝou echon" (SEL 1:296/135–36). Bokenham's Margaret, by contrast, explains why she is to be envied rather than pitied, proclaims her faith, and urges the bystanders to turn from their error, promising "my counsel if ye wyl do, / My soule for yours, ye shul saf be" (624–25).

Through his representation of virgin martyrs as zealous reformers, Bokenham reshapes the conflict between saints and their adversaries. Instead of dis-

---

³³ *The South English Legendary*, ed. Charlotte D'Evelyn and Anna J. Mill, 3 vols., EETS.OS 235, 236, 244 [henceforth cited as SEL] (London: Oxford University Press, 1956, 1959), 1:317/53–54.

³⁴ Jacobus de Voragine, *The Golden Legend: Readings on the Saints*, 2 vols., trans. William Granger Ryan (Princeton: Princeton University Press, 1993), 1:369.

missing their persecutors as *deuelles limes*, Bokenham's heroines use lengthy arguments to coax them into the fold. "Leue þine erroure & yiue credens" (9377), Lucy urges Paschasius. Margaret condemns Olibrius only because he "wylt not" be saved (626). Even after he has tried to bake, poison, and mutilate her, Christine assures Julian, "Knowst þou not, wreche . . . / Þat goddys pacience þe to penytence / Abydyth lenger & gladly wold inclyne?" (3043–45). In a similar spirit, Faith's companion Caprasius tells Dacian:

> Moor heleful counsel I wyl yiue þe,
> By wych þou mayst escheu þe peyn
> That þe is ordeynyd endles certeyn.
> Wurshepe my god & forsaak synne,
> And þou shalt han ioye wych neuer shal blyn.
>
> (3890–94)

In their desire to reform rather than simply to revile their persecutors, Bokenham's saints emerge as agents of God sent to restore an order that has been violated by men who have rebelled against their creator and are unjust even by heathen standards. Their adversaries are not the stock villains of hagiography— fiendish thugs who are damned as a matter of course. Rather, they are men who choose to be evil, who ignore the obvious, and who condemn themselves through "frowerd negligence" (3046) and "wylful resystence" (3049). Bokenham's narratives deliver a warning, which is stated explicitly at the end of his life of Agatha:

> Lo, þis ys euere þe ende of pryde,
> And of hem wych oute of here mynde
> Puttyn here creatour, & ben vnkynde
> To hys goodnesse, & euere debate
> Wyth hys seruauntys & hem doon hate,
> And lyst in no wyse here god knowe,
> Tyl þei in peyn be plounchyd lowe.
>
> (8876–82)

The emphasis on faith, prayer, and teaching that marks so many fifteenth-century legends—including the lives of St. Katherine that I will discuss in the next chapter—coheres with the introspective character of contemporary lay piety.[35] Seeking to cultivate satisfying personal relationships with Christ,

---

[35] For an especially good overview of this phenomenon, see Colin Richmond, "Religion and the Fifteenth-Century English Gentleman," in *The Church, Politics, and Patronage in the Fifteenth Century*, ed. Barrie Dobson (New York: St. Martin's, 1984), 193–208.

laypeople were adopting many of the practices associated with those traditional bastions of religious life, the monasteries. Books of Hours adapted monastic offices to the busy schedules of merchants and housewives, while some large households followed, insofar as possible, the routines of religious communities.[36] An anonymous early-fifteenth-century set of instructions written for a middle-class layman encourages mealtime reading for the same reason that reading was prescribed in monastic refectories, namely, to prevent frivolous chatter and worldly thoughts: "Let the book be brought to the table as readily as the bread. And lest the tongue speak vain or hurtful things, let there be reading, now by one, now by another, and by your children as soon as they can read."[37] Accounts of the daily routines of Edward IV's mother, Cicely of York, and Henry VII's mother, Margaret Beaufort, likewise attest to the importance of mealtime devotional readings in fifteenth-century households.[38]

During the fifteenth century, a wide range of literature that had been written by and for professional religious was being translated into the vernacular and disseminated to a lay audience.[39] Among the most popular adaptations of these "classics of spirituality" were meditative lives of Christ, such as Love's *Myrrour*, and translations of the Latin writings of Walter Hilton and Richard Rolle.[40] Not surprisingly, the laypeople who were consuming these works of contemplative literature were also adopting the reading practices associated with monks and anchorites. A rubric from MS Harley 1706 in the British Museum, a late-fifteenth-century religious miscellany that belonged to Elizabeth Vere (related by marriage to Bokenham's patron of the same name), advises:

> We schulde rede and use bokes in to this ende and entente. for formys of preysynge and preyynge to god. to oure lady seynte marye and to alle the seyntes.

[36] Kate Mertes, *The English Noble Household, 1250–1600: Good Governance and Politic Rule* (New York: Basil Blackwell, 1988), 139–60; Ann M. Hutchison, "Devotional Reading in the Monastery and in the Late Medieval Household," in *De Cella in Seculum: Religious and Secular Life and Devotion in Late Medieval England*, ed. Michael G. Sargent (Wolfeboro, N.H.: D. S. Brewer, 1989), 215–27; C. A. J. Armstrong, "The Piety of Cicely, Duchess of York: A Study in Late Mediaeval Culture," in *England, France, and Burgundy in the Fifteenth Century* (London: Hambledon, 1983), 135–56; Michael K. Jones and Malcolm G. Underwood, *The King's Mother: Lady Margaret Beaufort, Countess of Richmond and Derby* (Cambridge: Cambridge University Press, 1992), 171–201.

[37] W. A. Pantin, "Instructions for a Devout and Literate Layman," in *Medieval Learning and Literature: Essays Presented to Richard William Hunt*, ed. Jonathan G. Alexander and Margaret T. Gibson (Oxford: Clarendon, 1976), 399.

[38] See Armstrong, "Piety of Cicely," and Jones and Underwood, *The King's Mother.*

[39] Vincent Gillespie, "Vernacular Books of Religion," in *Book Production and Publishing in Britain, 1375–1475*, ed. Jeremy Griffiths and Derek Pearsall (Cambridge: Cambridge University Press, 1989), 317–44; and Anne Clark Bartlett, *Male Authors, Female Readers: Representation and Subjectivity in Middle English Devotional Literature* (Ithaca: Cornell University Press, 1995), 115–41.

[40] On the popularity of Love's *Myrrour* and related works, see Elizabeth Salter, *Nicholas Love's "Myrrour of the Blessed Lyf of Jesu Christ,"* Analecta Cartusiana 10 (Salzburg: Institut für Englische Sprache und Literatur, Universität Salzburg, 1974).

that we myghte have by the forseyd use of redynge understondynge of god of hys
benyfetys of hys lawe. of hys servyce or sume other goodly and gostely trowthis. or
ellys that we myghte have good affeccyon toward god and hys seyntes and hys
servyce to be gendryd and geten. (212v)[41]

This description of reading bears a striking resemblance to the characterization of reading as "good prayer" that we find in the *Ancrene Wisse*.[42] As Ann M.
Hutchison observed, the rubric also expresses "in a more elementary form . . .
the same aims of devotional reading as those expressed by the author of *The
Myroure of Oure Ladye*," a guide composed for the nuns of Syon during the
first half of the fifteenth century.[43] The author of the *Myroure* admonishes
readers that they should dispose themselves to reading as they dispose themselves to prayer: "with meke reuerence and deuocyon." He continues his long
exposition on reading by advising that "when ye rede by your selfe alone, ye
oughte not to be hasty to rede moche at ones, but ye oughte to abyde thervpon,
& som tyme rede a thynge ageyne twyes, or thryes, or oftener tyl ye vnderstonde
yt clerely."[44] With their meditations on the saints' virtues and their lengthy
passages of prayer and exposition, the legends of Bokenham and Lydgate assume an audience that will "abyde thervpon" and treat reading as a form of
"preysynge and preyynge to god."

Decorum and Politics

Like Love's *Myrrour* and other contemplative treatises on the life of Christ,
fifteenth-century saints' lives supply not only religious teachings for the pious
Christian to reflect on but models of conduct as well.[45] Lydgate's narratives, in

---

[41] Quoted in A. I. Doyle, "Books Connected with the Vere Family and Barking Abbey," *Transactions of the Essex Archaeological Society*, n.s., 25 (1958): 231.

[42] *The Ancrene Riwle*, trans. M. B. Salu (Notre Dame: University of Notre Dame Press, 1956), 127.

[43] Hutchison, "Devotional Reading," 224. A. I. Doyle has also commented on the "peculiarly religious" character of this passage ("Books," 231). John C. Hirsh discusses this rubric and other texts
that encourage meditative reading in "Prayer and Meditation in Late Mediaeval England: MS Bodley 789," *Medium Ævum* 48 (1979): 55–66.

[44] *Myroure of Oure Ladye*, ed. John Henry Blunt, EETS.ES 19 (London: Trübner, 1873), 66–67.
William Caxton disseminates identical instructions for reading in the prologue to his 1481 translation to *Reynart the Foxe*: "Thenne who that wyll haue the very vnderstandyng of this mater / he
muste ofte and many tymes rede in thys boke and ernestly and diligently marke wel that he redeth
/ ffor it is sette subtylly / lyke as ye shal see in redyng of it and not ones to rede it / ffor a man shal
not wyth ones ouer redyng fynde the ryght vnderstandyng ne comprise it wel / but oftymes to rede
it shal cause it wel to be vnderstande." See *The Prologues and Epilogues of William Caxton*, ed.
W. J. B. Crotch, EETS.OS 176 (1929; reprint, London: Oxford University Press, 1956), 60.

[45] Sarah Beckwith discusses how lives of Christ model social behavior in "A Very Material Mysticism: The Medieval Mysticism of Margery Kempe," in *Medieval Literature: Criticism, Ideology, and
History*, ed. David Aers (Brighton: Harvester, 1986), 34–57; and in her *Christ's Body: Identity, Culture, and Society in Late Medieval Writings* (London: Routledge, 1993).

particular, are informed by an unprecedented emphasis on decorum, both in their characterization of the saint and in their plots. Petronilla's refinement actually leads to her martyrdom, for "hir port and womanly noblesse, / Hir demenynge and gracious visage" (77–78) bring her to the attention of Count Flaccus. Both she and Margaret prevail over their adversaries not through defiance and invective but through "sleȝtez of þewez / And . . . teccheles termes of talkyng noble" that rival Gawain's achievements at Hautdesert.[46] Petronilla defends her virginity through discretion and "demure . . . langage": when Flaccus proposes marriage, she takes the count aside "oute of all the prees," then "benygnely" asks him to assemble a large company of matrons, wives, and virgins to conduct her to the wedding (81–88). As the happy bridegroom hastens to do her bidding, Petronilla prays for a speedy death and expires just before her escort arrives. Margaret is equally anxious to avoid confrontation, and Lydgate underscores her restraint in this lengthy description of how she pauses before answering the prefect's questions about her background:

> She, not to Rekel for noon hastynesse,
> But ful demure and sobre of contenaunce,
> Gan looke on him, by grete avisenesse,
> Dressyng to God hir hertes remembraunce,
> Of chere nor colour ther was no variaunce;
> Constaunt of herte, this holy blyssed mayde
> To the Prefecte euene thus she saide . . .
>
> (148–54)

Unable to avert a prolonged and violent encounter with Olibrius, Margaret nonetheless remains a paragon of courtesy throughout her trial. Her consistently moderate language sets her apart from the more combative heroine of Lydgate's acknowledged source, the *Legenda aurea*. Jacobus's Margaret debates Olibrius: when he rebukes her for worshiping a crucified man, she asks him how he knows of Christ; when he admits that his knowledge derives "from the Christians' books," she berates him for not being a better reader.[47] By contrast, when Lydgate's Olibrius derides Margaret's beliefs, the saint replies:

> "Certes," quod she, "what euer that thou seye,
> He wilfully suffred passioun,
> And humbely liste for mankynde deye
> And sched his blode for oure redempcioun

---

[46] *Sir Gawain and the Green Knight*, lines 916–17, in *The Poems of the Pearl Manuscript*, ed. Malcolm Andrew and Ronald Waldron (London: Edward Arnold, 1978), 207–300.

[47] Jacobus de Voragine, *Golden Legend*, 1:369.

To make vs fre, and payen oure raunsoun,
Of his Ioye that we ne sholde mysse
Where now he regneth eternaly in blysse."
(183–89)

It is hard to imagine a more tactful response. Setting aside her opponent's charge ("what euer that thou seye"), Margaret goes on to iterate her own convictions. As the scene progresses, she continues to profess her faith, never debating and only once attacking her adversary: "O gredy hounde, lyoun insaciable," the blood-ied saint calls from the gibbet, adding, "On my body thou maiste welle taken wrake, / But the soule shal perseuere stable" (261–63). Nowhere is her courtesy better attested than in the moments preceding her execution, when she requests "of humble affeccyoun" (442) that the judge who has tortured and goaded her now allow her a few moments to pray. After praying "of parfite charite" (449) for both her admirers and her enemies, she fondly summons her executioner ("myn oune brother dere" [484]) and beseeches him to strike off her head.

Margaret is as benign toward demons as she is toward her human adver-saries. Indeed, Lydgate carefully reworks her encounter with the dragon and devil so as to divest the scene of its sensational violence and to highlight the saint's gracious restraint. As in his rendition of Margaret's trial, Lydgate em-phasizes his heroine's faith rather than her aggressiveness. Feeling herself in the jaws of the dragon, Margaret crosses herself "in hir mortal drede" (291), and before she realizes what has happened ("or she toke hede" [292]), the dragon bursts. Victory is something that *happens to* her. Whereas the heroines of earlier legends bound their adversaries with chains (or, in one case, with a wimple), Lydgate's Margaret restrains her foe with the "invisible bonde" (304) of prayer. Only once does she assault an enemy (the devil in human form), and Lydgate presents her struggle in a manner designed to recall its typological association with Mary's triumph over the serpent in *Revelation*:

And she aroos with-oute fere or drede,
This cely ma[i]de, this tendre creature,
By grace of God hent him by the hede
And cast him doun, for all his felle armure,
Vnder hir fete—he myght[e] not recure;
And on this serpent for to do more wrake,
Hir ryght fote she sette upon his bake.
(309–15)

He further moderates Margaret's aggressiveness by having the devil testify that he was conquered by "Innocence" (327) and "holynesse" (342) rather than by might. Lydgate concludes the scene by emphasizing the saint's forbearance in dealing with her vanquished enemy. Having obtained the information she had sought of him, "she with-drowe to done him more duresse" (396). Margaret fights, in essence, like a good Christian knight, entrusting herself to God and showing mercy toward those she conquers.

Margaret and Petronilla provide heroic examples of the gracious comportment that was so assiduously cultivated by bourgeois and gentle readers eager to emulate their "betters." The saints epitomize the courtesy and discretion that contemporary writers of conduct literature associate with *gentilesse*. As Geoffroy de la Tour-Landry tells his daughters, "Ye must be meke and curteys, for there nis none so gret a vertu to gete the grace of God and the loue of all peple; for humilite and curtesie ouercomithe all proude hertys."[48] Graciousness and humility, Geoffroy goes on to illustrate, are potent weapons for men and women alike: "Ther was a lorde that y knew, that conquered the knightes and squiers by his curtesie and humilite to do hem [more] plesaunce in the tyme of his werre, than other lordes couthe gete with her gold and siluer or ani other yeftes. And also y haue know mani ladies and gentill women that haue gote hem moche loue of gret and smale for her curtesie and humilite."[49] In a similar vein, Peter Idley admonishes his son Thomas, "Restreyne and kepe well thy tonge."[50] Instead of arguing, Idley contends, the wise man strives for conciliation: "A softe worde swageth Ire / And causeth grete rest, it is no nay; / Who can suffre, hath his desire."[51] The importance of courtesy to fifteenth-century readers may partly explain why Lydgate's Margaret legend was so well anthologized, whereas Chaucer's "Second Nun's Tale" was extracted only twice—despite the apparent popularity of Chaucer's other moral and didactic tales among readers of this period.[52] Such readers as Idley, who urged his son, "Thoughe thy feelowe in defaute be founde, / Make therof no laugheng, sporte, ne Iape," may have considered denouncing and mocking a judge (even a bad judge) as signs of ill breeding rather than of heroism.[53] Margaret's legend implies that restraint and good manners are not only proper but also holy, allowing ambitious *gentils* to imagine themselves as mirrors of the blessed.

[48] Geoffrey de la Tour-Landry, *Book of the Knight*, 14.

[49] Ibid.

[50] *Peter Idley's Instructions to His Son*, ed. Charlotte D'Evelyn (London: Oxford University Press, 1935), 82, line 69. D'Evelyn estimates that this popular conduct book was composed sometime between 1445 and 1450 (58).

[51] Ibid., 84, lines 190–92.

[52] Daniel S. Silvia, "Some Fifteenth-Century Manuscripts of the *Canterbury Tales*," in *Chaucer and Middle English Studies in Honour of Rossell Hope Robbins*, ed. Beryl Rowland (London: George Allen and Unwin, 1974), 153–63. Margaret's behavior, by contrast, resembles the conduct of protagonists in Chaucer's more frequently copied tales—the Clerk's Griselda, for example.

[53] *Idley's Instructions*, 82, lines 92–93.

Lydgate also uses his legends to model proper social relationships. For example, Petronilla's eagerness "to do seruise with humble diligence" to her father (142) illustrates the unquestioning allegiance children should show their parents. After describing how Peter cures his infirm daughter and then orders her to serve his dinner guests, Lydgate dwells on the saint's obedience:

> She lyke a virgyn, of port moost agreable,
> What euer he bad she alwey diligent
> Of humble wyll, by tokenes moost notable,
> Lowly to accomplissh his commaundement.
>
> (53–56)

Commanded by Peter to return to her sickbed, Petronilla again "fulfylled his byddynge . . . / Withoute grutchinge, of virgynall mekenesse" (57–58). Peter, for his part, is portrayed as an ideal parent. Though Lydgate's narrative is much longer than Jacobus's, he omits a detail that had been crucial in the *Legenda aurea* and in all previous renditions of the Petronilla legend, namely, that Peter asked God to make his daughter sick, to test her faith and to preserve her from suitors. Lydgate is silent on the origin of Petronilla's disease, focusing instead, as we have seen, on how she deals with her affliction. He portrays Peter as a fond parent whose teaching gave his "doughter dere" (4) the strength to become "the clere myrroure of all perfection" (13). Where the Peter of the *Legenda aurea* cures Petronilla for the spiritual benefit of his disciples, Lydgate's apostle is moved by "faderly pyte" (49). Lydgate thus sacralizes those attributes of the father-daughter relationship that fifteenth-century readers—parents, at least—would surely approve: benevolence on his part, submissiveness on hers.

Less directly, Lydgate's heroines provide examples of proper conduct for wives. Discreet in speech and modest in demeanor, the saints act toward their persecutors as conduct book writers insisted that good wives should act toward their husbands—not humiliating them in public and chastening them "with fairnesse rather thanne with rudenesse."[54] Margaret's studied pause before responding to Olibrius illustrates Geoffroy de la Tour-Landry's advice, "Yef ye make a litell rest in youre ansuere, ye shall ansuere the beter and the more wisely and suerly," and her submission to physical abuse accords with his exhortation to "suffre and endure paciently" one's husband's anger.[55] Implicit is this message: If the saint could meekly endure the verbal and physical abuse of a godless sadist, how much more patiently should wives endure their own, (presumably) lesser tribulations at the hands of the Christian men whom they have vowed to obey?

[54] Geoffrey de la Tour-Landry, *Book of the Knight*, 24.
[55] Ibid., 17, 23.

Underlying these paradigms of domestic relationships is a political paradigm, for the saints display the respect that all people should have toward their
superiors in a well-ordered society. A privileged member of one of the chief
landholding institutions and most eminent centers of power within Suffolk,
Lydgate had an interest in promoting such respect. The abbey largely controlled
the town of Bury and its suburbs, regulating markets, collecting taxes, impos-
ing fees, minting coin, appointing parish priests, and running the courts.[56] Its
abbot, William Curteys, had powers and responsibilities of a great temporal
lord: he was a member of Parliament and presided over his own court, which
was responsible for dispensing royal justice. Moreover, he was immersed in
political conflicts against secular and ecclesiastical adversaries alike: on the one
hand, he worked to preserve the abbey's ancient exemption from episcopal
control; on the other hand, he struggled to maintain the abbey's control over
the town of Bury, which had become deeply resentful of the abbey's interfer-
ence in civic affairs.

As one might expect, given the abbey's diverse interests and close ties with
the secular world, Bury monks did not lead a strictly cloistered life but frequently left home to conduct abbey business, to visit relatives, or go on pilgrim-
ages (as Lydgate portrays himself doing in the *Siege of Thebes*).[57] Such excur-
sions gave them ample opportunities to cultivate friendships with magnates,
gentlepeople, and well-to-do burghers. Those opportunities were augmented
by the fact that many rich and powerful people were eager to forge personal associations with the prestigious abbey. Among those who entered into confra-
ternity with the abbey during the fifteenth century were Henry VI; Humphrey
of Gloucester and his wife, Eleanor; Richard Beauchamp, earl of Warwick; Elizabeth Vere, countess of Oxford; and William Paston.[58]

From all indications, Lydgate took full advantage of the freedom that monastic life offered him.[59] He probably left Bury for some years during the early
1400s to pursue a degree at Oxford. During the 1420s, he spent time in London
and Paris on business pertaining to the royal court. A headnote to Lydgate's
Gaude Virgo Mater Christi in one of John Shirley's anthologies claims that Lydgate composed that work "by night as he lay in his bedde at London"—perhaps
in the abbot's townhouse.[60] Thus immersed in the world, Lydgate had much in

---

[56] For extensive studies of the abbey, its jurisdiction, and its ongoing conflict with the town, see
M. D. Lobel, *The Borough of Bury St. Edmunds: A Study in the Government and Development of
a Monastic Town* (Oxford: Clarendon, 1935); and Robert S. Gottfried, *Bury St. Edmunds and the
Urban Crisis, 1290–1539* (Princeton: Princeton University Press, 1982).

[57] See Derek Pearsall, *John Lydgate* (London: Routledge, 1970), 24–29.

[58] Ibid., 27.

[59] Ibid., 28–29.

[60] Lydgate, *Minor Poems*, 1:288.

common with the wealthy merchants and aristocrats who numbered among his patrons and friends. It is little wonder that, instead of emphasizing virtues such as celibacy and contempt for the world that separate the clergy from the laity, he highlights such values as propriety, courtesy, patience, and filial obedience, whose promotion reinforces lay and clerical authority alike. Personal memories would probably have reminded him how deeply his interests were linked to the preservation of social harmony and respect for traditional hierarchies. At age eleven, he was old enough to remember the 1381 attack on the abbey of Bury, which was located only miles from his hometown of Lydgate. Not only was the abbey plundered, but its prior was also executed and his head displayed on a pike in the Bury marketplace. Derek Pearsall has suggested that at the time of these events, Lydgate may already have been recruited to Bury.[61]

During the fifteenth century, the interests of church and state were generally coalescing, as these institutions united against the heresies that were perceived to threaten the hegemony of both.[62] A series of statutes enacted during the first two decades of the fifteenth century ordained that secular and ecclesiastical authorities should join forces to find, prosecute, and punish heretics. The first of these statutes, *De heretico comburendo* (1401), decreed that unlicensed preachers should be arrested by diocesan authorities; if the offenders proved recalcitrant, they were to be turned over to the king's officers for execution. The statute's 1406 supplement charged church and state officials with actively seeking out and punishing Lollards in their districts. During the Leicester Parliament of 1414, another statute was passed, which, among other things, authorized still more officers of the state—including justices of the King's Bench and justices of peace and assize—to take part in the hunt for Lollards. These measures had dramatic consequences. At Henry IV's instigation, the parish priest and relapsed heretic William Sawtry was burned at Smithfield by special edict weeks before *De heretico comburendo* was officially promulgated. In 1410, the Evesham tailor John Badby became the first layperson to be executed for Lollardy, in a spectacle that was apparently designed to showcase the cooperation of the Church and the Crown to the widest possible audience.[63] Subsequent burnings performed under the new laws included the executions of such

---

[61] Pearsall, *John Lydgate*, 22–24.

[62] Aston, *Lollards and Reformers*, 1–47; Peter McNiven, *Heresy and Politics in the Reign of Henry IV: The Burning of John Badby* (Wolfeboro, N.H.: Boydell, 1987); E. F. Jacob, *The Fifteenth Century, 1399–1485* (1961; reprint, Oxford: Oxford University Press, 1993), 94–98. For a discussion of Lydgate's complex collaboration with Henry V's political and religious agendas, see Lee Patterson, "Making Identities in Fifteenth-Century England: Henry V and John Lydgate," in *New Historical Literary Study: Essays on Reproducing Texts, Representing History*, ed. Jeffrey N. Cox and Larry J. Reynolds (Princeton: Princeton University Press, 1993), 69–107.

[63] McNiven, *Reign of Henry IV*, 199–219.

"high-profile" figures as the popular teacher William White (1428) and Henry
V's personal friend, Sir John Oldcastle (1417). Following the exhumation, burning, and dispersal of Wyclif's supposed remains in 1428, a rash of heresy trials
was conducted under the auspices of church and state.

Lydgate composed his legends of Margaret and Petronilla at times when
concerns about heterodoxy ran especially high. He wrote his life of Margaret
during or just after the notorious "Oldcastle affair" of 1413–17.[64] Having been
tried and sentenced to death for heresy in 1413, Oldcastle escaped from prison,
orchestrated an uprising against the Crown in 1414, and remained at large for
three years before being captured and duly executed. Though Oldcastle's coup
failed, the rebellion provided incontrovertible evidence that Lollardy could
threaten the state as well as the Church—a view that anti-Lollard polemicists
had been promoting for some time. Spurred by this evidence of the dangers of
heterodoxy, secular and ecclesiastical authorities throughout the country re-
doubled their efforts to detect and punish heresy. Lydgate's Petronilla legend
(circa 1434) was the product of an equally anxious period: the most serious Lollard rising since the Oldcastle rebellion had been quelled only a couple of years
earlier, in 1431.[65] Moreover, two and a half years of proceedings against some
60–120 suspected heretics had just come to a conclusion in nearby Norwich,
proceedings that proved just how deeply heterodox views had penetrated East
Anglia.[66]

During the years Lydgate was writing his virgin martyr legends, reports and
rumors of what Lollards were saying, both during their interrogations and privately among their friends and acquaintances, probably circulated widely. Orthodox Christians such as Lydgate may well have discerned troubling echoes
of traditional martyr legends in the rhetoric and logic of the heretics, who, for
example, derided the veneration of relics and images for the same reasons the
martyrs had scorned idols. As William White reportedly put it during his 1428
trial, "Trees growing in a forest have more power and vigor . . . than a rock or
dead branch carved in the likeness of a man."[67] Also reminiscent of popular

---

[64] For a discussion of the crackdown on heretics following the Oldcastle rebellion, see Edward
Powell, *Kingship, Law, and Society: Criminal Justice in the Reign of Henry V* (Oxford: Clarendon,
1989), 161–66.

[65] For a discussion of the Oldcastle revolt and the 1431 rising, see Aston, *Lollards and Reformers,*
23–38.

[66] These proceedings have been edited by Norman P. Tanner in *Heresy Trials in the Diocese of
Norwich, 1428–31,* Camden Society, 4th ser., vol. 20 (London: Royal Historical Society, 1977).

[67] "Nam arbores crescentes in silva sunt majoris virtutis et vigoris . . . quam lapis vel lignum
mortuum ad similitudinem hominis sculptum," quoted by Aston, *Lollards and Reformers,* 90 (my
translation).

martyr legends is the blunt and often profane language that Lollards used to ridicule ecclesiastical authorities and their teachings. When asked his opinion of the pope during his 1413 trial before Archbishop Arundel, Oldcastle reportedly answered, "Þe pope is Antecrist; bischoppis be his membris, and freris be his tayl."[68] Equally frank, Margery Baxter scorned the consecrated host, which, she declared, is no more than bread that priests by the thousands consume and excrete daily.[69] Despite their professed disdain for saints, the Lollards' rhetoric of dissent was very much in the tradition of such martyrs as Cecilia, who compared her judge's power to "a bladdre ful of wynd" and ridiculed him for worshiping rocks.[70] It seems likely that, directly or indirectly, the performances of Lollards such as William White and Margery Baxter prompted Lydgate and other hagiographers to depart from the long-standing tradition of representing the saints as mettlesome rebels who make fools of religious authorities.

During the late fourteenth and early fifteenth centuries, heresy was increasingly linked with reading and teaching—particularly on the part of the laity. As one late-fourteenth-century preacher complained, "Behold now we see so great a dissemination of the Gospel, that simple men and women . . . write and learn the Gospel, and, as far as they can and know how, teach and scatter the word of God."[71] *De heretico comburendo* denounced Lollards because, among other things, "they hold and exercise schools, they make and write books, they do wickedly instruct and inform people."[72] When procedures for investigating suspected heretics were drawn up at the convocation of 1416, officials were specifically enjoined to look for vernacular writings. That injunction is hardly surprising, given the central place that books actually occupied within Lollard circles. Several Norwich Lollards admitted to possessing or circulating "libros continentes hereses."[73] Others acknowledged that they participated in reading

---

[68] John Capgrave, *Abbreuiacion of Cronicles,* ed. Peter J. Lucas, EETS.OS 285 (Oxford: Oxford University Press, 1983), 241.

[69] Tanner, *Heresy Trials,* 44–45.

[70] Geoffrey Chaucer, "Second Nun's Tale," in *Riverside Chaucer,* 268, line 439. On Lollard views of saints, see Anne Hudson, *The Premature Reformation: Wycliffite Texts and Lollard History* (Oxford: Clarendon, 1988), 302–3. The influence of hagiography is also evident in the "Testimony of William Thorpe." In describing his interrogation before Arundel, Thorpe portrays the archbishop as the stock villain of martyr legends, who calls his prisoner names, threatens him with "scharpe ponyschinge," and pounds a cupboard "fersli" with his fist when he finds himself outargued. See *Two Wycliffite Texts,* ed. Anne Hudson, EETS.OS 301 (Oxford: Oxford University Press, 1993), 76, 88. Hudson discusses Thorpe's *Testament* as "in some senses a substitute saint's life" in her introduction, lvi.

[71] Quoted in Aston, *Lollards and Reformers,* 50 (Aston's translation).

[72] Henry Bettenson, ed., *Documents of the Christian Church* (1943; reprint, London: Oxford University Press, 1963), 252.

[73] See Tanner, *Heresy Trials,* 39, 41, 47–48, 60, 69, 75, 99, 102.

groups or in *scolas* at which the contents of suspect books were doubtless discussed.[74] John Oldcastle was initially investigated because he was found to possess heretical tracts.[75] Moreover, as Oldcastle's associations suggest, quite a few Lollards appear to have been in the business of producing written documents. Of the three friends who brought about the condemned lord's 1413 escape from prison, one was a scrivener, another was a parchment maker, while a third friend, from whom Oldcastle sought refuge after the failed uprising, also made parchment for a living.[76]

Concerns about lay learning commonly found expression in representations of unruly female "scholars."[77] The Wife of Bath, of course, is the quintessential example of a "monstrous" female reader, a "noble prechour" who flamboyantly appropriates biblical and patristic texts to her own ends.[78] The Friar's counsel to Alison—"lete auctoritees, on Goddes name, / To prechyng and to scoles of clergye"—reverberated in various sources of the period.[79] Writing early in the fifteenth century, one anonymous preacher exhorts women to "tak þe to þi distaff, coveyt not to be a prest ne prechour, schal never cloc henne be wel crowing cok."[80] The outspoken Margery Kempe received the same advice from many "men of þe cuntre," who urged her to "forsake þis lyfe þat þu hast, & go spynne & carde as oþer women don."[81] During her 1417 visit to York, the archbishop worried that Kempe would "techyn" or "chalengyn þe pepil in my diocyse,"

[74] For a summary of the many references to schools in the proceedings, see ibid., 28.

[75] Jacob, *The Fifteenth Century*, 130.

[76] Ibid., 130–32. Anne Hudson comments on the apparent involvement of scribes and *parchemyners* in the Lollard movement in *Lollards and Their Books*, 182. See also her "Lollard Book Production," in *Book Production and Publishing in Britain*, ed. Griffiths and Pearsall, 125–42.

[77] For a provocative discussion of the perceived relationship of gender, heresy, and the vernacular in fifteenth-century England, see Rita Copeland, "Why Women Can't Read: Medieval Hermeneutics, Statutory Law, and the Lollard Heresy Trials," in *Representing Women: Law, Literature, and Feminism*, ed. Susan Sage Heinzelman and Zipporah Batshaw Wiseman (Durham: Duke University Press, 1994), 253–86. See also Ruth Shklar, "Cobham's Daughter: *The Book of Margery Kempe* and the Power of Heterodox Thinking," *Modern Language Quarterly* 56 (1995): 277–304; and Ralph Hanna III, "The Difficulty of Ricardian Prose Translation: The Case of the Lollards," *Modern Language Quarterly* 55 (1990): 319–40.

[78] *Riverside Chaucer*, 107, line 165. Mark Amsler explores the relationship between power and literacy and discusses the "disorderly woman" as an extreme representation of the threat the literate laity posed to clerical authority; see "The Wife of Bath and Women's Power," *Assays* 4 (1987): 67–83. See also Alcuin Blamires, "The Wife of Bath and Lollardy," *Medium Ævum* 58 (1989): 224–42. For a discussion of paradoxes in the Church's attitude toward women preaching, see Alcuin Blamires, "Women and Preaching in Medieval Orthodoxy, Heresy, and Saints' Lives," *Viator* 26 (1995): 135–52.

[79] *Riverside Chaucer*, 122, lines 1276–77.

[80] Cited in Roy Martin Haines, "'Wilde Wittes and Wilfulnes': John Swetstock's Attack on Those 'Poyswunmongeres,' the Lollards," in *Popular Belief and Practice*, ed. G. J. Cuming and Derek Baker (Cambridge: Cambridge University Press, 1972), 152.

[81] *Book of Margery Kempe*, 129.

and a "gret clerke" quoted to her the apostle Paul's admonition "þat no woman xulde prechyn."[82] To her detractors, the unconventional Norwich wife was the conventional product of Lollard teachers, who were accused—as Friar Daw put it—of transforming "mennes wyues" into "scolers of þe newe scole."[83]

Nowhere is the association of women, reading, heresy, and social disorder more vehemently stated than in Thomas Hoccleve's "Address to Sir John Old-castle" (1415). In this often venomous diatribe, Hoccleve caricatures women who presume to discuss the Bible:

> Some wommen eeke, thogh hir wit be thynne,
> Wole argumentes make in holy writ!
> Lewde calates! sittith doun and spynne,
> And kakele of sumwhat elles, for your wit
> Is al to feeble to despute of it!
> To Clerkes grete apparteneth þat aart
> The knowleche of þat, god hath fro yow shit;
> Stynte and leue of for right sclendre is your paart.[84]

Hoccleve denounces Oldcastle himself in similar terms:

> Bewar Oldcastel & for Crystes sake
> Clymbe no more in holy writ so hie!
> Rede the storie of Lancelot de lake,
> Or Vegece of the aart of Chiualrie,
> The seege of Troie or Thebes thee applie
> To thyng þat may to thordre of knyght longe!
> To thy correccioun now haaste and hie,
> For thow haast been out of ioynt al to longe.[85]

Inappropriate reading makes people forget their place. Just as the "scholarly" wives neglect their household chores, men such as Oldcastle discard the re-sponsibilities that were happily discharged by knights of old.[86]

Fashioned at a time when unregulated religious enthusiasm seemed to jeop-ardize orthodoxy and traditional values alike, Lydgate's saints exemplify the virtues not only of proper gentlewomen but of those worthy knights whose

[82] Ibid., 125–26.
[83] *Jack Upland, Friar Daw's Reply, and Upland's Rejoinder*, ed. P. L. Heyworth (London: Oxford University Press, 1968), 76, lines 100–101.
[84] *Hoccleve's Works*, 13, lines 145–52.
[85] Ibid., 14, lines 193–200.
[86] Shklar examines a very different conflation of Oldcastle with the "unruly woman" in "Cob-ham's Daughter," wherein she persuasively shows how "the political gendering of heresy and trea-son transforms [Kempe] into a stand-in for Oldcastle" (301).

passing Hoccleve laments in his "Address." "Stidefast . . . in Crystes feith" without being argumentative, they epitomize the "tendrenesse," "obedience," and "buxumnesse" that Hoccleve commends.[87] As a writer whose work was widely appreciated during his lifetime, Lydgate knew that his legends might circulate among a broad readership, and his narratives seem designed to provide that broad public with models of Christian heroism that were both attractive and "safe."[88] Readers could admire the saints' beauty and imitate their decorous piety; they could applaud the martyrs' courage and faith, while being gently reminded that saints are modest creatures—"Softe of . . . speche, and but of wordys fewe."[89]

Bokenham's similar concern with decorum may reflect a comparable desire to curb radical interpretations of saints' lives by laypeople such as Margery Kempe. Yet this desire cannot have been foremost in his mind, for we do not find in his legends the near obsession with the saints' passivity that marks Lydgate's narratives. If anything, his portrayal of the saints as intellectuals, who not only profess their faith but argue passionately for it, reaches out to readers with heterodox proclivities.[90] Though Bokenham does indicate that his heroines' speech is within the bounds of decorum,[91] his representation of the saints preaching on a range of theological topics, including the Incarnation and the Trinity, suggests that he was not overly concerned with discouraging future Margery Kempes.

Indeed, Bokenham was writing in a less anxious environment than was Lydgate. By the 1440s, the Norwich heresy trials were more than a decade in the past, and the Oldcastle revolt was a distant memory. Kempe, hounded for her bold speech during the years Lydgate was writing, had since been admitted to the prestigious Guild of the Trinity in King's Lynn and felt comfortable enough to record her *Book*. As Gail McMurray Gibson has observed, East Anglia was, as a rule, tolerant toward religious beliefs and practices that would have been

---

[87] *Hoccleve's Works*, 15, lines 209–16.

[88] For a discussion of the social diversity of Lydgate's audience, see A. S. G. Edwards, "Lydgate Manuscripts: Some Directions for Future Research," in *Manuscripts and Readers in Fifteenth-Century England*, ed. Derek Pearsall (Cambridge: D. S. Brewer, 1981), 15–26.

[89] Lydgate, "Margaret," in *Minor Poems*, 177, line 105.

[90] Ritchie D. Kendall discusses the importance of intellectual contests to Lollard ideals of heroism in *The Drama of Dissent: The Radical Poetics of Nonconformity, 1380–1590* (Chapel Hill: University of North Carolina Press, 1986), 14–89. See also Rita Copeland's discussion of William Thorpe as a "triumphant intellectual martyr-hero" in "William Thorpe and His Lollard Community: Intellectual Labor and the Representation of Dissent," in *Bodies and Disciplines: Intersections of Literature and History in Fifteenth-Century England*, ed. Barbara A. Hanawalt and David Wallace (Minneapolis: University of Minnesota Press, 1996), 199–221 (quote on 208).

[91] For example, his rather tame statement that St. Katherine "coude comune" intelligently with clerks (6395–97) contrasts with Capgrave's corresponding account of Katherine's showing up scholars (*Life of St. Katharine*, 1.400–427).

considered alarming elsewhere, so long as those beliefs and practices did not threaten the state.[92] In keeping with that general spirit of tolerance, Bokenham's legends are less concerned with regulating piety than with catering to a discriminating readership.

Customized Hagiography

Like so many writers of the period, fifteenth-century hagiographers were obsessed with their readers.[93] As I discussed earlier, Capgrave begins his life of Augustine with an extensive account of how an unnamed gentlewoman induced him to write, and Symon Wynter provides detailed instructions for circulating his life of Jerome. Lydgate introduces his Margaret legend with a tribute to Ann Mortimer, explaining how Lady March commanded him to compile a narrative from Latin and French sources (66–77); he concludes by addressing the broader audience of women whom he expects to read his legend. Bokenham's lives of Margaret, Katherine, Agatha, Mary Magdalene, Anne, Dorothy, Cecilia, and Elizabeth include autobiographical passages and tributes to patrons, ranging in length from a few lines to several pages. These passages reveal that hagiographers were at least as concerned with pleasing readers as with edifying them.

In his legends, Bokenham provides especially clear examples of two strategies that hagiographers often employed to provide for the "plesauns and consolation" of contemporary audiences: first, he celebrates readers along with the saints by integrating into their legends tributes to and prayers for his patrons; and second, he pays more attention to secular affairs. These two strategies complement the one I just discussed, namely, the transformation of the saints into model gentils—mirrors of middle- and upper-class readers.

Bokenham's frequent references to his readers and their eagerness for his work convey the image of a much-admired hagiographer whose friends and acquaintances kept him busy with commissions. In the prologue to the life of St. Margaret, he explains that he is writing at the "inportune and besy preyere /

---

[92] Gibson, *Theater of Devotion*, 30–31. Norman P. Tanner has likewise observed that the local church in Norwich shows every indication of having been "rich and varied, and sufficiently tolerant towards what might be called the left wing of orthodoxy" to please most of the faithful, in *The Church in Late Medieval Norwich, 1370–1532* (Toronto: Pontifical Institute of Mediaeval Studies, 1984), 166.

[93] Seth Lerer has discussed this phenomenon in relation to fifteenth-century courtly love literature. He points out that this literature frequently contains "fables of patronage," recounting the circumstances of its commission. He relates the frequency of such accounts to the social aspirations of regional magnates and gentlepeople, who were eager to advertise their participation in practices of commission that prevailed at court. See *Chaucer and His Readers*, 57–84.

Of oon whom I loue wyth herte entere," a friend "whos request to me is a comaundement" (177–78, 182); in his legend of St. Dorothy, he writes at the "request & humble supplycacyoun" (4979) of John and Isabel Hunt; while in his *Mappula Angliae*, he refers to an unidentified "englische boke . . . of legenda aurea and of oþer famous legendes," which was written "at the instaunce of my specialle frendis."[94]

The friar's most colorful testimony to his own popularity occurs in the pro-logue to his life of Mary Magdalene. At a Twelfth Night party given by the Countess of Eu, he and his hostess spend some time discussing his legends of female saints. They talk about the works he has already completed—legends of Anne, Margaret, Dorothy, Faith, Christine, Agnes, and Ursula—and Boken-ham tells the countess about his work-in-progress, a life of Elizabeth of Hun-gary undertaken at the request of Elizabeth Vere. If this account is any indica-tion of the actual conversation, Bokenham spends quite a bit of time praising the Countess of Oxford:

> . . . hyr to whom sey nay
> I nethyr kan, ne wyl, ne may,
> So mych am I boundon to hyr goodnesse,
> I mene of Oxenforthe þe countesse,
> Dame Elyzabeth ver by hyr ryht name,
> Whom god euere kepe from syn & shame,
> And of good lyf so hyr auaunce
> Here in þis werd wyth perseueraunce,
> That, whan she chaungyth hir mortal fate,
> Of lyf eterne she may entryn þe gate,
> Ther-ynne to dwellyn wythowten endyng.
> (5051–61)

Perhaps motivated, as Gibson has suggested,[95] by a sense of competitiveness with her fellow countess, Isabel puts in her own request:

> "I haue," quod she, "of pure affeccyoun
> Ful longe tym had a synguler deuocyoun
> To þat holy wumman, wych, as I gesse,
> Is clepyd of apostyls þe apostyllesse;
> Blyssyd Mary mawdelyn y mene,
> Whom cryste from syn made pure & clene,

---

[94] "*Mappula Angliae* von Osbern Bokenham," ed. Carl Horstmann, *Englische Studien* 10 (1887): 6.
[95] Gibson, "Saint Anne," 102–3.

As þe clerkys seyn, ful mercyfully,
Whos lyf in englysshe I desyre sothly
To han maad, & for my sake
If ye lykyd þe labour to take,
& for reuerence of hyr, I wold you preye."

(5065–75)

Though flattered, Bokenham hesitates to accept the commission. With what his friends might have recognized as false modesty (he has just mentioned seven completed verse legends!), he pleads: "My lytyl experyence in rymy[n]gs art, / My labyl mynde, & þe dulnesse / Of my wyt" (5078–80). Unable to resist "a-statys preyer" (5083), however, he ultimately accepts; indeed, Isabel is so importunate that he apparently sets aside his life of Elizabeth to carry out her wishes. As a further compliment to his hostess, he includes a long recitation of Isabel's lineage as well as a digression establishing the claim of her brother, Richard, Duke of York, to the crown of Spain (and, implicitly, as Sheila Delany notes, to the throne of England).[96]

There is no reason to doubt that Bokenham worked within a congenial milieu, surrounded by appreciative friends. That milieu, however, certainly generated its peculiar anxieties. During the first half of the fifteenth century, East Anglia was a region rich in poet-hagiographers: Bokenham was competing for the admiration of a limited circle of readers with Capgrave and Lydgate, both of whom were well-connected writers, whose patrons included Humphrey of Gloucester and Henry VI. Lydgate, indeed, had a national reputation. Faced with such competition, Bokenham takes every opportunity to bolster his own repute. We have seen how he drops the names of prominent patrons such as the Countesses of Eu and Oxford. Knowing he will inevitably be compared with Capgrave and Lydgate, he endeavors to control the terms of that comparison through a strategy of polite self-promotion. Acknowledging Lydgate's superior artistry, he consistently places "þe munk of bery" (10532) within a trinity of "fresh rethoryens" that also includes Gower and Chaucer: "I dwellyd neuere wyth the fresh rethoryens, / Gower, Chauncers, ner wyth lytgate, / Wych lyuyth yet, lest he deyed late" (416–18). Though still alive (Bokenham presumes), Lydgate resides among the dead masters, while Bokenham communes with the living. Bokenham may lack "cunnyng and eloquens" (1401), but his legends please his readers, and they are custom-made for the solace of his

[96] Delany, introduction to *Legend*, xiv–xv. For more on Bokenham's Yorkist sympathies, see Sheila Delany, "Bokenham's Claudian as Yorkist Propaganda," *Journal of Medieval History* 22 (1996): 83–96.

friends. Bokenham similarly distinguishes himself from his "maystyr Ioon Capgraue" (6356). He acknowledges that Capgrave's recently completed life of St. Katherine is more extensive than his own rendition of the virgin martyr's legend; moreover, it is written "in balaadys rymyd ful craftyly" (6359). Yet, he muses, Capgrave's text "is rare / And straunge to gete, at myn estymacyoun" (6361–62). It is therefore up to Bokenham to provide for the "gostly consolacyoun" and "conforte" of his friends Katherine Howard and Katherine Denston by producing a new version of the legend, "if grace my wyt wyl illumyne" (6365–67).[97]

A desire to please his friends may well have prompted Bokenham to supply far more detail about the backgrounds and circumstances of his characters than had the Middle English hagiographers who wrote a generation earlier. He describes persons and places, relates events to local customs, and offers philosophical observations. His best-known amplification is this description of Margaret through Olibrius's eyes, which echoes the language of courtly literature:

> Hyr forheed lely-whyht,
> Hyr bent browys blake, & hyr grey eyne,
> Hyr chyry chekys, hyr nose streyt & ryht,
> Hyr lyppys rody, hyr chyn, wych as pleyne
> Pulshyd marbyl shoon, & clouyn in tweyne.
>
> (449–53)

Bokenham manifests his interest in worldly affairs not only through such descriptions but also through his frequent apologies for not going into more detail about a subject. For example, although Jacobus claims that Agatha is of noble kindred, Bokenham notes that he cannot locate any exact information on her genealogy (8359–63). After describing Margaret's birth, he writes: "I kan in no wyse remembre me / That euere I red in the hethene gyse / What rytys were vsyd & what royalte / In namys yeuyng" (365–68). These apologies suggest that by the middle of the fifteenth century, people were reading virgin martyr legends with different expectations and that writers had new ideas about what details were appropriate to these narratives. Before the fifteenth century, hagiographers routinely claimed that the virgin martyr was noble, but they

[97] Sheila Delany has argued that Bokenham also tailored his Katherine legend to the political interests of a patron unnamed in that legend by "transforming it into a miniature mirror for magistrates, a plea for social justice, and a subtle statement of support for . . . Richard duke of York." "Bokenham's 'Katherine' as Yorkist Propaganda," paper presented at the Convention of the Modern Language Association, San Diego, California, 30 December 1994. I thank Professor Delany for allowing me to quote from her paper, which is taken from her forthcoming book, *Impolitic Bodies: Poetry, Saints, and Society in Fifteenth-Century England* (New York: Oxford University Press, in press).

rarely bothered with the details of her pedigree; they asserted that she was beautiful but did not worry about the color of her eyes. Earlier hagiographers expressed no concern that readers would wonder which malady afflicts Lucy's mother, why Maxentius leaves town for a few days, or how the people of Antioch celebrate Margaret's birth. Such particulars were irrelevant to the universal paradigm of sanctity, which earlier hagiographers sought to construct and which earlier readers had expected. Bokenham's narratives assume an audience with a taste for history and romance and a keen interest in social and political contexts. Indeed, so important did Bokenham consider such "peripherals" that he composed an entire volume, the *Mappula Angliae*, as a sort of readers' guide to his legends of English saints, so that "hit shalle byne easy ynoughe to vnderstande alle þat is towched þer-of in the seyd legende."[98]

With their attention to history, local customs, family relationships, and current events, Bokenham's legends capture the worldliness that permeated virtually all aspects of religious life, marking even the most private and personal expressions of piety. Beautifully illuminated Books of Hours, for example, served both as aids to private devotion and as status symbols. While prayers and illustrations express the personal piety of the men and women who commissioned these works, coats of arms, mottoes, and individual or family portraits advertise the owner's position in society.[99] Likewise, the organization of many late medieval households into "religious as well as . . . domestic" communities served social as well as spiritual ends.[100] As Kate Mertes has pointed out, "Magnificent buildings and their accoutrements were one way of advertising one's splendour," while daily services reaffirmed the place of individual members within the hierarchy of the household.[101] Similarly, the preference among members of the gentry for private pews and enclosed "closetts" in their parish churches both satisfied a desire for greater privacy in their communication with God and suggested to humbler parishioners that "the secular hierarchy was . . . ordained by God and not made by man."[102]

Bokenham's tributes to his patrons have much in common with the inscriptions in parish churches and the family portraits in finely crafted Books of Hours. In a passage that serves much as would a portrait, Bokenham uses metaphor to extol the colorful clothing worn by Isabel Bourchier's dancing sons:

[98] Bokenham, "*Mappula Angliae*," 6.

[99] See especially Lawrence R. Poos, "Social History and the Book of Hours," in *Time Sanctified: The Book of Hours in Medieval Art and Life*, ed. Roger S. Wieck (New York: Braziller, 1988), 33–38; and John Harthan, *Books of Hours and Their Owners* (London: Thames and Hudson, 1977).

[100] Mertes, *English Noble Household*, 139.

[101] Ibid., 147–48.

[102] Nigel Saul, *Scenes from Provincial Life: Knightly Families in Sussex, 1280–1400* (Oxford: Clarendon, 1986), 159.

Was neuyr [wyth] flouris [whyt], blewe & grene,
Medewe motleyid freshlyere, I wene,
Than were her garnementys; for as it semyd me
Mynerue hyr-self, wych hath þe souereynte
Of gay texture, as declaryth Ouyde,
Wyth al hire wyt ne coude prouyde
More goodly aray þow she dede en[cl]os
Wyth-ynne oo web al methamorphosyos.

(5027–34)

Bokenham's long prayers committing Agatha Flegge to the protection of St. Agatha, and John and Isabel Hunt to the keeping of St. Dorothy, likewise recall the paintings of saints presenting patrons to Christ that were so common in churches and Books of Hours, while his tributes to Katherine and John Denston discreetly adorn his legends of Saints Katherine and Anne much as their images glistened in the stained-glass windows of Long Melford's Holy Trinity Church.[103] These literary tributes, like the portraits and inscriptions in churches, are not intended merely—or even, perhaps, primarily—for the patrons' pleasure; rather, they serve as monuments to the patrons, monuments that are more broadly directed at that audience of readers whose presence Bokenham implicitly assumes throughout his writing.[104] These "monuments," as I noted earlier, also serve as a form of self-advertisement for the poet whose talents were so eagerly sought after by such distinguished persons. Bokenham, his patrons, and the saints, "hys valentyns" (8278), thus mingle comfortably in texts that testify to the worthiness of them all.

[103] Gibson, "Saint Anne," 104–7, figure 4.

[104] Maureen Novak points to several indications that Bokenham was aware that his legends might reach an audience extending beyond his immediate circle of patrons; see "Agency and Mobility in Fifteenth-Century Representations of Female Sanctity," paper delivered at the 29th International Congress on Medieval Studies, Western Michigan University, Kalamazoo, 7 May 1994. This paper also contains a provocative discussion of how Bokenham used correspondences between the saints and his patrons to promote his own role as translator.

4

The Politics of Reading

In an altar panel dating from the mid-1400s, Robert Campin pictures St. Barbara seated on a cushioned bench before a fire, turning the pages of a small illuminated manuscript (figure 24). Unlike martyrs depicted in previous centuries, who bear books as conventional emblems, Campin's Barbara is engrossed in the text before her.[1] Her book, along with her sumptuous clothing and the room's expensive appointments, marks her as a woman of leisure and refinement.

Campin's painting is one of countless images of reading saints produced on the Continent during the fifteenth century. Such images occur in group portraits of the saints, such as the Bruges altar panel (figure 1) discussed in the introduction to this volume, and they abound in Books of Hours, whose illustrators shared Campin's taste for domestic detail.[2] In one such miniature, from a Flemish *Horae*, an aproned Petronilla cradles a book as she tends her cauldron (figure 25). Hair pulled back tidily from her round face and cooking utensils in hand, she looks more like a contented housewife than the patron saint of the infirm. The broom propped against the wall behind her suggests that dust does not gather on St. Peter's tiled floors. Though virgin martyrs rarely read in their kitchens, artists routinely locate them in other familiar settings: in gardens, parlors, or courtyards and by brooks or in meadows.

Far from encouraging contempt for the world, these images of saints and their books convey the joys of living: the pleasure of reading outside on a sunny afternoon or the satisfaction of performing household tasks well. They even invite viewers to admire material possessions — elegant clothing, a finely bound book, a splendid manor. In surrounding their martyrs with careful representations of

[1] There may be counterexamples to this generalization, but I cannot recall any. It is, in any case, safe to say that images of reading virgin martyrs produced before the fifteenth century are rare.

[2] For other examples of saints reading within groups, see Ellen Muller, "Saintly Virgins: The Veneration of Virgin Saints in Religious Women's Communities," in *Saints and She-Devils: Images of Women in the Fifteenth and Sixteenth Centuries,* ed. Lène Dresen-Coenders (London: Rubicon, 1987), 83–100. Susan Groag Bell discusses a related phenomenon in fifteenth-century Books of Hours — the popularity of images of the Virgin Mary reading — in her "Medieval Women Book Owners: Arbiters of Lay Piety and Ambassadors of Culture," *Signs* 7 (1981/82): 742–68. See also Diana M. Webb, "Woman and Home: The Domestic Setting of Late Medieval Spirituality," *Studies in Church History* 27 (1990): 159–73.

24. St. Barbara, by Robert Campin, by permission of the Museo del Prado, Madrid.

25. St. Petronilla, MS 349, fol. 56, by permission of Queen's College, Oxford.

the minutiae of everyday life, fifteenth-century artists suggest that living comfortably is no barrier to holiness, so long as one is *willing* to sacrifice life and property for God's sake.

Happily, sacrifice and suffering seem remote, even for the saints. It is hard to imagine Campin's decorous Barbara stripped and beaten by her angry father and harder still to imagine the robust Petronilla wasted by illness. Without wholly expunging references to martyrdom, fifteenth-century artists dislodged the saints' passions from their once central place in iconography. Viewers of Campin's altar panel, for example, might overlook Barbara's execution taking place on the faraway hillside that is barely visible through the parlor window. And where Campin relegates Barbara's passion to the background, another artist marginalizes it: Barbara's father prepares to lop off her head amid the foliage that frames a miniature of the saint reading (figure 26). The emblems that once attested to the virgin martyr's singularity (in this case, Barbara's tower) are now incorporated within the landscape. In the Hours of Engelbert of Nassau, the white flowers denoting Barbara's virginity grow from an ordinary potted plant, and in another *Horae*, Katherine of Alexandria's upturned sword is more suggestive of monarchy than of martyrdom (figure 27).[3] When the saint's emblems are not naturalized, they are often diminished: one must look carefully indeed to see the sword pinning a tiny spiked wheel to the floor beneath Katherine's desk in a French miniature of the period (figure 28).

Images of reading saints would have been well known to prosperous English-people, who were avid consumers of Continental Books of Hours. Such images would hardly have seemed foreign to an English public, for they complemented native trends to reduce the brutality of virgin martyr legends and to create saints who resembled contemporary readers. What better way to associate saints with readers than to portray the saints *as* readers? The degree of identification that could be attained between reading saints and medieval readers is illustrated by a seal used by Margaret, Lady Hungerford (died 1478). By portraying herself in a posture then associated with virgin martyrs and the Virgin Mary, Margaret quite literally fashioned herself in the image of saints who had themselves been fashioned in the image of aristocrats such as herself (figure 29; compare Margaret with St. Katherine in figure 30).[4] Yet, despite the natural appeal of reading as a subject, surprisingly few representations of reading saints were actually produced in England. To be sure, many virgin martyrs *carry* books as emblems, but few saints actually read them (figure 23 is one exception; figure 13 is more typical). We find no reference to pious study in the catalogues of saintly habits furnished by Bokenham and Lydgate; indeed, Bokenham barely mentions Katherine of Alexandria's education.

I am not suggesting that English writers and artists consciously avoided portraying virgin martyrs as readers but rather that certain factors made such por-

[3] For the Engelbert of Nassau Barbara, see *The Master of Mary of Burgundy: A Book of Hours for Engelbert of Nassau* (New York: Braziller, 1970), plate 36.

[4] Carol M. Meale draws attention to the similarity between Margaret Hungerford and popular representations of Mary and other female saints in "'. . . alle the bokes that I haue of latyn, englisch, and frensch': Laywomen and Their Books in Late Medieval England," in *Women and Literature in Britain, 1150–1500*, ed. Meale (Cambridge: Cambridge University Press, 1993), 128–30.

26. St. Barbara, MS Auct. D. inf.2.13, fol. 47r, by permission of the Bodleian Library, Oxford.

27. St. Katherine, MS Douce 20, fol. 178v, by permission of the Bodleian Library, Oxford.

trayals unlikely. As I have discussed, reading was a charged issue in fifteenth-century England. Depicting the saint as a reader thus posed problems that portraying her as a stylish gentlewoman did not. What do virgin martyrs read: Books of Hours? Theological tracts? English Bibles? If their books are unidentified, what might laypeople *suppose* that they read? Moreover, if a pious laywoman identified with St. Katherine as a reader, might not she fancy herself a scholar, vested with the authority—indeed, with the responsibility—to speak out on political and spiritual issues?

28. St. Katherine, MS W.222, fol. 30v, by permission of the Walters Art Gallery, Baltimore.

29. Seal of Margaret, Lady Hungerford, Seal XCII 23, by permission of the British Library, London.

Reading provided an immediate way of identifying with the virgin martyrs—especially in Books of Hours, where the saint's behavior coincides exactly with that of her beholder. What is more, reading, as Margaret Hungerford's seal demonstrates, allowed the pious layperson actually to style herself a saint. English artists and writers may well have balked at promoting such a complete identification between saints and the laity—especially because that identification could be used to dubious worldly ends. Margaret Hungerford's seal is a case in point: the dowager probably did intend her seal as a "pious gloss" on her politicking, as Carol Meale has suggested.[5] During the years Margaret used the seal (1462–78), her struggle to preserve the Hungerford fortune embroiled her in the treacherous machinations of civil war England. Though a son and grandson were executed and she was thrice imprisoned, Margaret safeguarded the bulk of her estate. Her seal was suited to the maneuvering such a triumph required: even as Margaret presents herself as a paragon of proper feminine

[5] Ibid., 129. For more on Lady Hungerford's piety and political activities, see M. A. Hicks, "The Piety of Margaret, Lady Hungerford (d. 1478)," *Journal of Ecclesiastical History* 38 (1987): 19–38.

30. St. Katherine sitting on Maxentius, MS Gough Liturg. 15, fol. 68r, by permission of the Bodleian Library, Oxford.

humility, she seals her undertakings with a saint's authority and God's implied blessing.

However demure the reading saint might appear, she could all too easily become an emblem of female authority—if only through appropriation by a beholder such as Margaret. The saint's mastery is sometimes manifest, as we see in a Flemish miniature dating from about the time of Lady Hungerford's seal (figure 30). Seated in the posture of humility that Margaret imitated, Katherine of Alexandria would epitomize genteel femininity—were Maxentius not glowering beneath her skirts. The prostrate emperor makes explicit the message that is implicit in images of other holy readers (including Margaret Hunger-ford): the pious scholar does not need male authority; she is herself an authority. Modishly dressed and armed with a book, Katherine is a potent incarnation of the "woman on top" precisely because she seems so harmless.

In this chapter I examine two popular lives of St. Katherine that are unusual for their exploitation of the virgin martyr's identity as a reader. The first is an anonymous prose *Lyf of Seynt Katerine*, composed circa 1420 and later incorporated into the 1438 *Gilte Legende;* the second is John Capgrave's eight-thousand-line legend, written circa 1445 for a general audience "of man, of mayde, of wyf."[6] Both works have close affinities with Continental depictions of reading saints. In fact, both hagiographers conjure up the very scenes that abound in Books of Hours—Katherine relaxing in her study or reading beneath a tree in her "grete gardeyn."[7] Like contemporary artists, Capgrave and the writer of the *Lyf* situate the saint's life in a world that would have seemed familiar to fifteenth-century readers. Domestic details embellish both texts, as do considerations of a variety of historical, political, social, and moral issues. Katherine's martyrdom is less central to these narratives than is her love of Christ, cultivated through study and contemplation. The two hagiographers, however, offer divergent interpretations of Katherine's studies. The *Lyf* uses Katherine to provide a straightforward model for pious lay readers. Capgrave, by contrast, explores the social and political ramifications of Katherine's scholarship, at once encouraging lay learning and warning of its dangers. These interpretations were shaped by the very different political environments in which the legends were produced.

The *Lyf of Seynt Katerine* and the Mixed Life

The *Lyf of Seynt Katerine* was composed during a period of national euphoria.[8] Henry V had achieved stunning victories in France—among them the tri-

---

[6]I am using the following editions: *The Life and Martyrdom of St. Katherine of Alexandria*, ed. Henry Hucks Gibbs (London: Nichols, 1884); and John Capgrave, *The Life of St. Katharine of Alexandria*, ed. Carl Horstmann, EETS.OS 100 (1893; reprint, Millwood, N.Y.: Kraus, 1987). Subsequent references are to pages of the prose *Lyf* and to books and line numbers of Capgrave's narrative. For the quotation from Capgrave, see Prol. 66. Both these unusual Katherine legends claim to be based on Latin sources, but their sources—if they existed—have not survived. To my knowledge, only one Latin legend resembles these vernacular works, but that legend may have been produced after the Middle English texts and may indeed have been based on them. For a discussion and partial transcription of that Latin *vita*, see Auvo Kurvinen, "The Source of Capgrave's *Life of St. Katharine of Alexandria*," *Neuphilologische Mitteilungen* 61 (1960): 268–324.

[7]Capgrave, *St. Katharine*, 1.343–50.

[8]Though the earliest surviving manuscripts of the *Lyf* date from the second quarter of the fifteenth century, the incipit to the legend in MS 390/610, Gonville and Caius College, Cambridge,

umph at Agincourt in 1415 and the conquest of Normandy four years later—
which were taken as evidence that the English were a new Israel, a people chosen by God.[9] The Treaty of Troyes, concluded in 1420, made Henry heir to the
kingdom of France and regent of that country until Charles VI's death. Henry's
short reign was, of course, hardly trouble free. As discussed in the previous
chapter, anxieties about heresy surged, particularly after the Oldcastle revolt.
Yet those anxieties were attended by a widespread confidence that the alliance
between church and state would match the English triumph abroad by the defeat
of error on the home front. Perhaps inspired by Agincourt, Thomas Hoccleve
styled the king a new Constantine in a *Balade* composed circa 1416:

> O Lige lord, þat han eek the liknesse
> Of Constantyn, thensaumple and the mirour
> To Princes alle, in loue & buxumnesse
> To holy chirche o verray sustenour
> And piler of our feith, and werreyour
> Ageyn the heresies bittir galle,
> Do foorth do foorth continue your socour!
> Holde vp Crystes Baner lat it nat falle!
> This yle, or this, had been but hethenesse,
> Nad been of your feith the force & vigour![10]

claims that it was composed during the reign of Henry V. Auvo Kurvinen estimates that the earliest
version of the *Lyf* was written just before 1420 and then revised in 1420 and again in 1422 (the historical introduction that I will discuss was first included in the 1420 version and expanded in the
1422 revision); she hypothesizes that the fullest version of the legend (reproduced in the Gibbs edition) was written in honor of Henry V's marriage to Katherine of Valois in 1422. Given the nation-
alist themes of the *Lyf*'s historical sections, the expansion of those sections would support Kurvinen's association of the 1422 revision with Henry's marriage. For the dating of the *Lyf*, see Auvo
Kurvinen, "The Life of St. Catharine of Alexandria in Middle English Prose," Doctoral diss., Oxford University, 1960. Saara Nevanlinna and Irma Taavitsainen summarize and supplement Kurvinen's findings in their edition of a 1500 version of the prose legend, *St. Katherine of Alexandria: The
Late Middle English Prose Legend in Southwell Minster MS 7* (Cambridge: D. S. Brewer, 1993),
21–35.

[9] For useful overviews of Henry's accomplishments and contemporary views of the king, see
G. L. Harriss, "Introduction: The Exemplar of Kingship," and C. T. Allmand, "Henry V the Soldier, and the War in France," both in *Henry V: The Practice of Kingship*, ed. G. L. Harriss (Oxford:
Oxford University Press, 1985), 1–29, and 117–35, respectively; and Edward Powell, *Kingship, Law,
and Society: Criminal Justice in the Reign of Henry V* (Oxford: Clarendon, 1989). Of course, I am
not claiming the optimism was universal. See Lynn Staley's interpretation of the *Book of Margery
Kempe* as a critical commentary on England during the reign of Henry V, *Margery Kempe's Dissenting Fictions* (University Park: Pennsylvania State University Press, 1994).

[10] *Hoccleve's Works: The Minor Poems*, ed. Frederick J. Furnivall and Sir I. Gollancz, EETS.ES 61,
73 (London: Oxford University Press, 1892, 1925), 41, lines 9–18. I am using J. A. Burrow's dating in
Thomas Hoccleve (Brookfield, Vt.: Variorum, 1994), 21–22, 32. Burrow does note, however, that the
Balade may have been written as early as 1414.

The anonymous *Gesta Henrici Quinti* (1416) likewise celebrated Henry as a soldier of Christ who promoted God's honor by defeating Oldcastle and the French.[11]

The *Lyf of Seynt Katerine* resonates with the nationalism that was vigorously promoted during Henry V's reign. The work opens with a chapter that purports to demonstrate Katherine's relation through her father to the emperors of Rome; in fact, the hagiographer seems more concerned with associating famous Romans (and, by extension, Katherine herself) with England. Only a few sentences into the chapter, the hagiographer abruptly begins to write of "þe Brytons whiche come of þe noble blood of Troye and were cosyns to þe Romayns" (4). He recounts how the British were conquered by Julius Caesar and how they eventually came under the lordship of a Roman senator, Constance, who was sent to the island to quell a rebellion against Rome. Constance married Helen, daughter of the British king Coel, and governed Britain until he died "at 3ork in Englond and ther he was buryed." The son of Constance and Helen was "worthy Constantyn þat by vertu of þe holy crosse ouercome his enemys" (6). By associating the English with such illustrious figures from early Christian history, the hagiographer enhances his nation's stature. That same use of history is found in the writings of professional propagandists, such as Thomas Polton, an English representative to the Council of Constance (1417).[12] Faced with French efforts to rescind England's status as a voting member of the council by denying its importance as a Christian nation, Polton argued that key triumphs of the early Church were accomplished by members of the English royal family, namely, Constantine and Helen: the recovery of Christ's cross, the endowment of the Church, the foundation of St. Peter's and other churches, and the formation of "general councils for the extirpation of heresies and schisms" (in other words, the precursors of the Council of Constance).[13]

Evidence of a specifically Lancastrian bias may be discerned in the hagiographer's preoccupation with political legitimacy. In explaining how Constance became sovereign first of Armenia and later of England, the writer invokes the favorite themes of Lancastrian apologists—that is, right, might, and popular acclaim.[14] Though the parallels between Henry IV and Constance are by

---

[11] *Gesta Henrici Quinti: The Deeds of Henry the Fifth*, ed. and trans. Frank Taylor and John S. Roskell (Oxford: Clarendon, 1975). Allmand discusses contemporary views of Henry as a soldier of Christ waging military and spiritual battles in "Henry V the Soldier," 119–21.

[12] J.-P. Genet, "English Nationalism: Thomas Polton at the Council of Constance," *Nottingham Mediaeval Studies* 28 (1984): 60–78.

[13] John Hine Mundy and Kennerly M. Woody, eds., *The Council of Constance: The Unification of the Church*, trans. Louise Ropes Loomis (New York: Columbia University Press, 1961), 341–42.

[14] For a discussion of these themes, see Frank Grady, "The Lancastrian Gower and the Limits of Exemplarity," *Speculum* 70 (1995): 552–75; Alan S. Ambrisco and Paul Strohm, "Succession and

no means exact, they are nonetheless noteworthy. Constance's mission—to reclaim kingdoms that had been driven to rebellion by the emperor's tyranny and ineptitude—echoes Henry's own claim before the 1399 Parliament that he had come to "recover" a realm that was "in poynt to ben undoo for defaute of governance and undoying of the good lawes."[15] Constance arrives with an army, prepared to enforce imperial rule; however, the hagiographer emphasizes that he had no need to use force, having so impressed the Armenians with his "manly and vertuouse gouernaunce" that "the kynge and all þe puple desired that he schuld wedde his doughter and heyr of that lond" (5). Likewise, Constance's "vertu and prudence" make him "also acceptable to þe kynge of Brytayn . . . and to all þe peple of þe londe þat þe peple with o voys required þe kynge to ʒeue hym hys doughter and his heyre in mariage" (6). Lancastrian apologists similarly emphasized that Henry IV's control of the realm was ratified by overwhelming popular support rather than enforced by might. In the words of the *Brut* chronicler, "alle þe lordeʒ of þe Reme, with þe comyns assent, and by one accorde, chosyn þis worthi lorde, Ser Henry of Bolyngbroke, Erle of Derby, Duk of Herford and Duke of Lancastre be riʒt lyne and heritage; and for his myʒtful manhode þat þe peple founde yn hym, before al oþer þei choson hym, & made hym King of Engelonde."[16] Or, as John Gower succinctly put it in his address to Henry IV: "Thi title is knowe upon thin ancestrie, / The londes folk hath ek thy riht affermed; / So stant thi regne of god and man confermed."[17] Similar themes later shape the hagiographer's account of how Constantine drove Maxentius from Rome. According to the *Lyf*, Constantine was pressed into invading Rome at the "great instaunce" of "bothe knyghtes and other puple," who, having been oppressed by Maxentius's "greet cruelte and extorsioun," urged him "to take heede of þe ryght þat he hym felf [sic] had to þempire and of þe wronges doo to hem by þe tyraunt Maxence sturyng hym to labour booth for hys owne ryght and for heres." Constantine "atte last" consented, and after defeating Maxentius, "myghtyly occupied þempire" (23).

Sovereignty in Lydgate's Prologue to *The Troy Book*," *Chaucer Review* 30 (1995): 40–57; Paul Strohm, "Saving the Appearances: Chaucer's 'Purse' and the Fabrication of the Lancastrian Claim," in *Hochon's Arrow: The Social Imagination of Fourteenth-Century Texts* (Princeton: Princeton University Press, 1992), 75–94; and Caroline Barron, "The Deposition of Richard II," in *Politics and Crisis in Fourteenth-Century England*, ed. John Taylor and Wendy Childs (Wolfeboro Falls, N.H.: Alan Sutton, 1990), 132–49.

[15] From "Document A" (Stowe MS. 66, British Library), in G. O. Sayles, ed., "The Deposition of Richard II: Three Lancastrian Narratives," *Bulletin of the Institute of Historical Research* 54 (1981): 266.

[16] *The Brut, or The Chronicles of England*, pt. 2, ed. Friedrich W. D. Brie, EETS.OS 136 (1908; reprint, Millwood, N.Y.: Kraus, 1987), 359.

[17] John Gower, "To King Henry the Fourth, in Praise of Peace," in *The English Works of John Gower*, vol. 2, ed. G. C. Macaulay, EETS.ES 82 (London: Oxford University Press, 1900), 481, lines 12–14. See Grady's discussion of the complex politics of this poem ("The Lancastrian Gower"). Grady postulates that this poem was composed circa 1402.

The *Lyf* also highlights details that might have prompted a 1420s reader to think that the current king, Henry V, had much in common with Constance and Constantine. The hagiographer's point that Constance's sovereignty over first Armenia and then England was secured through marriage was immediately relevant to Henry V, for by the terms of the Treaty of Troyes, Henry's position as heir to the kingdom of France would be ratified through his marriage to Charles VI's daughter, Katherine of Valois. The *Lyf*, moreover, repeatedly identifies Constance and Constantine as kings of England and France. The hagiographer explains that although Constance was entitled to govern all of western Europe, he "held himself content wyth Fraunce Spayne and Engelond" (6; the reference to Spain is not irrelevant to Lancastrian political interests, for in 1388 John of Gaunt had claimed the kingdom of Spain by virtue of his marriage to Constance of Castile). Upon his father's death, Constantine "regned aftur hym vppon Englond and Fraunce not oonly as kyng of Englond by ryght of hys moder bot also as Emperour vppon booth reaumes by ryght of his Fader" (6). In his introduction to Katherine's passion, the hagiographer again mentions Constantine's sovereignty over England and France when he relates how the Roman emperor Maxentius was driven from power by the king "þat worthyly and manfully regned þat tyme vppon Englond and Fraunce" (23). It can be no coincidence that one of the two earliest copies of the *Lyf* occurs in a collection of saints' legends that, according to George R. Keiser, shows signs of having been produced by the Carthusians of Sheen "for the use of a member of the Lancastrian court."[18]

With its politicized introduction followed by its detailed account of Katherine's spiritual development, the *Lyf* encapsulates the peculiar blend of contemplation and politics that Henry V sponsored.[19] Profoundly religious himself, Henry favored introspective forms of devotion, which he deftly turned to public ends. For example, he encouraged the development of ritual and music that gave expression to affective devotion; those liturgical innovations were then used in services celebrating Henry's military victories and in the growing number of feasts honoring national and military saints—George, for example—whose cults promoted Henry's own image as a soldier of Christ.[20] The king's dedication to introspective modes of spirituality is also evident in his foundation in 1415 of the Carthusian house at Sheen and a Brigittine house just across the Thames at Syon. Though the Carthusians, with their commitment to a rigorous life of prayer and contemplation, epitomized the private orientation of

---

[18] George R. Keiser, "Patronage and Piety in Fifteenth-Century England: Margaret, Duchess of Clarence, Symon Wynter, and Beinecke MS 317," *Yale University Library Gazette* 60 (1985): 42.

[19] Jeremy Catto, "Religious Change under Henry V," in *Henry V*, ed. Harriss, 97–115.

[20] Ibid., 107.

fifteenth-century piety, Sheen also had an eminently public function, for it served, to use M. B. Tait's formulation, as a "gigantic power-house of prayer" for the Lancastrians.[21] That function is clearly illustrated in the *Gesta Henrici Quinti*'s account of the events preceding the 1416 engagement with French forces at the mouth of the Seine:

> And in order that, by increasing the number of those making intercession, he [the king] might the better obtain from God's bountifulness a favourable outcome to his prayer, he sent word on the following morning to the man of God, the hermit at Westminster, and to the saintly monks of the London Charterhouse and his own house at Sheen, that among their private prayers and lamentations, and especially at the altar of Christ where the Son is offered up as a sacrifice to the Father for the salvation of His people, they should pray with all possible tenderness and devotion.[22]

The Carthusians were also partners in another of Henry's politico-religious policies, namely, the propagation of a literature that would satisfy the laity's desire for a personal relationship with Christ without encouraging ideas and behavior that might undermine the state.[23] The *Lyf of Seynt Katerine* formed part of that literature.

The *Lyf* depicts Katherine at the center of a loving family and at the head of state. Katherine's parents are described as people of "vertuous gouernaunce" who, despite being pagans, "lyued a blessed lyf in as muche as longeth to þe world" (7). Katherine, for her part, is an affectionate daughter who recognizes that the behavior society expects of her is not contemptible, even when it conflicts with spiritual pursuits. When her widowed mother joins with her male relatives and the lords of her realm in a parliament to urge her to marry, she tries to appease them rather than to defy them in the usual hagiographical manner. Realizing that she cannot expect her lords or mother to understand her commitment to celibacy, she uses diplomacy and political arguments to postpone discussion of her marriage. Her response is larded with flattering references to the "greet wysdom of my lady my moder" and the "greet trouthe and kyndenesse" of her advisers (9). She appeals to her subjects' nationalism in declaring there is no need to "seke a straunge lorde" to rule over them, and she asserts her confidence in their own "good trouthe and wysdom" to guide her (10). Only when such diplomacy fails does she flatly refuse to marry. In refusing,

---

[21] M. B. Tait, "The Brigittine Monastery at Syon," Doctoral diss., Oxford University, 1975, 55.
[22] *Gesta Henrici Quinti*, 147.
[23] Catto, "Religious Change," 110–11; Michael G. Sargent, "The Transmission by the English Carthusians of Some Late Medieval Spiritual Writings," *Journal of Ecclesiastical History* 27 (1976): 225–40; and James Hogg, "Mount Grace Charterhouse and Late Medieval English Spirituality," *Analecta Cartusiana* 82.3 (1980): 1–43.

however, she displays a discomfort we would not expect of a virgin martyr: she "kaste hir eyen doun mekely and held hir stille" (11); when her mother angrily admonishes her to "do as ȝour noble eldres haue doo afore ȝou," Katherine defends her decision with a "pytous syghynge voys" (12).

Katherine's unhappy encounter with her mother and her lords illustrates a dilemma that many pious laypeople of the later Middle Ages were facing—that is, how to reconcile their temporal obligations with the pursuit of an absorbing personal relationship with God. That dilemma was the subject of numerous treatises, among the most popular of which was Walter Hilton's "Epistle on the Mixed Life," composed during the 1370s. Hilton, addressing "a deuout man in temperal estate," declares that God himself "haþ ordeyned þe & set þe in þe stat of souereynte ouur oþur men . . . and lente þe abundaunce of worldli godes for to rule & susteyne speciali alle þo þat are vnder þi gouernaunce & þi lordschipe in þi miȝt & þi cunnyng." [24] Indeed, Hilton continues, God would frown on a lord who abandoned the world for a life of contemplation:

> Wite þou wel, ȝif þou leue nedful bisynes of actyf lyf, & be recheles & take no kepe of þi worldly godes, hou þei be kept & spended, ne haue no force of þi soiettes & of þin euencristen, be cause of desyre & wille þat þou hast only for to ȝeue þe to gostly ocupacion, wenyng þat þou art þerbi excused: ȝif þou do so, þou dost not wysli. What are alle þi werkes worþ, wheþer þei be bodili or gostli, but ȝif þei be don riȝtfulli & resonably, to þe worschipe of god & at his biddyng? [25]

The pious layman should rather combine "werkes of actif lyf wiþ gostly werkes of contemplatyf lyf." [26]

Hilton's congenial advice was echoed in a variety of texts, including not only other spiritual treatises but also popular romances and saints' lives such as the *Lyf of Seynt Katerine*.[27] Notwithstanding her uncompromising stand on marriage, in other areas Katherine offers a model of how one can live in this world and transcend it as well. As much as she wishes to devote herself entirely to contemplation following her conversion and mystical marriage, she does not neglect her duties as a ruler: "The puple þat was lefte vnder hir cure by enheritaunce She gouerned wyth gret entendaunce. Not for thy þat she delited hir ih

---

[24] Walter Hilton, "Epistle on Mixed Life," in *Yorkshire Writers*, ed. Carl Horstmann (London, 1895), 1:264, 271.

[25] Ibid., 271.

[26] Ibid., 267.

[27] For a discussion of this literature, see Jonathan Hughes, *Pastors and Visionaries: Religion and Secular Life in Late Medieval Yorkshire* (Wolfeboro, N.H.: Boydell, 1988), 251–97; and the essays collected in Michael G. Sargent, ed., *De Cella in Seculum: Religious and Secular Life and Devotion in Late Medieval England* (Wolfeboro, N.H.: D. S. Brewer, 1989).

[*sic*] gret seruyce of men and wommen bot for she thought þat she myght not wyth oute synne kepe to hir self hir faders lyflode and suffre þe puple peryshe for defaute namely syth she had caste hir to haue ryght nought a doo wyth the world" (22). Instead of withdrawing from the world, she maintains "hir household in hir paleys wyth fulle cristen gouernaunce" (22) and channels her longing for God into productive social action—defending Christianity against skeptics, converting and instructing her people, and performing charitable deeds. Following the advice of many late medieval spiritual advisers, she avoids "playes or iapes or eny veyn or worldly wordes or songes" (22), and she devotes her leisure to prayer, contemplation, and reading.[28] At the end of the *Lyf*, Katherine is praised for virtues associated with both the active and the contemplative life (64): her wisdom consists in governing justly as well as in pursuing God through contemplation; her "clennes" is especially commendable because she maintains it despite her position in the world.

In exploring Katherine's spiritual development and in describing her relationship with Christ, the writer of the *Lyf* uses language and motifs associated with the large body of literature that advised readers on how to arrive at an intimate relationship with God through contemplation. During the fourteenth and fifteenth centuries, that literature took, broadly speaking, two directions. Some writers—Richard Rolle and the anonymous author of the *Cloud of Unknowing*, for example—explained how to achieve a mystical union with God through meditation. Writers of this literature chiefly address a spiritual elite of monks, nuns, and recluses.[29] Though they occasionally refer to a wider audience that includes the secular clergy and the laity, they make few concessions, if any, to the needs of that wider audience. The *Cloud* writer, indeed, shudders at the thought that his treatise might reach the hoi polloi:

> Fleschly iangelers, glosers & blamers, roukers & rouners, & alle maner of pynchers, kept I neuer þat þei sawe þis book; for myn entent was neuer to write soche þing to hem. & þerfore I wolde not þat þei herde it, neiþer þei ne none of þees corious lettrid ne lewid men, 3e! alþof þei be ful good men in actyue leuyng; for it acordeþ not to hem.[30]

---

[28] For example, one fifteenth-century layman is admonished by his spiritual adviser: "I forbid you for ever all spectacles, that is to say, dances (*choreas*), buckler-play, dicing, wrestling, and the like." See W. A. Pantin, "Instructions for a Devout and Literate Layman," in *Medieval Learning and Literature: Essays Presented to Richard William Hunt,* ed. Jonathan G. Alexander and Margaret T. Gibson (Oxford: Clarendon, 1976), 400.

[29] S. S. Hussey, "The Audience for the Middle English Mystics," in *De Cella in Seculum,* 109–22.

[30] *"The Cloud of Unknowing" and Related Treatises,* ed. Phyllis Hodgson (Exeter, England: Catholic Records Press, 1982), 73.

Rolle merely doubts that it is possible for people involved in secular affairs to experience the joys available to those who devote their lives to contemplation. In the *Incendium amoris* he writes:

> If any man could achieve both lives at once, the contemplative and the active, and sustain and fulfill them, he would be great indeed. He would maintain a ministry with his body, and at the same time experience within himself the song of heaven, absorbed in melody and the joy of everlasting love. I do not know if anybody has ever done this: it seems to me impossible to do both at once.[31]

By the time the *Lyf of Seynt Katerine* was composed, the fears of the writer of the *Cloud of Unknowing* were realized, as mystical tracts originally intended for monks and recluses came into the hands of grocers, lawyers, merchants, and housewives.[32] Worried that these lay enthusiasts might isolate themselves from their communities and disregard pastoral teachings in their desire to achieve a "mystical" union with God, some clerics supported the dissemination of literature promoting a more serene communion with God through the contemplation of Christ's life and passion.[33] This impetus toward a socially conservative contemplative literature was especially strong in the fifteenth century, when concerns about Lollardy led to a general constriction of theological writing in English.[34] Nicholas Love's adaptation of the *Meditationes vitae Christi* encourages readers to imagine scenes from the Bible "as þou were present" and to share the joys and sorrows of the Holy Family.[35] Far from isolating individuals from their earthly communities, the exercises proposed in the *Myrrour of the Blessed Lyf of Jesu Christ* and similar texts valorize social relationships—friendship, family, marriage—by showing how important those relationships were in Jesus's life.[36]

Love explicitly intended his treatise as an alternative to the writings of Rolle and others, designing it for those "symple" practitioners of the mixed life for whom "contemplacion of þe monhede of cryste is more likyng more spedefull

---

[31] Richard Rolle, *The Fire of Love*, trans. Clifton Wolters (New York: Penguin, 1972), 112.

[32] This process is surveyed by Hussey, "Middle English Mystics."

[33] Hughes, *Pastors and Visionaries*, 251–97.

[34] For an analysis of the conservatism of fifteenth-century theological writings, see Nicholas Watson, "Censorship and Cultural Change in Late-Medieval England: Vernacular Theology, the Oxford Translation Debate, and Arundel's Constitutions of 1409," *Speculum* 70 (1995): 822–64.

[35] Nicholas Love, *Mirror of the Blessed Life of Jesus Christ*, ed. Michael G. Sargent (New York: Garland, 1992), 21.

[36] Sarah Beckwith discusses this process in Love's *Myrrour* and related texts in *Christ's Body: Identity, Culture, and Society in Late Medieval Writings* (London: Routledge, 1993), and in "A Very Material Mysticism: The Medieval Mysticism of Margery Kempe," in *Medieval Literature: Criticism, Ideology, and History*, ed. David Aers (Brighton: Harvester, 1986), 34–57.

& more sykere þan is hyʒe contemplacion of þe godhed."[37] Actual lay readers, however, turned to both traditions of contemplative writings. Margery Kempe, for example, read (or heard read) "þe Bybyl wyth doctowrys þer-up-on, Seynt Brydys boke, Hyltons boke, Bone-ventur, Stimulus Amoris, Incendium Amoris, & swech oþer."[38] The *Lyf* is suited to the eclectic reading habits of people such as Kempe, for it folds themes from such esoteric tracts as Rolle's *Incendium amoris* and the *Cloud* into a narrative that owes much to the affective tradition associated with Nicholas Love. The governing tendency of the *Lyf* is to personalize Katherine's heavenly experience, rendering the sublime familiar, even cozy. When Katherine arrives in heaven, a congregation of martyrs welcomes their "dere suster," and the Virgin Mary endeavors to put her "beloued doughter" at ease in her unfamiliar surroundings (18). Christ, described as "þe semlyest ʒong kyng" (19), acts the devoted bridegroom, taking Katherine's hand, asking for her love, and speaking to her "in frendly wyse" (20). The hagiographer makes it easy to imagine "as þou were present" Katherine and Christ pledging their love in a marriage ceremony that takes place in a monastery and concludes with the Mass.

To reach her spouse, however, Katherine struggles toward spiritual fulfillment along the paths mapped out in arcane mystical tracts. The *Cloud of Unknowing* explains that the soul's "nakid entent vnto God" is frustrated by "a derknes, & as it were a cloude of vnknowyng."[39] Katherine speaks in similar terms of being separated from her beloved by "derkenesse" and by "derke cloudes of ignoraunce" (12). The *Cloud* advises readers, "Schap þee to bide in þis derknes as longe as þou maist, euermore criing after him þat þou louest."[40] Katherine does exactly that: her "hert was soo sette a fyre with thys husbond þat she had soo descryued þat she coude nothyng doo ne thenke bot alle hir mynde and hir entencioun was oonly in hym. Wherfore she studyed and mused contynuely how she myght fynde hym" (12). For the writer of the *Lyf*, as for most mystical writers, only God's grace can illuminate the soul shrouded in darkness, and that grace comes only through desire.[41] That lesson is clearly stated by the Virgin Mary, when she tells her messenger, the hermit Adrian, that he will find Katherine "allone in hir studie bysieng hir fulle sore to fynde

---

[37] Love, *Mirror*, 10. Love explicitly directs readers to Hilton's "Epistle" in *Mirror*, 124.

[38] *The Book of Margery Kempe*, ed. Sanford Brown Meech, EETS.OS 212 (Oxford: Oxford University Press, 1940), 143.

[39] *Cloud*, 9.

[40] Ibid.

[41] For a discussion of these themes, particularly in Hilton's *Scale of Perfection*, see Joseph E. Milosh, *"The Scale of Perfection" and the English Mystical Tradition* (Madison: University of Wisconsin Press, 1966), 51–110.

by hir wyttes that þat wyl not be. *Wherfore my sone hath compassion on hir labour and for hir good wylle* she shalle be soo specialle wyth his grace þat þere was neuer noon lyke to hir out take myn owne persone þat am his owen chosen moder" (14; emphasis mine). Allusions to Katherine's "brennyng fyre of loue" (12) echo the language of Rolle's popular *Incendium*, and mystical language also pervades the account of Katherine's marriage, where assertions that words cannot describe Katherine's experience alternate with reports of deathlike swoons and sensations of being ravished.[42]

By using the language of esoteric mystical tracts to describe his heroine's experiences, the Middle English hagiographer makes the ideas of a literature intended for professional contemplatives more accessible to amateur consumers of that literature. Katherine's story shows the spiritual states described in such treatises as the *Incendium* or the *Cloud* as they are experienced by a woman who, like ordinary laypeople, must reconcile her spiritual ambitions with her earthly duties. The *Lyf*, in effect, provides a model for assimilating the contemplative literature that was so popular among fifteenth-century readers, at the same time locating that literature securely within the boundaries of social relations and temporal responsibilities.

In contrast to Capgrave's Katherine legend, which I will discuss shortly, the *Lyf* never contests the value of reading. The anonymous hagiographer praises unequivocally Katherine's zeal for knowledge: "Noo wonder þough sche dronke plenteuously of þe welle of wysdom for she was ordeyned in tyme to come to be a techer and an enformer of þe euerlastynge wysdom" (8). Though study alone cannot lead Katherine to God, it does precipitate God's intervention in her life. Moreover, Katherine's training in the seven liberal arts, combined with her diligent study of holy scripture, gives her the wherewithal to defend her faith: "From hir childhode hir fader had sette hir to liberal studyes . . . in whiche she was soo sufficiantly taught þat she myght not be deceyued wyth no craft of sotilte or of argumentes. For thaugh many grete clerkes assayed hir wyth sotilte of questions and obiections ʒet þey proued hem self bot

---

[42] For a discussion of comparable language in the writings of the mystics, see Wolfgang Riehle, *The Middle English Mystics,* trans. Bernard Standring (Boston: Routledge and Kegan Paul, 1981), 92–96, 134–41. When Katherine first sees the company of virgins at the gates of heaven, she "al rauysshed fille doun before hem wyth greet drede" (17). As a host of martyrs greets her, she is so "rauysshed wyth so gret ioye and meruaylle" that she is speechless (17). The author declines to describe the Virgin Mary's "rychesse" for "hit excedith euery mannes mynde," but he writes that when the Virgin approached Katherine, the saint "was so fulfylled wyth heuenly ioye þat she lay a greet whyle as deed" (18). After she has addressed Mary, "alle hir spirites were shett vp soo fast þat she lay as deed" (18). Not surprisingly, Christ's presence is unbearable for the earthly queen. When he speaks to her, "so gret a swetnesse entred in to hir soule þat she fel doun as deed lyynge before hym" (20). Only when he endows her with "a noble strengthe þat passed kynde" (20) can she endure his presence.

foles and ydiotes" (22–23). Her learning makes her receptive to Christian doctrine but not self-willed. Thus, when Adrian explains the tenets of Christianity, the scholarly queen listens with the utmost respect: "She asked hym many an hye questioun and he answered hir sufficiantly and enformede hir in alle þe poyntes of þe feyth and she receyued plenteuously his doctrine and enformacioun and vndirstode hym merveylously" (16). Nor is the *Lyf*'s Katherine distracted from her duties as a monarch, as is Capgrave's heroine. The writer of the *Lyf* indicates that Katherine presides regularly over Parliament (the dispute about her marriage occurs when "þe queen on a day saat in hir parlement" [9]), where she is eager to deliberate all matters pertaining to "þe good reule and gouernaunce of oure reaumes" (10), except, of course, her own marriage.[43]

In transforming the saint into an exemplar of the mixed life, the writer of the *Lyf* does open the door to questions that previous Middle English Katherine legends did not invite: Is there a relationship between Katherine's behavior as a monarch and her martyrdom? What business has a woman governing a kingdom? Is it advisable for a woman to be such a scholar? Focusing resolutely on the exemplary aspects of Katherine's behavior—her concern for "good reule and gouernaunce," her esteem for her mother and advisers, her devotion—the hagiographer skirts these troublesome issues. Only once does he hint that Katherine's pious learning may have unfortunate social ramifications. When Katherine declares that she will marry only an infinitely wise and rich immortal who was born of a virgin, her mother retorts: "Allas doughter ys this ȝour greet wysdom þat is talked of so fer. Muche sorowe be ȝe lyke to do to me and to alle ȝoures. Allas who sawe euer any womman forge hir an husband wyth wordys suche on as ȝe haue deuysed was þer neuer noon ne neuer shal be and therfor gode doughter leue þis greet folye and do as ȝour noble eldres haue doo afore ȝou" (11–12). The disturbing themes of this passage fade quickly, however, as Katherine respectfully insists that reason assures her that the spouse she has stipulated really *does* exist. The saint's impassioned response neatly deflects attention from the social consequences of her scholarship to the spiritual acuity that her study has engendered. As we will see, the quickly silenced complaints of Katherine's mother resound through Capgrave's legend.

Capgrave's Katherine and the Politics of Reading

Written more than two decades after the prose *Lyf,* Capgrave's Katherine legend was the product of a very different climate, one conditioned by humiliat-

---

[43] As we will see, Capgrave's Katherine is taken from her studies for a special session of Parliament, called to discuss her marriage.

ing losses abroad and rampant lawlessness at home.[44] Henry VI was showing what would later be cited as signs of sanctity, and some of those signs were quite alarming—indifference to government, for example, and a rumored aversion to sex. The uncertainties of the 1440s find expression in Capgrave's ambivalence toward virtually everything—politics, sainthood, learning, and history, including the Constantine myth.

Capgrave passes up the opportunity to exploit the relationship between Katherine and Constantine for nationalist/royalist ends. His prologue deals not with England's illustrious past but with the literary genealogy of his purported source, which he scrupulously traces back to the eyewitness account of Katherine's disciple, Athanasius. Constantine is not mentioned until book 4, when Capgrave reports the events leading up to Maxentius's arrival in Alexandria. As in the *Lyf*, Capgrave identifies Constantine with "brytayn, the lond in whiche we dwelle" (4.111), but he makes no effort to represent the future Roman emperor as a national hero. After recounting Constantine's expulsion of Maxentius from Rome, he forcefully conveys Maxentius's opinion that Constantine was a "traytour" who "as a fals intrusore entred in to his lande" (4.288–89). Capgrave's own opinion of Constantine's victory is ambiguous: at first he seems almost to side with Maxentius, criticizing the Romans who betrayed their emperor—"Be this exaumple wyse men may weel leere / To truste on the puple; for thei wil faile at nede" (4.180–81). Only a few lines later, he contradicts himself, explaining that Maxentius was "deceyued rightfully thus be her trayn—/ Right for his leuyng, that was soo vicyous" (4.185–86). The only trace of national pride in Capgrave's legend is Maxentius's reference to "hem of Bretayn and frans" as "a grete puple and a statly powere" (4.285–87)—dubious praise, given the source.

In its chronicle of the fall of a once great empire under the stewardship of a virtuous incompetent, Capgrave's narrative registers the pessimism evoked by the current state of England. Capgrave begins his narrative with an account of the happy reign of Katherine's father, detailing the king's policies and accomplishments in terms reminiscent of contemporary tributes to Henry V. He praises Costus as a just and prudent monarch and a protector of trade, and he pays particular attention to the king's success as a military commander:

> Was no lord be-syde þat wold do hym wrake,
> ffor what man that dede, he shulde it sone wayle;

[44] For surveys of these developments, see Ralph A. Griffiths, *The Reign of King Henry VI: The Exercise of Royal Authority, 1422–1461* (London: Ernest Benn, 1981); Bertram Percy Wolffe, *Henry VI* (London: Methuen, 1981); and R. L. Storey, *The End of the House of Lancaster* (New York: Stein and Day, 1967).

> Whan he gan vengeavns to take,
> Prayer as þan wolde non a-vayle;
> To many a kyngdam made he asayle,
> And many a castell beet he ryght dovn
> Whan thei to his lawes wolde not be boun.
>
> (1.29–35)

Capgrave even suggests Henry's famed piety when he observes of Costus, "Synne hated he hertely, harlotry and vys" (1.49).

Costus's death—like Henry's—leaves his realm in a state of apprehension. Dismayed at the prospect of being governed by a young woman, Costus's bereaved subjects lament: "Weelaway, allas! what shal we doo? / Oure lord is now goo, we gete hym no moo. / ho shal bere the crovne, now he is deed?" (1.452–54). Without a strong leader, lawlessness plagues the realm: "Ther is no revle in lord ne in Iustyse, / They sette the shire, þe cessyons and the Cyse / Ryght as hem lest; will for resoun gooth now" (1.893–95). Such worries mirror those of the chronicler John Hardyng, who wonders what will become of England, left in the hands of a child: "O lorde, who shall Englond now defende? / Seth he is gone that was our hiegh Iustyse."[45] Capgrave's lament in his 1446 biography of Henry VI—"We who were accustomed to conquering all people are now conquered by all"—is echoed in the complaints of Katherine's subjects: "We bounde somtyme, nov mote we suffre bondes" (1.462).[46] As I have shown elsewhere, Capgrave endows Katherine with attributes that he and contemporaries such as Hardyng lamented in Henry VI, including excessive mercy, liberality, and devotion to chastity, and insufficient attention to affairs of state.[47] It seems reasonable to suppose that Capgrave's account of the disintegration of Costus's empire, which culminates in Katherine's execution, embodies his concern for the fate of his own country as it staggered toward civil war.

Capgrave's political worries go hand in hand with his troubled view of reading, which was surely affected by mounting anxieties about lay access to vernacular texts among church and state officials.[48] During the reign of Henry VI, denunciations of vernacular texts increasingly embraced not only Lollard tracts and English Bibles but English books generally. One anti-Lollard ordinance from circa 1426 actually attributed heresy to "possessing and reading

[45] "Extracts from the First Version of Hardyng's Chronicle," ed. C. L. Kingsford, *English Historical Review* 27 (1912): 744.

[46] John Capgrave, *Liber de illustribus Henricis,* ed. Francis Charles Hingeston (London, 1858), 135. The Latin reads, "Qui solebamus victores esse omnium populorum ab omnibus jam populis vincimur."

[47] Karen Winstead, "Capgrave's Saint Katherine and the Perils of Gynecocracy," *Viator* 25 (1994): 367–71.

[48] On this development, see Watson, "Censorship and Cultural Change."

books that are written in our vulgar tongue,"[49] while in 1430, Robert Bert of
Bury St. Edmunds was accused of, among other things, owning *Dives and Pauper,* which was said to "contain many errors and multiple heresies."[50] Though,
as I noted in the preceding chapter, 1440s East Anglia was relatively tolerant of
risqué ideas, Capgrave was clearly affected by the hysteria that was at large in
the country. His situation—writing within a relatively tolerant community at a
time of broad intolerance—helps account for the curious blend of conservatism and radicalism that marks his narrative.

In contrast to the writer of the *Lyf of Seynt Katerine,* Capgrave looks critically
at Katherine's reading. At the beginning of his legend, he unequivocally commends his protagonist's devotion to books. Looking forward to the day when
her arguments will confound fifty pagan philosophers, he exhorts her to study
hard: "Lerne sore, þou yovnge goddys scolere" (1.285). Her knowledge, bolstered by God's grace, will defeat the Church's enemies: "She shal so be lerned
þat alle her assayle / Shal fayle" (1.299–300). As Katherine's story unfolds, however, Capgrave shows his protagonist applying her knowledge in ways that
fifteenth-century readers would have found more controversial than trounc-
ing fifty pagan philosophers. The first two books of his narrative delineate the
troubles that Katherine's bookishness brings on her kingdom. Soon after her
father's death, her subjects complain that she is so engrossed in her books that
she ignores the state of her realm:

> We haue a qveen, she cometh a-mong no men,
> She loveth not ellis but bookys and scole;
> Lete alle oure enemys in londe ryde or ren,
> She is euere in stody and euere-more soole.
> This wil turne vs alle to wrake and to doole!
>
> (1.862–66)

Capgrave substantiates these charges, for he relates that, following her corona-
tion, Katherine spends her days reading within her palace and that she resents
being interrupted, especially with bad news (1.778–94).

To Katherine's subjects, bookishness is wrong in a sovereign, but especially
wrong in a queen. As her mother puts it: "To leue allone in stody, it was neuer
seyn / That ony lady ony tyme dede soo" (1.976–77). When Katherine's mother
and the lords of her realm assemble in the "Marriage Parliament," they insist
that Katherine has an obligation to put aside her books and marry so that a

[49]"Librorum possessio et lectura, qui scribunter in vulgari idiomate nostro," quoted in Anne
Hudson, *Lollards and Their Books* (London: Hambledon, 1985), 149.

[50]"Multi errores et hereses quamplures"; see Norman P. Tanner, ed., *Heresy Trials in the Diocese
of Norwich, 1428–31,* Camden Fourth Series 20 (London: Royal Historical Society, 1977), 102.

husband can take charge of the realm and that she may produce heirs to her line. In the words of the Parliament's speaker: "Ye must now leue your stody and your bookes / And take yowre solace be feeldes and be brookes" (2.125–26). Katherine is uninterested in marriage, however, in part because she realizes that the duties of a wife are incompatible with a scholar's life (2.183–87). Though she has no strong desire to govern (2.157–58), she argues to her lords at length that a queen can rule as effectively as can a king and that she therefore has no reason to marry.

Katherine's reading threatens social stability not only because it distracts her from her duties but also because it gives her the skill to defend positions that even she does not fully believe. When the speaker explains why she must marry, she silently acknowledges that he is right; recognizing that her desire to remain single is "ageyn my owne lawe, / Whiche I am swore to kepe and to defende" (2.176–77), she admits that "I ne wot ne can / Voyde the sentens of þis ilke wyse man" (2.158–59). She nonetheless answers the speaker and his fellows with clever language, equivocation, and plausible arguments, freely contradicting herself and taking advantage of her lords' rhetorical awkwardness by restating their arguments in forms that are easy to refute or to mock. For example, though she first agrees to marry—but not yet (2.198–231)—she later declares that she merely promised to appoint a regent (2.778–833). When one lord insists that she must marry because women lack the physical strength to govern, she promises to marry the man who can defeat his enemies single-handedly (2.995-1001). Thus bolstered by rhetoric, Katherine prevails against her subjects' appeals to tradition and social convention in order to follow a course that, from a worldly point of view, is demonstrably wrongheaded. When Maxentius occupies Alexandria, Capgrave reminds readers that the fall of her kingdom was the predicted consequence of Katherine's willfulness, as one of her subjects laments:

> . . . now is come that hour
> That was dred tho of youre freendes alle
> Whan that ye wolde receyue no counseillour,
> ffor no thyng that men myght on-to [you] calle.
> I amful soory, for now are lykly to falle
> all tho myshappes whiche that were seyde before.
> (4.463–68)

Other comments by Katherine's subjects emphasize that her radical opinions and conduct have resulted from her reading. The Marriage Parliament, indeed, begins and ends with references to Katherine's books: as the debate opens, the speaker tells Katherine that she must put aside her books and take up hunting, a more seemly pursuit, while the council concludes with Katherine's lords returning home, "cursyng hir bookis alle" (2.125–26, 1479). During the debate, the lords, stymied at every turn by Katherine's smooth rhetoric, damn her books and her teachers. "He þat taught yow first þis scole, I pray / he mote be hanged," one declares (2.470–71). They implore her to forgo the pernicious counsel of her books:

> ffor goddys loue, and for youre puples sake,
> Chaunge now your lyf and lete youre book be stille,
> Looke no lengere vp-on tho letterys blake!
> ffor, be my wytte, stody shal yow spylle.
>
> (2.477–80)

Yet in the end there is nothing they can do but sputter: "Youre wordes arn sharpe, thei can bynde and knytte. / But had ye ben as other women are, / Thanne shulde ye a ferde as other women fare" (2.838–40).

Capgrave not only draws attention to the disastrous worldly consequences of Katherine's studiousness but also dissociates her learning from her saintly triumphs. In book 3, he indicates that Katherine's learning is part of the past she must discard if she is to become Christ's bride. When the Virgin Mary sends the hermit Adrian to convert Katherine and escort her to her heavenly wedding, she describes the future saint as "a right grete clerk" (3.211) who will abandon her books for Christ: "Hir book, hir stody shal she leeue ryght than" (3.318). Sure enough, Adrian finds Katherine poring over a book (3.386) and eventually persuades her to leave "bookys alle" (3.778). When she is later brought to debate Maxentius's philosophers, she declares, "I haue lefte alle myn auctouris olde, / I fond noo frute in hem but eloquens; / My bookis ben goo, ʒouen or ellis solde" (4.1324–26). Persuaded by Katherine's arguments, the philosophers, too, "despise her bookis alle" (4.1220).

One might easily conclude that Capgrave is using the Katherine of Alexandria legend to censure women's learning—and, by extension, lay learning generally—on both social and religious grounds. Capgrave's East Anglia had a tradition of notorious female scholars.[51] The Norwich heresy trials of the late 1420s had exposed the activities of Lollard wives like Hawisia Mone, who ad-

---

[51] The careers of many of these women are described in Margaret Aston, "Lollardy and Literacy," in *Lollards and Reformers: Images and Literacy in Late Medieval Religion* (London: Hambledon, 1984), 193–217; and Claire Cross, "'Great reasoners in scripture': The Activities of Women Lollards, 1380–1530," in *Medieval Women*, ed. Derek Baker (Oxford: Basil Blackwell, 1978), 359–80. See also Ralph Hanna III's discussion of Margery Baxter, Hawisia Mone, Margery Kempe, and Julian of Norwich, in "Some Norfolk Women and Their Books, ca. 1390–1440," in *The Cultural Patronage of Medieval Women*, ed. June Hall McCash (Athens: University of Georgia Press, 1996), 288–305.

mitted that she participated in "scoles of heresie" at which she "herd, conceyved, lerned and reported" various "errours."[52] Joan White carried on her husband William's "missionary" work following his 1428 burning.[53] One of William White's disciples, Margery Baxter, circulated White's writings within Norfolk and harangued her friends on Church doctrine.[54] Baxter owned one of White's books, and her servant Alice possessed a New Testament. Still closer to home, Capgrave may have known Margery Kempe, a fellow inhabitant of King's Lynn; in any case, he surely knew *of* her. Katherine embodies stereotypes that had become associated with women who, like Kempe and the "Lollard wives," aspired to learning. Dismissing social convention and tradition to embrace values derived from logic and scholarship, she scorns marriage, rejects the advice of friends, and even quotes Scripture. When Adrian first tries to teach her about Christianity, she is not immediately receptive, as was the Katherine of the *Lyf*; rather, she voices objections of the type that the Lollards were denounced for. For example, with all the pragmatism of a Margery Baxter, she insists that Christ's mother could not possibly be a virgin because "knowe I weel, and ilke man knoweth, / hoo wil haue a child, seed somtyme he soweth" (3.643–44).

The conservative message of Capgrave's legend is complicated, however, for if Capgrave criticizes Katherine's reading, he also criticizes her piety, which has the same deleterious political consequences. After her mystical marriage, Katherine retreats to her study, where, having discarded her pagan books, she devotes herself to prayer and contemplation. While she is thus occupied, Maxentius invades her kingdom, harasses her subjects, overturns her laws, and occupies her capital (4.204–427). Katherine learns of these events only when the racket from the emperor's birthday celebration interrupts her meditations (4.428–38). Though she eventually confronts the intruder, her leadership comes too late to save herself or her people. I must point out that Katherine is personally exonerated for neglecting her kingdom after her conversion, insofar as she is merely following the Virgin Mary's orders: "Keepeth ȝoure chaunbre wyth leuyng virtuous, / With preyng, fastynge, and elmesse-dede" (3.1482–83). Yet we must bear in mind that behavior that is acceptable in a character who, by generic exigency, must die at the end of the narrative is not necessarily advisable for secular leaders generally. The Virgin is, in effect, reaffirming what Katherine's subjects have said: if Katherine remains withdrawn and does not worry about "rychesse," an enemy is bound to attack within a couple of years (3.1478–87). For the prince who does not aspire to martyrdom—Henry VI, for

[52] Tanner, *Heresy Trials*, 140.
[53] Aston, *Lollards and Reformers*, 87.
[54] Tanner, *Heresy Trials*, 41–51.

instance—the message is clear: studiousness and devotion are commendable so long as one does not neglect one's kingdom. Or, as Walter Hilton put it, "ȝif þou leue nedful bisynes of actyf lyf . . . þou dost not wysli." [55]

A second reason we cannot read the *Life of St. Katherine* as a simple indictment of Katherine's learning is that Capgrave challenges his own readers to engage in the very freethinking that got his protagonist into such trouble. To begin with, he presents even Katherine's most radical opinions about gender and government with passion and eloquence. [56] Though Katherine is a pagan when she expresses those opinions, her sainthood still lends authority to them—especially because Capgrave maintains that she was a "very seynt" even before her conversion (1.803–4). During the second half of his narrative, Capgrave moves from sociopolitical issues into the more dangerous terrain of theology. As I mentioned earlier, his account of Katherine's conversion includes an extensive conversation between Katherine and Adrian, in which Katherine plies her teacher with practical objections to Christian doctrine (3.463–770). Her debate with the fifty philosophers involves an equally rigorous interrogation of dogma. Spanning a thousand lines, Capgrave's version of the debate is the longest I know of in Latin or the vernacular, and he uses it to discuss topics, such as the Incarnation, that many ecclesiastical authorities felt should not be discussed in English. [57] Perhaps twitting conservative clerics, Capgrave even admits that it is "ful hard" to expound topics like the Incarnation "pleynly in langage of oure nacyon"—especially when one is trying to rhyme (4.2194–95). On two occasions, he transgresses the bounds of orthodoxy and invites readers to consult Scripture: in explaining why he will not report what Katherine tells the philosophers about original sin, he says that "this dilatacyon / . . . occupieth ny al the newe testament, / That men myght plod in her, if þat hem lyst" (4.2278–81); earlier he bolstered his statement that God often chooses unlikely servants with the comment, "paule seith þis best / In his epystoles, hoo þat wil hem reede" (3.369–70). [58]

Such comments were risky indeed. Since the beginning of the century, secular and clerical authorities had been attacking the unsupervised reading of the

[55] Hilton, "Epistle," 271.

[56] I have discussed the persuasiveness of Katherine's arguments in Winstead, "Gynecocracy," 363–65.

[57] On fifteenth-century attitudes toward the vernacular, see Rita Copeland, "Why Women Can't Read: Medieval Hermeneutics, Statutory Law, and the Lollard Heresy Trials," in *Representing Women: Law, Literature, and Feminism*, eds. Susan Sage Heinzelman and Zipporah Batshaw Wiseman (Durham: Duke University Press, 1994), 253–86.

[58] Further evidence of Capgrave's apparent endorsement of lay Bible reading is his praise of St. Cecilia for carrying "þe gospel materialy wrytyn in hir bosum þat sche myth rede it whan sche wold"; see John Capgrave, *Ye Solace of Pilgrimes*, ed. C. A. Mills (London: Oxford University Press, 1911), 110.

Bible as a threat to church and state. John Badby was burned at Smithfield in 1410 for, among other things, propagating heresies derived from his interpretation of Scripture.[59] As Archbishop Arundel reportedly charged in his 1407 interrogation of the Lollard preacher William Thorpe, "Whi, losel, wolt þou not and oþer þat ben confedrid wiþ þee sechen out of holy writt and of þe sentence of doctours as scharpe auctoritees aȝens lordis and knyȝtis and squyeris and aȝens oþer secular men, as ȝe done aȝens preestis?"[60] As Nicholas Watson has shown, Arundel's 1409 Constitutions effectively stifled discussion of a wide variety of theological issues not only by prohibiting certain kinds of teaching but also by "creating an atmosphere in which self-censorship was assumed to be both for the common good and (for one's own safety) prudent."[61] By mid-century, it could be dangerous for even the most orthodox thinker to argue matters of faith in the vernacular. So Bishop Reginald Pecock of Chichester discovered in 1457, when he was convicted of error and his substantial corpus of anti-Lollard books was burned.[62] Convinced that the best way to fight error is through reason, Pecock had produced works in English aimed not at scholars but at ordinary Christians of the sort that were examined at Norwich—craftspeople and entrepreneurs, housewives and servants. He wrote to contradict *libros hereticos* and to compete with them in satisfying the desire for intellectual stimulation that drove people like Hawisia Mone and her husband, Thomas, to "scoles of heresie."[63] In doing so, however, he ran afoul of those who believed it more effective to ban objectionable ideas than to refute them. To these authorities, his enthusiasm for vernacular books must have "seemed dangerously akin to that of the heretics," as Margaret Aston observed.[64] Forced to abjure his ideas and resign his bishopric, Pecock spent his last years in confinement at Thorney Abbey, Cambridgeshire. Long after his abjuration, he continued to be associated with the man whose ideas he had labored to discredit, John Wyclif.

Though Capgrave inveighs against Lollards in his *Abbreuiacion of Cronicles* and elsewhere, his ambiguous position between orthodoxy and heterodoxy is signaled by his depiction of Katherine's *passio*, which makes it easy to see the

---

[59] Peter McNiven, *Heresy and Politics in the Reign of Henry IV: The Burning of John Badby* (Wolfeboro, N.H.: Boydell, 1987), 202.

[60] "The Testimony of William Thorpe," in *Two Wycliffite Texts*, ed. Anne Hudson, EETS.OS 301 (Oxford: Oxford University Press, 1993), 72.

[61] Watson, "Censorship and Cultural Change," 831; see also Anne Hudson, "Lollardy: The English Heresy?" in *Lollards and Their Books*, 141–63.

[62] For more on Pecock, see Margaret Aston, *Faith and Fire: Popular and Unpopular Religion, 1350–1600* (London: Hambledon, 1993), 73–93; and Roy Martin Haines, "Reginald Pecock: A Tolerant Man in an Age of Intolerance," *Studies in Church History* 21 (1984): 125–37.

[63] Haines discusses Pecock's intended audience in "Reginald Pecock," 129–30.

[64] Aston, *Lollards and Reformers*, 208.

virgin martyr not as the conventional champion of the Church but as a brave heretic struggling against an orthodoxy that burns those it cannot convince.[65] He presents Maxentius's persecution of Christians as a war against "a newe errour" (4.1417), undertaken for the national good (4.315–36) and implemented through an alliance of church and state: Maxentius orders his officers to arrest and punish Christians (4.234–38), while a "bysshop . . . with myter and wyth croos" (4.309) preaches a "grete sermoun" in support of his sovereign's policy, determined that no heretic will escape "but he wil to þe rak / And on the same ly with a broken bak" (4.351, 354–55). One of the emperor's philosophers boasts that he has "brent with brond" many Christians because "that thei calle feith, we calle delirament" (4.1419, 1421). Worried that Katherine will corrupt "lewde foolkis" with "apparent resons," the philosopher reminds his fellows that "to suffre swiche prechouris it is agayn oure lawe" (4.1431–35)—a possible reference to the current prohibition in England against unlicensed preaching. At one point, Capgrave explicitly associates Christians with Lollards: as Adrian sets out on his mission to Alexandria, the Virgin Mary assures him, "Though thei you calle lollard, wytche or elue, / Beth not dismayed" (3.327–28). The parallels I have just rehearsed may have occurred to the sixteenth-century Protestant reader who placed a "nota bene" mark beside the line "that thei calle feith, we calle delirament" in one manuscript of Capgrave's legend.[66]

Capgrave's portrayal of his villains as fonts of anti-Lollard rhetoric is the mirror image of Margery Kempe's portrayal of herself, under examination for heresy, as a "new" Saint Katherine. Like his Lynn neighbor, Capgrave decried the terms on which the war against heterodoxy was waged, intimating that even one of the Church's most venerated martyrs would not escape persecution at the hands of contemporary zealots.[67] Capgrave was surely alarmed at how the definition of heresy had shifted in the past fifty years (in the early 1400s, the view that the faithful should have ready access to Scripture, though controversial, had been within the bounds of orthodoxy).[68] Like the Lollards—and Reginald Pecock—he champions an informed, examined faith, even though

---

[65] For examples of Capgrave's anti-Lollard invective, see *Abbreuiacion of Cronicles*, ed. Peter J. Lucas, EETS.OS 285 (Oxford: Oxford University Press, 1983), 204–5, 220.

[66] Arundel 168, fol. 48r, British Library; the same annotator writes "Bale fol. 522" on 16r, where Capgrave identifies his hometown as Lynne (Prol., 240).

[67] Ruth Shklar discusses Kempe's "critique of the prevailing discourses that would define heresy" in "Cobham's Daughter: *The Book of Margery Kempe* and the Power of Heterodox Thinking," *Modern Language Quarterly* 56 (1995): 277–304. See also Staley, *Margery Kempe's Dissenting Fictions*.

[68] For a useful discussion of the narrow dividing line between orthodoxy and heterodoxy, see J. A. F. Thomson, "Orthodox Religion and the Origins of Lollardy," *History* 74 (1989): 39–55. See also Hudson, "Lollardy: The English Heresy?"

he recognizes that intellectual inquiry may have deleterious consequences. Where such conservatives as Thomas Hoccleve ridiculed Lollards for asking, "'Why stant this word heere?' and 'why this word there?' / 'Why spake god thus and seith thus elles where?'"[69] Capgrave expects and encourages orthodox Christians to ask such questions. By recording such extensive debates between Adrian and the unconverted Katherine and between Katherine and the philosophers, he affirms that reason can indeed prevail over error. Without endorsing heresy, he censures a regime that burns books and prohibits inquiry. Hagiography provided an ideal venue for such social criticism—as well as for theological deliberation: what safer place to flirt with dangerous ideas than within a genre whose uncontested authority and orthodoxy would deflect the sort of attacks that eventually ruined Pecock? And what better way to register uncertainties about traditional values than by sabotaging the conventional pieties of hagiography?[70]

Capgrave's narrative proffers a gloomy rejoinder to the prose *Lyf*. Except during its relatively brief Marriage Parliament, the *Lyf* sharply distinguishes right from wrong, heroes from villains. Like conventional virgin martyr legends, it comforts readers by, among other things, confidently reconciling worthy pursuits that seem at odds with each other: politics and spirituality, the active and the contemplative lives, and "affective" and "mystical" approaches to contemplation. The hagiographer's audacious use of a virgin martyr as an exemplar of the mixed life stands as a tribute to a king whose career seemed to testify that piety, military prowess, and responsible leadership were not incompatible virtues. Capgrave, by contrast, eschews certitudes in a narrative that seems determined to perplex its readers. Even the legend's conclusion is problematic, for instead of offering a conventional tribute to the martyr, Capgrave worries about the fate of his legend in the hands of a skeptical public (5.1965–81).[71] The ambiguity and open-endedness of his narrative may well be attributable to the too many uncertainties—political, moral, social, dynastic—in 1440s England. Capgrave could only incite readers to think, then leave them to their own devices.

---

[69] Thomas Hoccleve, "Address to Sir John Oldcastle," in *Hoccleve's Works*, 13, lines 156–57.

[70] Capgrave's *Life of St. Katherine* can thus be read as supporting Nicholas Watson's proposed "'underground' fifteenth-century theological tradition, carried on mainly through the processes of translation and compilation" ("Censorship and Cultural Change," 836). For more on Capgrave as a translator and compiler, see my "John Capgrave and the Chaucer Tradition," *Chaucer Review* 30 (1996): 389–400.

[71] The scribe of MS Arundel 20, British Library, was apparently so unsatisfied with Capgrave's ending that he omitted the final stanzas of the legend, replacing them with his own tribute to St. Katherine.

❀ Virgin Martyrs ❀

You shall be a saint yourself...

The power of virgin martyrs as cultural symbols during the later Middle Ages is manifest not only in the continual refashioning of the saints themselves but in their use in constructing alternative paradigms of holiness. As we saw in Chapter 1, Christina of Markyate's twelfth-century biographer valorized his heroine by recounting her attempt to emulate St. Cecilia in a dangerous and frightening contemporary world. With the expansion of the lay reading public in the thirteenth and fourteenth centuries, Middle English romance writers began borrowing the rhetoric and motifs of virgin martyr legends to extol virtuous laywomen. Like the virgin martyrs, Emaré, Florence, Constance, and other heroines of "pious romance" perform miracles, suffer tribulations, and repulse sexual advances, but their ordeals end not in death but in recovery of their wealth, reintegration within their communities, and reunion with their earthly spouses. Pious romances thus impart the reassuring message that the holy woman need not renounce family, property, and life itself for God's love.[72] Likewise, Margery Kempe recasts traditional indicators of sainthood, particularly virginity and martyrdom, to allow a wife and mother like herself to participate in the vita sanctorum. Though she dreads becoming a martyr and cannot be a virgin, God assures her that she need not be either to enjoy the same privileges as "classic" saints such as Margaret and Katherine. When Kempe imagines the "most soft deth" she would suffer for God's love, God thanks her for her good intentions and avers that merely desiring martyrdom guarantees her "þe same mede in Heuyn as þow þu suffredyst þe same deth."[73] God responds in the same strain to Kempe's laments for her lost virginity: "For-asmech as þu art a mayden in þi sowle . . . so xalt þu dawnsyn in Hevyn wyth oþer holy maydens & virgynes."[74] Significantly, Kempe does not restrict her broadened definition of sainthood to herself. Thus, when a devout man asks her to pray for him "yf euyr þu be seynt in Heuyn," she responds, "Sir, I hope ʒe xal be a seynt ʒowr-selfe & euery man þat xal come to Heuyn."[75]

To varying degrees, fifteenth-century hagiographers refashioned their virgin martyr legends along similar lines, Capgrave and the writer of the *Lyf* being the extreme cases. Going beyond Lydgate and Bokenham, Capgrave and the prose hagiographer not only endow their heroine with imitable virtues but also cast her in roles—reader, contemplative, daughter, wife, governor, head of house-

---

[72] For a more detailed discussion of how pious romances reformulate traditional ideals of sainthood, see Karen A. Winstead, "Saints, Wives, and Other 'Hooly Thynges': Pious Laywomen in Middle English Romance," *Chaucer Yearbook* 2 (1995): 137–54.

[73] *Book of Margery Kempe*, 30.

[74] Ibid., 52.

[75] Ibid., 130.

hold—that fifteenth-century laypeople could identify with. Like the biographers of "modern" saints such as Christina of Markyate and Margery Kempe, the Middle English hagiographers go out of their way to show that their heroines are neither omnipotent nor omniscient—indeed, at times they seem pathetic, even silly. The protagonist of the *Lyf* seems singularly unheroic defending her virginity with a "pytous syghynge voys" (12). As I have shown elsewhere, Capgrave gently mocks his heroine as she tries to finagle her way out of marriage by stipulating a mate she knows cannot be produced (immortal, son of a virgin, and so on).[76]

Most surprising, however, is the Katherine legends' treatment of those staples of virgin martyr legends, virginity and martyrdom. Both hagiographers place less emphasis on Katherine's virginity than on her loving relationship with Christ. Significantly, her union with her spouse occurs not upon her death, in the conventional fashion, but while she is alive, thus demonstrating that it is possible to enjoy a fulfilling relationship with Christ in this world. The legends' depictions of Katherine's mystical marriage, moreover, seem designed to stimulate readers' fantasies in various ways. Readers could simply imagine themselves in Katherine's place, pledging their love to Christ. Margery Kempe, in fact, describes her own mystical marriage to the Godhead in terms similar to Katherine's.[77] Those widows who took chastity vows in formal wedding ceremonies, of course, would find it especially easy to see themselves as Katherine.[78] Yet readers would not need to think of themselves as Christ's brides to identify with Katherine as a fellow wife who defends home and property in her husband's absence.[79] As for martyrdom, the heroines of these two Katherine legends are no more eager to give up life's pleasures than is Kempe. Blenching at the prospect of being thrown into a "hote cawdron of bras" (4.488), Capgrave's Katherine responds to the news of Maxentius's arrival by pacing her chamber, "fful sore astoyned what hir is beste for to doo" (4.498). She enjoys life, as she later admits to the emperor ("Though that my lyf bee ful swete to me" [5.1038]), but will die if she must. Similarly, though willing to suffer poverty, she is in no hurry: "If it come, I wil obeye þer-tille" (5.564). And despite her earlier indifference to government, she jealously asserts her prerogative when it

---

[76] Karen Winstead, "Piety, Politics, and Social Commitment in Capgrave's *Life of St. Katherine,*" *Medievalia et Humanistica,* n.s., 17 (1990): 66–67.

[77] *Book of Margery Kempe,* 87.

[78] Joel T. Rosenthal discusses chastity vows in "Fifteenth-Century Widows and Widowhood: Bereavement, Reintegration, and Life Choices," in *Wife and Widow in Medieval England,* ed. Sue Sheridan Walker (Ann Arbor: University of Michigan Press, 1993), 44–47, and in his *Patriarchy and Families of Privilege in Fifteenth-Century England* (Philadelphia: University of Pennsylvania Press, 1991), 229–30.

[79] I develop this point in "Gynecocracy," 374–75.

is threatened: "It is not onknowen to al the orient / That bothe be descens and be testament / This citee is myn" (4.914–16). The heroine of the *Lyf* lives just as comfortably as Capgrave's protagonist "in here paleys ful of richesse and of seruauntes." She, too, goes to Maxentius's temple with a few attendants, not looking for a spectacular death but hoping that "wyth free auctorite she wolde dampne þat unlefful sacrifice" (24–25).

With their devout yet strangely worldly saints, it is little wonder that both Katherine legends were popular among consumers of hagiography: as a free-standing legend or as part of the 1438 *Gilte Legende,* the prose *Lyf* survives in twenty-four manuscripts.[80] It was included in Caxton's *Golden Legend* and printed twice as an independent narrative during the sixteenth century.[81] Manuscript evidence indicates an immediate demand for Capgrave's narrative in East Anglia, and Osbern Bokenham takes it for granted that his lay readers will be able to obtain a copy, should they so desire.[82] It is also little wonder that orthodox hagiographers did not rush to produce similar legends, for these Katherine legends undercut the very premise of hagiography, namely, the saint's singularity. Bokenham may have realized as much when, with Capgrave's narrative "but newly compylyd,"[83] he retold the Katherine of Alexandria legend, omitting Katherine's *vita* and retaining just a passing reference to her scholarship. Admittedly, the passiones and the Katherine Group texts also encouraged a direct and intimate association between reader and saint, but it is one matter to encourage professional religious to identify with the saints and quite another to make such an intimate identification available to everybody. Paradoxically, as they crafted their richly detailed portrayals of Katherine, Capgrave and his anonymous contemporary rubbed elbows with those increasingly vocal critics of the Church who were erasing the saints' faces. Even as both hagiographers profess an appropriate reverence for St. Katherine through prayers and tributes, their narratives encourage what might best be termed a proto-Protestant view of the saint: admirable, imitable, but certainly not venerable.

[80] For the most recent listing, see *St. Katherine of Alexandria,* ed. Nevanlinna and Taavitsainin, xi–xii.

[81] For a discussion of the freestanding printed versions, see Auvo Kurvinen, "Two Sixteenth-Century Editions of *The Life of St. Catharine of Alexandria,*" in *English and Medieval Studies Presented to J. R. R. Tolkien,* ed. Norman Davis and C. L. Wrenn (London: Allen and Unwin, 1962), 269–79.

[82] Jane C. Fredeman, "The Life of John Capgrave, O.E.S.A. (1393–1464)," *Augustiniana* 29 (1979): 229; A. I. Doyle, "Publication by Members of the Religious Orders," in *Book Production and Publishing in Britain, 1375–1475,* ed. Jeremy Griffiths and Derek Pearsall (Cambridge: Cambridge University Press, 1989), 118. For Osbern Bokenham's comments, see *Legendys of Hooly Wummen,* ed. Mary S. Serjeantson, EETS.OS 206 (1938; reprint, Millwood, N.Y.: Kraus, 1988), lines 6347–60.

[83] Bokenham, *Legendys,* line 6357.

✵
Bibliography

Primary Sources

Acta Sanctorum. Brussels [etc.], 1643 –.

Aelred of Rievaulx. "De Sanctimoniali de Watun." *Patrologia cursus completus: Series latina,* ed. J. P. Migne, vol. 195, cols. 784 – 96. Paris: Migne, 1861 – 64.

——. *Treatises: The Pastoral Prayer.* Spencer, Mass.: Cistercian Publications, 1971.

The Ancrene Riwle. Trans. M. B. Salu. Notre Dame: University of Notre Dame Press, 1956.

Ancrene Wisse. Ed. J. R. R. Tolkien. EETS.OS 249. London: Oxford University Press, 1962.

The English Text of the "Ancrene Riwle." Ed. Mabel Day. EETS.OS 225. London: Oxford University Press, 1952.

The Apocryphal New Testament: A Collection of Apocryphal Christian Literature in an English Translation Based on M. R. James. Ed. J. K. Elliott. Oxford: Clarendon, 1993.

Bettenson, Henry, ed. *Documents of the Christian Church.* 1943. Reprint, London: Oxford University Press, 1963.

Bokenham, Osbern. *Legendys of Hooly Wummen.* Ed. Mary S. Serjeantson. EETS.OS 206. 1938. Reprint, Millwood, N.Y.: Kraus, 1988.

——. "*Mappula Angliae* von Osbern Bokenham." Ed. Carl Horstmann. *Englische Studien* 10 (1887): 1 – 34.

Bozon, Nicholas. *Seven More Poems by Nicholas Bozon.* Ed. and trans. M. Amelia Klenke. St. Bonaventure, N.Y.: Franciscan Institute, 1951.

——. *Three Saints' Lives by Nicholas Bozon.* Ed. and trans. M. Amelia Klenke. St. Bonaventure, N.Y.: Franciscan Institute, 1947.

The Brut, or The Chronicles of England. Ed. Friedrich W. D. Brie. EETS.OS 131 and 136. 1906 and 1908. Reprint, Millwood, N.Y.: Kraus, 1987.

Capgrave, John. *Abbreuiacion of Chronicles.* Ed. Peter J. Lucas. EETS.OS 285. Oxford: Oxford University Press, 1983.

——. *Liber de illustribus Henricis.* Ed. Francis Charles Hingeston. London, 1858.

——. *The Life of St. Katharine of Alexandria.* Ed. Carl Horstmann. EETS.OS 100. 1893. Reprint, Millwood, N.Y.: Kraus, 1987.

——. *Lives of St. Augustine and St. Gilbert of Sempringham, and a Sermon.* Ed. J. J. Munro. EETS.OS 140. 1910. Reprint, Millwood, N.Y.: Kraus, 1987.

——. *Ye Solace of Pilgrimes.* Ed. C. A. Mills. London: Oxford University Press, 1911.

Caxton, William. *The Prologues and Epilogues of William Caxton.* Ed. W. J. B. Crotch. EETS.OS 176. 1929. Reprint, London: Oxford University Press, 1956.

Chaucer, Geoffrey. *The Riverside Chaucer.* 3d ed. Ed. Larry D. Benson. Boston: Houghton Mifflin, 1987.

The Life of Christina of Markyate. Ed. and trans. C. H. Talbot. Oxford: Clarendon, 1959.

❀ Bibliography ❀

"The Cloud of Unknowing" and Related Treatises. Ed. Phyllis Hodgson. Exeter, England: Catholic Records Press, 1982.

Dives and Pauper. Ed. Priscilla Heath Barnum. 2 vols. EETS.OS 275, 280. London: Oxford University Press, 1976, 1980.

Eusebius. *History of the Church.* Trans. G. A. Williamson. New York: Penguin, 1965.

Garmonsway, G. N., and R. R. Raymo. "A Middle-English Prose Life of St.Ursula." *Review of English Studies,* n.s., 9 (1958): 353–61.

Geoffroy de la Tour-Landry. *The Book of the Knight of La Tour-Landry.* Ed. Thomas Wright. EETS.OS 33. 1906. Reprint, New York: Greenwood, 1969.

Gesta Henrici Quinti: The Deeds of Henry the Fifth. Ed. and trans. Frank Taylor and John S. Roskell. Oxford: Clarendon, 1975.

The Book of St. Gilbert. Ed. and trans. Raymonde Foreville and Gillian Keir. Oxford: Clarendon, 1987.

Gower, John. *The English Works of John Gower.* Ed. G. C. Macaulay. EETS.ES 81–82. London: Oxford University Press, 1900.

Gregory of Tours. *Life of the Fathers.* Trans. Edward James. Liverpool: Liverpool University Press, 1985.

Gregory the Great. *Dialogues,* bk. 2, *Saint Benedict.* Trans. Myra L. Uhlfelder. Indianapolis: Bobbs-Merrill, 1967.

Hali Meiðhad. Ed. Bella Millett. EETS.OS 284. London: Oxford University Press, 1982.

Hardyng, John. "Extracts from the First Version of Hardyng's Chronicle." Ed. C. L. Kingsford. *English Historical Review* 27 (1912): 740–53.

Hilton, Walter. "Epistle on Mixed Life." In *Yorkshire Writers,* ed. Carl Horstmann. London, 1895.

Hoccleve, Thomas. *Hoccleve's Works: The Minor Poems.* Ed. Frederick J. Furnivall and Sir I. Gollancz. EETS.ES 61, 73. London: Oxford University Press, 1892, 1925. Rev. Jerome Mitchell and A. I. Doyle and reprinted as one volume. London: Oxford University Press, 1970.

Horstmann, Carl, ed. *Altenglische Legenden: Neue Folge.* Heilbronn: Henninger, 1881.

———. *Sammlung Altenglischer Legenden.* Heilbronn: Henninger, 1878.

Idley, Peter. *Peter Idley's Instructions to His Son.* Ed. Charlotte D'Evelyn. London: Oxford University Press, 1935.

Jack Upland, Friar Daw's Reply, and Upland's Rejoinder. Ed. P. L. Heyworth. London: Oxford University Press, 1968.

Jacobus de Voragine. *The Golden Legend: Readings on the Saints.* 2 vols. Trans. William Granger Ryan. Princeton: Princeton University Press, 1993.

Jean de Mailly. *Abrégé des gestes et miracles des saints.* Trans. Antoine Dondaine. Paris: Cerf, 1947.

A Book of Showings to the Anchoress Julian of Norwich. Ed. Edmund Colledge and James Walsh. Toronto: Pontifical Institute of Mediaeval Studies, 1978.

Þe Liflade ant te Passiun of Seinte Iuliene. Ed. S.R.T.O. d'Ardenne. EETS.OS 248. London: Oxford University Press, 1961.

Seinte Katerine. Ed. S.R.T.O. d'Ardenne and E. J. Dobson. EETS.SS 7. Oxford: Oxford University Press, 1981.

The Life and Martyrdom of St. Katherine of Alexandria. Ed. Henry Hucks Gibbs. London: Nichols, 1884.

St. Katherine of Alexandria: The Late Middle English Prose Legend in Southwell Minster MS 7. Ed. Saara Nevanlinna and Irma Taavitsainen. Cambridge: D. S. Brewer, 1993.

❀ Bibliography ❀

Kempe, Margery. *The Book of Margery Kempe.* Ed. Sanford Brown Meech. EETS.OS 212. Oxford: Oxford University Press, 1940.

Knighton, Henry. *Knighton's Chronicle, 1337–1396.* Ed. and trans. G. H. Martin. Oxford: Clarendon, 1995.

Love, Nicholas. *Mirror of the Blessed Life of Jesus Christ.* Ed. Michael G. Sargent. New York: Garland, 1992.

The Luttrell Psalter: Two Plates in Colour and One Hundred and Eighty-Three in Monochrome from Additional Manuscript 42130 in the British Museum. London: British Museum, 1932.

Lydgate, John. *The Minor Poems of John Lydgate.* 2 vols. Ed. Henry Noble MacCracken. EETS.ES 107, EETS.OS 192. London: Oxford University Press, 1911, 1934.

"The Legend of St. Margaret." Ed. Frederic Spencer. Parts 1 and 2. *Modern Language Notes* 4 (1889): 197–201; 5 (1890): 107–111.

Seinte Marherete. Ed. Frances M. Mack. EETS.OS 193. 1934. Reprint, London: Oxford University Press, 1958.

The Master of Mary of Burgundy: A Book of Hours for Engelbert of Nassau. New York: Braziller, 1970.

Mirk, John. *Mirk's Festial.* Ed. Theodor Erbe. EETS.ES 96. 1905. Reprint, Millwood, N.Y.: Kraus, 1987.

Mombritius, Boninus. *Sanctuarium, seu Vitae Sanctorum.* 2 vols. Hildesheim: Georg Olms Verlag, 1978.

Mundy, John Hine, and Kennerly M. Woody, eds. *The Council of Constance: The Unification of the Church.* Trans. Louise Ropes Loomis. New York: Columbia University Press, 1961.

Myroure of Oure Ladye. Ed. John Henry Blunt. EETS.ES 19. London: Trübner, 1873.

North English Legendary. In *Altenglische Legenden: Neue Folge,* ed. Carl Horstmann, 3–173. Heilbronn: Henninger, 1881.

Pantin, W. A. "Instructions for a Devout and Literate Layman." In *Medieval Learning and Literature: Essays Presented to Richard William Hunt,* ed. Jonathan G. Alexander and Margaret T. Gibson, 398–422. Oxford: Clarendon, 1976.

Paris, William. "Cristine." In *Sammlung Altenglischer Legenden,* ed. Carl Horstmann, 183–90. Heilbronn: Henninger, 1878.

Passio Kiliani, Ps. Theotimus, Passio Margaretae, Orationes. Ed. Cynthia Hahn. Graz, Austria: Akademische Druck-U. Verlagsanstalt, 1988.

Paston Letters and Papers of the Fifteenth Century. 2 vols. Ed. Norman Davis. Oxford: Clarendon, 1971.

The Poems of the Pearl Manuscript. Ed. Malcolm Andrew and Ronald Waldron. London: Edward Arnold, 1978.

Queen Mary's Psalter: Miniatures and Drawings by an English Artist of the Fourteenth Century Reproduced from Royal MS.2B.VII in the British Museum. London: Oxford University Press, 1912.

Rolle, Richard. *The Fire of Love.* Trans. Clifton Wolters. New York: Penguin, 1972.

Rüttgers, Severin, ed. *Der Heiligen Leben und Leiden, anders genannt das Passional.* 2 vols. Leipzig, 1913.

Sayles, G. O., ed. "The Deposition of Richard II: Three Lancastrian Narratives." *Bulletin of the Institute of Historical Research* 54 (1981): 257–70.

The Early South-English Legendary. Ed. Carl Horstmann. EETS.OS 87. 1887. Reprint, Millwood, N.Y.: Kraus, 1987.

The South English Legendary. Ed. Charlotte D'Evelyn and Anna J. Mill. 3 vols. EETS.OS 235, 236, 244. London: Oxford University Press, 1956, 1959.

❀ Bibliography ❀

Speculum Sacerdotale. Ed. Edward H. Weatherly. EETS.OS 200. 1936. Reprint, Millwood, N.Y.: Kraus, 1971.

Tanner, Norman P., ed. *Heresy Trials in the Diocese of Norwich, 1428–31.* Camden Fourth Series 20. London: Royal Historical Society, 1977.

Thorpe, William. "The Testimony of William Thorpe." In *Two Wycliffite Texts,* ed. Anne Hudson. EETS.OS 301. Oxford: Oxford University Press, 1993.

The Towneley Plays. Ed. George England. EETS.ES 71. 1897. Reprint, Millwood, N.Y.: Kraus, 1966.

William of Saint-Thierry. *The Golden Epistle: A Letter to the Brethren at Mont Dieu.* Trans. Theodore Berkeley. Spencer, Mass.: Cistercian Publications, 1971.

Wycliffe, John. *Trialogus cum supplemento trialogi.* Ed. G. V. Lechler. Oxford: Clarendon, 1869.

Wynter, Symon. "S. Hieronymus." In *"Prosalegenden."* Ed. Carl Horstmann. *Anglia* 3 (1880): 328–60.

Secondary Sources

Aers, David. *Community, Gender, and Individual Identity: English Writing, 1360–1430.* New York: Routledge, 1988.

——, ed. *Medieval Literature: Criticism, Ideology, and History.* Brighton: Harvester, 1986.

Allmand, Christopher. *Henry V.* Berkeley: University of California Press, 1992.

——. "Henry V the Soldier, and the War in France." In *Henry V,* ed. Harriss, 117–35.

Ambrisco, Alan S., and Paul Strohm. "Succession and Sovereignty in Lydgate's Prologue to *The Troy Book.*" *Chaucer Review* 30 (1995): 40–57.

Amsler, Mark. "The Wife of Bath and Women's Power." *Assays* 4 (1987): 67–83.

Armstrong, C. A. J. "The Piety of Cicely, Duchess of York: A Study in Late Mediaeval Culture." In *For Hilaire Belloc,* ed. Douglas Woodruff, 73–94. London: Sheed and Ward, 1942. Reprinted in Armstrong, *England, France, and Burgundy in the Fifteenth Century,* 135–56. London: Hambledon, 1983.

Ashley, Kathleen M. "Medieval Courtesy Literature and Dramatic Mirrors of Female Conduct." In *The Ideology of Conduct: Essays in Literature and the History of Sexuality,* ed. Nancy Armstrong and Leonard Tennenhouse, 25–38. New York: Methuen, 1987.

Ashley, Kathleen M., and Pamela Sheingorn, eds. *Interpreting Cultural Symbols: Saint Anne in Late Medieval Society.* Athens: University of Georgia Press, 1990.

Aston, Margaret. *Faith and Fire: Popular and Unpopular Religion, 1350–1600.* London: Hambledon, 1993.

——. *Lollards and Reformers: Images and Literacy in Late Medieval Religion.* London: Hambledon, 1984.

Baker, Derek, ed. *Medieval Women.* Oxford: Basil Blackwell, 1978.

Baker, John. *English Stained Glass.* New York: Harry N. Abrams, 1960.

Barron, Caroline. "The Deposition of Richard II." In *Politics and Crisis in Fourteenth-Century England,* ed. John Taylor and Wendy Childs, 132–49. Wolfeboro Falls, N.H.: Alan Sutton, 1990.

Bartlett, Anne Clark. *Male Authors, Female Readers: Representation and Subjectivity in Middle English Devotional Literature.* Ithaca: Cornell University Press, 1995.

Beadle, Richard. "Prolegomena to a Literary Geography of Later Medieval Norfolk." In *Regionalism in Late Medieval Texts: Essays Celebrating the Publication of "A Linguistic Atlas of Late Mediaeval English,"* ed. Felicity Riddy, 89–108. Cambridge: D. S. Brewer, 1991.

❀ Bibliography ❀

Beckwith, Sarah. *Christ's Body: Identity, Culture, and Society in Late Medieval Writings*. London: Routledge, 1993.

——. "A Very Material Mysticism: The Medieval Mysticism of Margery Kempe." In *Medieval Literature*, ed. Aers, 34–57.

Bell, Susan Groag. "Medieval Women Book Owners: Arbiters of Lay Piety and Ambassadors of Culture." *Signs* 7 (1981–82): 742–68. Reprinted in *Women and Power in the Middle Ages*, ed. Mary Erler and Maryanne Kowaleski, 149–87. Athens: University of Georgia Press, 1988.

Bennett, Judith M. "Medieval Women, Modern Women: Across the Great Divide." In *Culture and History, 1350–1600: Essays on English Communities, Identities, and Writing*, ed. David Aers, 147–75. Detroit: Wayne State University Press, 1992.

——. "Misogyny, Popular Culture, and Women's Work." *History Workshop* 31 (1991): 166–88.

——. *Women in the Medieval English Countryside: Gender and Household in Brigstock before the Plague*. New York: Oxford University Press, 1987.

Biscoglio, Frances M. "'Unspun' Heroes: Iconography of the Spinning Woman in the Middle Ages." *Journal of Medieval and Renaissance Studies* 25 (1995): 163–76.

Bjelland, Karen. "Franciscan versus Dominican Responses to the Knight as a Societal Model: The Case of the *South English Legendary*." *Franciscan Studies* 48 (1988): 11–27.

Blamires, Alcuin. "The Wife of Bath and Lollardy." *Medium Ævum* 58 (1989): 224–42.

——. "Women and Preaching in Medieval Orthodoxy, Heresy, and Saints' Lives." *Viator* 26 (1995): 135–52.

Bloch, R. Howard. *Medieval Misogyny and the Invention of Western Romantic Love*. Chicago: University of Chicago Press, 1991.

Blumenfeld-Kosinski, Renate, and Timea Szell, eds. *Images of Sainthood in Medieval Europe*. Ithaca: Cornell University Press, 1991.

Boléo, José de Paiva. *O Martírio de Santa Apolónia*. Porto, Portugal, n.d.

Bond, Francis. *Dedications and Patrons of English Churches: Ecclesiastical Symbolism, Saints, and Their Emblems*. London: Oxford University Press, 1914.

Bornstein, Diane. *The Lady in the Tower: Medieval Courtesy Literature for Women*. Hamden, Conn.: Archon, 1983.

Boureau, Alain. *La "Légende dorée": Le système narratif de Jacques de Voragine*. Paris: Cerf, 1984.

Braswell, Laurel. "The *South English Legendary* Collection: A Study in Middle English Religious Literature of the Thirteenth and Fourteenth Centuries." Ph.D. diss., University of Toronto, 1964.

Brieger, Peter. *English Art, 1216–1307*. Oxford: Clarendon, 1957.

Brown, Peter. *The Body and Society: Men, Women, and Sexual Renunciation in Early Christianity*. New York: Columbia University Press, 1988.

Brundage, James A. *Law, Sex, and Christian Society in Medieval Europe*. Chicago: University of Chicago Press, 1987.

Burrow, J. A. *Thomas Hoccleve*. Brookfield, Vt.: Variorum, 1994.

Burrus, Virginia. *Chastity as Autonomy: Women in the Stories of the Apocryphal Acts*. Lewiston, N.Y.: Edwin Mellen, 1987.

Bynum, Caroline Walker. "'. . . and Woman His Humanity': Female Imagery in the Religious Writing of the Later Middle Ages." In *Fragmentation and Redemption: Essays on Gender and the Human Body in Medieval Religion*, 151–79. New York: Zone, 1992.

——. *Holy Feast and Holy Fast: The Religious Significance of Food to Medieval Women*. Berkeley: University of California Press, 1987.

❀ Bibliography ❀

Caiger-Smith, Alan. *English Medieval Mural Paintings.* Oxford: Clarendon, 1963.

Carrasco, Magdalena Elizabeth. "An Early Illustrated Manuscript of the Passion of St. Agatha (Paris, Bibl. Nat., MS lat. 5594)." *Gesta* 24 (1985): 19–32.

Catto, Jeremy. "Religious Change under Henry V." In *Henry V,* ed. Harriss, 97–115.

Cavanaugh, Susan Hagen. "A Study of Books Privately Owned in England: 1300–1450." Ph. D. diss., University of Pennsylvania, 1980.

Cazelles, Brigitte. *The Lady as Saint: A Collection of French Hagiographic Romances of the Thirteenth Century.* Philadelphia: University of Pennsylvania Press, 1991.

Charles, Lindsey, and Lorna Duffin. *Women and Work in Pre-Industrial England.* London: Croom Helm, 1985.

Cheetham, Francis. *English Medieval Alabasters.* Oxford: Phaidon, 1984.

Clay, Rotha Mary. *The Hermits and Anchorites of England.* London: Methuen, 1914.

Coakley, John. "Friars as Confidants of Holy Women in Medieval Dominican Hagiography." In *Images of Sainthood,* ed. Blumenfeld-Kosinski and Szell, 222–46.

——. "Gender and the Authority of Friars: The Significance of Holy Women for Thirteenth-Century Franciscans and Dominicans." *Church History* 60 (1991): 445–60.

Coens, Maurice. "Une 'Passio S. Apolloniae' inédite suivi d'un miracle en Bourgogne." *Analecta Bollandiana* 70 (1952): 138–59.

Coleman, Janet. *Medieval Readers and Writers, 1350–1400.* New York: Columbia University Press, 1981.

Constable, Giles. "Aelred of Rievaulx and the Nun of Watton: An Episode in the Early History of the Gilbertine Order." In *Medieval Women,* ed. Baker, 205–26.

Copeland, Rita. "Why Women Can't Read: Medieval Hermeneutics, Statutory Law, and the Lollard Heresy Trials." In *Representing Women: Law, Literature, and Feminism,* ed. Susan Sage Heinzelman and Zipporah Batshaw Wiseman, 253–86. Durham: Duke University Press, 1994.

——. "William Thorpe and His Lollard Community: Intellectual Labor and the Representation of Dissent." In *Bodies and Disciplines: Intersections of Literature and History in Fifteenth-Century England,* ed. Barbara A. Hanawalt and David Wallace, 199–221. Minneapolis: University of Minnesota Press, 1996.

Crane, Susan. *Insular Romance: Politics, Faith, and Culture in Anglo-Norman and Middle English Literature.* Berkeley: University of California Press, 1986.

Cross, Claire. "'Great reasoners in scripture': The Activities of Women Lollards, 1380–1530." In *Medieval Women,* ed. Baker, 359–80.

Damrosch, David. "*Non Alia Sed Aliter:* The Hermeneutics of Gender in Bernard of Clairvaux." In *Images of Sainthood in Medieval Europe,* ed. Blumenfeld-Kosinski and Szell, 181–95.

Davies, Stevan L. *The Revolt of the Widows: The Social World of the Apocryphal Acts.* Carbondale: Southern Illinois University Press, 1980.

Davis, Natalie Zemon. "Women on Top." In *Society and Culture in Early Modern France,* 124–51. Stanford: Stanford University Press, 1975.

Deanesly, Margaret. "Vernacular Books in England in the Fourteenth and Fifteenth Centuries." *Modern Language Review* 15 (1920): 349–58.

Delany, Sheila. "Bokenham's Claudian as Yorkist Propaganda." *Journal of Medieval History* 22 (1996): 83–96.

——. "Bokenham's Katherine as Yorkist Propaganda." Paper presented at the Convention of the Modern Language Association, San Diego, California, 30 December 1994.

❀ Bibliography ❀

——. *Impolitic Bodies: Poetry, Saints, and Society in Fifteenth-Century England.* New York: Oxford University Press, in press.

——. Introduction to *A Legend of Holy Women: A Translation of Osbern Bokenham's "Legends of Holy Women."* Notre Dame: University of Notre Dame Press, 1992.

Delehaye, Hippolyte. *Étude sur le légendier romain: Les saints de Novembre et Décembre.* Subsidia hagiographica 23. Brussels: Société des Bollandistes, 1936.

D'Evelyn, Charlotte. "Saints' Legends." In *A Manual of the Writings in Middle English, 1050–1500,* ed. J. Burke Severs, vol. 2, 413–39, 556–635. Hamden, Conn.: Archon, 1970.

Dobson, E. J. *The Origins of the "Ancrene Wisse."* Oxford: Clarendon, 1976.

Dondaine, Antoine. "Le dominicain français Jean de Mailly et la *Légende dorée.*" *Archives d'histoire dominicaine* 1 (1946): 53–102.

Doyle, A. I. "Books Connected with the Vere Family and Barking Abbey." *Transactions of the Essex Archaeological Society,* n.s., 25 (1958): 222–43.

——. "Publication by Members of the Religious Orders." In *Book Production and Publishing in Britain,* ed. Griffiths and Pearsall, 109–23.

Duffy, Eamon. *The Stripping of the Altars: Traditional Religion in England, c. 1400–1580.* New Haven: Yale University Press, 1992.

Dunn-Lardeau, Brenda, ed. *"Legenda aurea": Sept siècles de diffusion.* Actes du colloque international sur la *Legenda aurea:* Texte latin et branches vernaculaires à l'université du Québec à Montréal, 11–12 Mai 1983. Montreal: Bellarmin, 1986.

Dutschke, C. W. *Guide to Medieval and Renaissance Manuscripts in the Huntington Library.* 2 vols. San Marino, Calif.: Huntington Library and Art Gallery, 1989.

Ebin, Lois A. *John Lydgate.* Boston: Twayne, 1985.

Edwards, A. S. G. "Lydgate Manuscripts: Some Directions for Future Research." In *Manuscripts and Readers in Fifteenth-Century England,* ed. Derek Pearsall, 15–26. Cambridge: D. S. Brewer, 1981.

——. "The Transmission and Audience of Osbern Bokenham's *Legendys of Hooly Wummen.*" In *Late-Medieval Religious Texts and Their Transmission: Essays in Honour of A. I. Doyle,* ed. A. J. Minnis, 157–67. Cambridge: D. S. Brewer, 1994.

Eggebroten, Anne. "*Sawles Warde:* A Retelling of *De Anima* for a Female Audience." *Mediaevalia* 10 (1988): 27–47.

Elkins, Sharon K. *Holy Women of Twelfth-Century England.* Chapel Hill: University of North Carolina Press, 1988.

Elliott, Dyan. *Spiritual Marriage: Sexual Abstinence in Medieval Wedlock.* Princeton: Princeton University Press, 1993.

Farmer, Sharon. "Persuasive Voices: Clerical Images of Medieval Wives." *Speculum* 61 (1986): 517–43.

Fredeman, Jane C. "The Life of John Capgrave, O.E.S.A. (1393–1464)." *Augustiniana* 29 (1979): 197–237.

Gehl, Paul F. "*Competens silentium:* Varieties of Monastic Silence in the Medieval West." *Viator* 18 (1987): 125–60.

Genet, J.-P. "English Nationalism: Thomas Polton at the Council of Constance." *Nottingham Mediaeval Studies* 28 (1984): 60–78.

Gerould, Gordon Hall. "The Legend of St. Christina by William Paris." *Modern Language Notes* 29 (1914): 129–33.

Gibson, Gail McMurray. "Saint Anne and the Religion of Childbed: Some East Anglian Texts and Talismans." In *Interpreting Cultural Symbols,* ed. Ashley and Sheingorn, 95–110.

❀ Bibliography ❀

——. *The Theater of Devotion: East Anglian Drama and Society in the Late Middle Ages.* Chicago: University of Chicago Press, 1989.

Gillespie, Vincent. "Vernacular Books of Religion." In *Book Production and Publishing in Britain,* ed. Griffiths and Pearsall, 317–44.

Glasser, Marc. "Marriage in Medieval Hagiography." *Studies in Medieval and Renaissance History,* n.s., 4 (1981): 3–34.

Goldberg, P. J. P. *Women, Work, and Life Cycle in a Medieval Economy: Women in York and Yorkshire, c. 1300–1520.* Oxford: Clarendon, 1992.

——, ed. *Woman Is a Worthy Wight: Women in English Society, c. 1200–1500.* Wolfeboro Falls, N.H.: Alan Sutton, 1992.

Goodich, Michael. *Vita Perfecta: The Ideal of Sainthood in the Thirteenth Century.* Stuttgart: Hiersemann, 1982.

Görlach, Manfred. *An East Midland Revision of the "South English Legendary."* Heidelberg: Carl Winter, 1976.

——. "The *Legenda aurea* and the Early History of *The South English Legendary.*" In *"Legenda aurea,"* ed. Dunn-Lardeau, 301–16.

——. *The Textual Tradition of the "South English Legendary."* Leeds: University of Leeds School of English, 1974.

Gottfried, Robert S. *Bury St. Edmunds and the Urban Crisis, 1290–1539.* Princeton: Princeton University Press, 1982.

Grady, Frank. "The Lancastrian Gower and the Limits of Exemplarity." *Speculum* 70 (1995): 552–75.

Graham, Helena. "'A Woman's Work . . .': Labour and Gender in the Late Medieval Countryside." In *Woman Is a Worthy Wight,* ed. Goldberg, 126–48.

Griffiths, Jeremy, and Derek Pearsall, eds. *Book Production and Publishing in Britain, 1375–1475.* Cambridge: Cambridge University Press, 1989.

Griffiths, Ralph A. *The Reign of King Henry VI: The Exercise of Royal Authority, 1422–1461.* London: Ernest Benn, 1981.

Grössinger, Christa. "Misericords." In *Age of Chivalry: Art in Plantagenet England, 1200–1400,* ed. Jonathan Alexander and Paul Binski, 122–24. London: Weidenfeld and Nicolson, 1987.

Hahn, Cynthia. "The Powers of Gesture in Illustrated Saints' Lives." Paper delivered at the Sewanee Medieval Colloquium, University of the South, 3 April 1993.

Haines, Roy Martin. "Reginald Pecock: A Tolerant Man in an Age of Intolerance." *Studies in Church History* 21 (1984): 125–37.

——. "'Wilde Wittes and Wilfulness': John Swetstock's Attack on Those 'Poyswunmongeres,' the Lollards." In *Popular Belief and Practice,* ed. G. J. Cuming and Derek Baker, 143–53. Cambridge: Cambridge University Press, 1972.

Hanna, Ralph, III. "The Difficulty of Ricardian Prose Translation: The Case of the Lollards." *Modern Language Quarterly* 55 (1990): 319–40.

——. "Some Norfolk Women and Their Books, ca. 1390–1440." In *Cultural Patronage,* ed. McCash, 288–305.

Harriss, G. L. "Introduction: The Exemplar of Kingship." In *Henry V: The Practice of Kingship,* 1–29. Oxford: Oxford University Press, 1985.

——, ed. *Henry V: The Practice of Kingship.* Oxford: Oxford University Press, 1985.

Harthan, John. *Books of Hours and Their Owners.* London: Thames and Hudson, 1977.

Head, Thomas. "The Marriages of Christina of Markyate." *Viator* 21 (1990): 75–101.

❀ Bibliography ❀

Heffernan, Thomas J. *Sacred Biography: Saints and Their Biographers in the Middle Ages.* New York: Oxford University Press, 1988.

Helmholz, R. H. *Marriage Litigation in Medieval England.* Cambridge: Cambridge University Press, 1974.

Hicks, M. A. "The Piety of Margaret, Lady Hungerford (d. 1478)." *Journal of Ecclesiastical History* 38 (1987): 19–38.

Hilton, R. H. "Small Town Society in England before the Black Death." *Past and Present* 105 (1984): 53–78.

Hirsh, John C. "Prayer and Meditation in Late Mediaeval England: MS Bodley 789." *Medium Ævum* 48 (1979): 55–66.

Hogg, James. "Mount Grace Charterhouse and Late Medieval English Spirituality." *Analecta Cartusiana* 82.3 (1980): 1–43.

Howell, Martha C. *Women, Production, and Patriarchy in Late Medieval Cities.* Chicago: University of Chicago Press, 1986.

Hudson, Anne. "Lollard Book Production." In *Book Production and Publishing in Britain,* ed. Griffiths and Pearsall, 125–42.

———. *Lollards and Their Books.* London: Hambledon, 1985.

———. *The Premature Reformation: Wycliffite Texts and Lollard History.* Oxford: Clarendon, 1988.

Hughes, Jonathan. *Pastors and Visionaries: Religion and Secular Life in Late Medieval Yorkshire.* Wolfeboro, N.H.: Boydell, 1988.

Hussey, S. S. "The Audience for the Middle English Mystics." In *De Cella in Seculum,* ed. Sargent, 109–22.

Hutchison, Ann M. "Devotional Reading in the Monastery and in the Late Medieval Household." In *De Cella in Seculum,* ed. Sargent, 215–27.

Hutton, Diane. "Women in Fourteenth Century Shrewsbury." In *Women and Work,* ed. Charles and Duffin, 83–99.

Jacob, E. F. *The Fifteenth Century, 1399–1485.* 1961. Reprint, Oxford: Oxford University Press, 1993.

Jambeck, Karen K. "Patterns of Women's Literary Patronage: England, 1200–ca. 1475." In *Cultural Patronage,* ed. McCash, 228–65.

Jankofsky, Klaus P. "Entertainment, Edification, and Popular Education in the *South English Legendary.*" *Journal of Popular Culture* 11 (1977/78): 707–17.

———. "*Legenda aurea* Materials in *The South English Legendary:* Translation, Transformation, Acculturation." In *"Legenda aurea,"* ed. Dunn-Lardeau, 317–29.

———. "National Characteristics in the Portrayal of English Saints in the *South English Legendary.*" In *Images of Sainthood,* ed. Blumenfeld-Kosinski and Szell, 81–93.

———, ed. *The "South English Legendary": A Critical Assessment.* Tübingen: Francke Verlag, 1992.

Jankowski, Eileen S. "Reception of Chaucer's *Second Nun's Tale:* Osbern Bokenham's *Lyf of S. Cycile.*" *Chaucer Review* 30 (1996): 306–18.

Jenkins, Jacqueline. "An English Life of St. Catherine and the Fifteenth-Century Female Audience." Paper delivered at the International Medieval Congress, University of Leeds, 4–7 July 1994.

Johnson, Lynn Staley. "Chaucer's Tale of the Second Nun and the Strategies of Dissent." *Studies in Philology* 89 (1992): 314–33.

Jones, Michael K., and Malcolm G. Underwood. *The King's Mother: Lady Margaret Beaufort, Countess of Richmond and Derby.* Cambridge: Cambridge University Press, 1992.

❀ Bibliography ❀

Jordan, Constance. "The Household and the State: Transformations in the Representation of an Analogy from Aristotle to James I." *Modern Language Quarterly* 54 (1993): 307–26.

Karras, Ruth Mazo. *Common Women: Prostitution and Sexuality in Medieval England.* New York: Oxford University Press, 1996.

Keiser, George R. "Patronage and Piety in Fifteenth-Century England: Margaret, Duchess of Clarence, Symon Wynter, and Beinecke MS 317." *Yale University Library Gazette* 60 (1985): 32–46.

Kendall, Ritchie D. *The Drama of Dissent: The Radical Poetics of Nonconformity, 1380–1590.* Chapel Hill: University of North Carolina Press, 1986.

Kieckhefer, Richard. *Unquiet Souls: Fourteenth-Century Saints and Their Religious Milieu.* Chicago: University of Chicago Press, 1984.

Kolve, V. A. "Chaucer's *Second Nun's Tale* and the Iconography of St. Cecilia." In *New Perspectives in Chaucer Criticism,* ed. Donald M. Rose, 137–58. Norman, Okla.: Pilgrim Books, 1981.

Kowaleski, Maryanne. "Women's Work in a Market Town: Exeter in the Late Fourteenth Century." In *Women and Work in Preindustrial Europe,* ed. Barbara A. Hanawalt, 145–64. Bloomington: Indiana University Press, 1986.

Kurvinen, Auvo. "The Life of St. Catharine of Alexandria in Middle English Prose." Doctoral diss., Oxford University, 1960.

——. "The Source of Capgrave's *Life of St. Katharine of Alexandria.*" *Neuphilologische Mitteilungen* 61 (1960): 268–324.

——. "Two Sixteenth-Century Editions of *The Life of St. Catharine of Alexandria.*" In *English and Medieval Studies Presented to J. R. R. Tolkien,* ed. Norman Davis and C. L. Wrenn, 269–79. London: Allen and Unwin, 1962.

Lacey, Kay E. "Women and Work in Fourteenth and Fifteenth Century London." In *Women and Work,* ed. Charles and Duffin, 24–82.

Leclercq, Jean. "L'écriture sainte dans l'hagiographie monastique du haut moyen âge." In *La Bibbia nell'Alto Medioevo,* 111–15. Spoleto, Italy, 1963.

——. *The Love of Learning and the Desire for God: A Study of Monastic Culture.* Trans. Catharine Misrahi. New York: Fordham University Press, 1961.

Lees, Clare A., ed. *Medieval Masculinities: Regarding Men in the Middle Ages.* Minneapolis: University of Minnesota Press, 1994.

Legge, M. Dominica. *Anglo-Norman Literature and Its Background.* Oxford: Clarendon, 1963.

Lerer, Seth. *Chaucer and His Readers: Imagining the Author in Late-Medieval England.* Princeton: Princeton University Press, 1993.

Lobel, M. D. *The Borough of Bury St. Edmunds: A Study in the Government and Development of a Monastic Town.* Oxford: Clarendon, 1935.

Maddocks, Hilary. "Illumination in Jean de Vignay's *Légende dorée.*" In *"Legenda aurea,"* ed. Dunn-Lardeau, 155–69.

Makowski, Elizabeth M. "The Conjugal Debt and Medieval Canon Law." *Journal of Medieval History* 3 (1977): 99–114.

Margherita, Gayle. *The Romance of Origins: Language and Sexual Difference in Middle English Literature.* Philadelphia: University of Pennsylvania Press, 1994.

McCash, June Hall, ed. *The Cultural Patronage of Medieval Women.* Athens: University of Georgia Press, 1996.

McNamara, Jo Ann. "The *Herrenfrage:* The Restructuring of the Gender System, 1050–1150." In *Medieval Masculinities,* ed. Lees, 3–29.

———. *A New Song: Celibate Women in the First Three Christian Centuries*. New York: Haworth, 1983.

McNiven, Peter. *Heresy and Politics in the Reign of Henry IV: The Burning of John Badby*. Wolfeboro, N.H.: Boydell, 1987.

Meale, Carol M. "'. . . alle the bokes that I haue of latyn, englisch, and frensch': Laywomen and Their Books in Late Medieval England." In *Women and Literature in Britain*, ed. Meale, 128–58.

———, ed. *Women and Literature in Britain, 1150–1500*. Cambridge: Cambridge University Press, 1993.

Mertes, Kate. *The English Noble Household, 1250–1600: Good Governance and Politic Rule*. New York: Basil Blackwell, 1988.

Millett, Bella. "The Audience of the Saints' Lives of the Katherine Group." *Reading Medieval Studies* 16 (1990): 127–55.

———. "The Saints' Lives of the Katherine Group and the Alliterative Tradition." *Journal of English and Germanic Philology* 87 (1988): 16–34.

———. "Women in No Man's Land: English Recluses and the Development of Vernacular Literature in the Twelfth and Thirteenth Centuries." In *Women and Literature in Britain*, ed. Meale, 86–103.

Milosh, Joseph E. *"The Scale of Perfection" and the English Mystical Tradition*. Madison: University of Wisconsin Press, 1966.

Mockridge, Diane L. "Marital Imagery in Six Late Twelfth- and Early Thirteenth-Century Vitae of Female Saints." In *That Gentle Strength: Historical Perspectives on Women in Christianity*, ed. Lynda L. Coon, Katherine J. Haldane, and Elisabeth W. Sommer, 60–78. Charlottesville: University Press of Virginia, 1990.

Moore, Samuel. "Patrons of Letters in Norfolk and Suffolk, c. 1450." Parts 1 and 2. *PMLA* 27 (1912): 188–207; 28 (1913): 79–105.

Muller, Ellen. "Saintly Virgins: The Veneration of Virgin Saints in Religious Women's Communities." In *Saints and She-Devils: Images of Women in the Fifteenth and Sixteenth Centuries*, ed. Lène Dresen-Coenders, 83–100. London: Rubicon, 1987.

Nevanlinna, Saara. Introduction to *The Northern Homily Cycle*, 3 vols., 1:5–17. Helsinki, 1972.

Newman, Barbara. "Flaws in the Golden Bowl: Gender and Spiritual Formation in the Twelfth Century." *Traditio* 45 (1989): 111–46. Reprinted in *From Virile Woman to Woman-Christ: Studies in Medieval Religion and Literature*, 19–45. Philadelphia: University of Pennsylvania Press, 1995.

Nicholls, Jonathan. *The Matter of Courtesy: Medieval Courtesy Books and the Gawain-Poet*. Woodbridge, Suffolk: D. S. Brewer, 1985.

Noonan, John T., Jr. "Power to Choose." *Viator* 4 (1973): 419–34.

Novak, Maureen. "Agency and Mobility in Fifteenth-Century Representations of Female Sanctity." Paper delivered at the 29th International Congress on Medieval Studies, Western Michigan University, Kalamazoo, 7 May 1994.

Pantin, W. A. *The English Church in the Fourteenth Century*. 1955. Reprint, Toronto: University of Toronto Press, 1980.

Parkes, M. B. "The Literacy of the Laity." In *The Medieval World*, ed. David Daiches and Anthony Thorlby, 555–77. London: Aldus, 1973.

Patterson, Lee. *Chaucer and the Subject of History*. Madison: University of Wisconsin Press, 1991.

———. "Making Identities in Fifteenth-Century England: Henry V and John Lydgate." In *New*

❀ Bibliography ❀

Historical Literary Study: Essays on Reproducing Texts, Representing History, ed. Jeffrey N. Cox and Larry J. Reynolds, 69–107. Princeton: Princeton University Press, 1993.

Pearsall, Derek. *John Lydgate.* London: Routledge, 1970.

Philippart, Guy. *Les légendiers latins et autres manuscrits hagiographiques.* Typologie des sources du moyen âge occidental 24–25. Turnhout, Belgium, 1977.

Poletti, Gian Battista. *Il Martirio di Santa Apollonia.* Rocca S. Casciano, 1934.

Poos, Lawrence R. "Social History and the Book of Hours." In *Time Sanctified,* ed. Wieck, 33–38.

Powell, Edward. *Kingship, Law, and Society: Criminal Justice in the Reign of Henry V.* Oxford: Clarendon, 1989.

Randall, Lilian M. C. *Images in the Margins of Gothic Manuscripts.* Berkeley: University of California Press, 1966.

Reames, Sherry L. "Artistry, Decorum, and Purpose in Three Middle English Retellings of the Cecilia Legend." In *The Endless Knot,* ed. M. Teresa Tavormina and R. F. Yeager, 177–99. Cambridge: D. S. Brewer, 1995.

———. "Attitudes toward the Cult of the Saints in the Late Middle Ages: The Light Shed by English Breviary Manuscripts." Paper presented at the 11th meeting of the Illinois Medieval Association, Loyola University, Chicago, 18–19 February 1994.

———. "The Cecilia Legend as Chaucer Inherited It and Retold It: The Disappearance of an Augustinian Ideal." *Speculum* 55 (1980): 38–57.

———. *The "Legenda aurea": A Reexamination of Its Paradoxical History.* Madison: University of Wisconsin Press, 1985.

———. "*Mouvance* and Interpretation in Late-Medieval Latin: The Legend of St. Cecilia in British Breviaries." In *Medieval Literature: Texts and Interpretation,* ed. Tim William Machan, 159–89. Binghamton, N.Y.: Medieval and Renaissance Texts and Studies, 1991.

———. "A Recent Discovery concerning the Sources of Chaucer's 'Second Nun's Tale.'" *Modern Philology* 87 (1990): 337–61.

Richmond, Colin. "Religion and the Fifteenth-Century English Gentleman." In *The Church, Politics, and Patronage in the Fifteenth Century,* ed. Barrie Dobson, 193–208. New York: St. Martin's, 1984.

Riddy, Felicity. "Mother Knows Best: Reading Social Change in a Courtesy Text." *Speculum* 71 (1996): 66–86.

———. "'Women Talking about the Things of God': A Late Medieval Sub-culture." In *Women and Literature in Britain,* ed. Meale, 104–27.

Riehle, Wolfgang. *The Middle English Mystics.* Trans. Bernard Standring. Boston: Routledge and Kegan Paul, 1981.

Robertson, Elizabeth. *Early English Devotional Prose and the Female Audience.* Knoxville: University of Tennessee Press, 1990.

Rosenthal, Joel T. "Fifteenth-Century Widows and Widowhood: Bereavement, Reintegration, and Life Choices." In *Wife and Widow in Medieval England,* ed. Sue Sheridan Walker, 33–58. Ann Arbor: University of Michigan Press, 1993.

———. *Patriarchy and Families of Privilege in Fifteenth-Century England.* Philadelphia: University of Pennsylvania Press, 1991.

Rubin, Miri. *Corpus Christi: The Eucharist in Late Medieval Culture.* Cambridge: Cambridge University Press, 1991.

Sadlek, Gregory M. "The Image of the Devil's Five Fingers in the *South English Legendary's* 'St. Michael' and in Chaucer's 'Parson's Tale.'" In *"South English Legendary": A Critical Assessment,* ed. Jankofsky, 49–64.

❀ Bibliography ❀

Saenger, Paul. "Silent Reading: Its Impact on Late Medieval Script and Society." *Viator* 13 (1982): 367–414.

Salter, Elizabeth. *Fourteenth-Century English Poetry: Contexts and Readings*. Oxford: Clarendon, 1983.

——. *Nicholas Love's "Myrrour of the Blessed Lyf of Jesu Christ."* Analecta Cartusiana 10. Salzburg: Institut für Englische Sprache und Literatur, Universität Salzburg, 1974.

Samson, Annie. "The *South English Legendary*: Constructing a Context." In *Thirteenth-Century England: I. Proceedings of the Newcastle upon Tyne Conference, 1985*, ed. P. R. Coss and D. S. Lloyd, 185–95. Wolfeboro, N.H.: Boydell, 1986.

Sargent, Michael G. "The Transmission by the English Carthusians of Some Late Medieval Spiritual Writings." *Journal of Ecclesiastical History* 27 (1976): 225–40.

——, ed. *De Cella in Seculum: Religious and Secular Life and Devotion in Late Medieval England*. Wolfeboro, N.H.: D. S. Brewer, 1989.

Saul, Nigel. *Scenes from Provincial Life: Knightly Families in Sussex, 1280–1400*. Oxford: Clarendon, 1986.

Savage, Anne, and Nicholas Watson. General introduction to *Anchoritic Spirituality: "Ancrene Wisse" and Associated Works*, 7–32. New York: Paulist, 1991.

Scarry, Elaine. *The Body in Pain: The Making and Unmaking of the World*. Oxford: Oxford University Press, 1985.

Schirmer, Walter F. *John Lydgate: A Study in the Culture of the Fifteenth Century*. Trans. Ann E. Keep. Westport, Conn.: Greenwood, 1961.

Schulenburg, Jane Tibbetts. "The Heroics of Virginity: Brides of Christ and Sacrificial Mutilation." In *Women in the Middle Ages and the Renaissance: Literary and Historical Perspectives*, ed. Mary Beth Rose, 29–72. Syracuse: Syracuse University Press, 1986.

——. "Sexism and the Celestial Gynaceum—from 500–1200." *Journal of Medieval History* 4 (1978): 117–33.

Seybolt, Robert Francis. "Fifteenth-Century Editions of the *Legenda aurea*." *Speculum* 21 (1946): 327–38.

——. "The *Legenda aurea*, Bible, and *Historia scholastica*." *Speculum* 21 (1946): 339–42.

Shklar, Ruth. "Cobham's Daughter: *The Book of Margery Kempe* and the Power of Heterodox Thinking." *Modern Language Quarterly* 56 (1995): 277–304.

Silvia, Daniel S. "Some Fifteenth-Century Manuscripts of the *Canterbury Tales*." In *Chaucer and Middle English Studies in Honour of Rossell Hope Robbins*, ed. Beryl Rowland, 153–63. London: George Allen and Unwin, 1974.

Smith, Richard M. "Geographical Diversity in the Resort to Marriage in Late Medieval Europe: Work, Reputation, and Unmarried Females in the Household Formation Systems of Northern and Southern Europe." In *Woman Is a Worthy Wight*, ed. Goldberg, 16–59.

Staley, Lynn. *Margery Kempe's Dissenting Fictions*. University Park: Pennsylvania State University Press, 1994.

Storey, R. L. *The End of the House of Lancaster*. New York: Stein and Day, 1967.

Stouck, Mary-Ann. "A Poet in the Household of the Beauchamp Earls of Warwick, c. 1393–1427." *Warwickshire History* 9 (1994): 113–17.

Strohm, Paul. *Hochon's Arrow: The Social Imagination of Fourteenth-Century Texts*. Princeton: Princeton University Press, 1992.

——. "*Passioun, Lyf, Miracle, Legende*: Some Generic Terms in Middle English Hagiographical Narrative." *Chaucer Review* 10 (1974/75): 62–75, 154–71.

——. *Social Chaucer*. Cambridge: Harvard University Press, 1989.

Tait, M. B. "The Brigittine Monastery of Syon." Doctoral diss., Oxford University, 1975

❀ Bibliography ❀

Tanner, Norman P. *The Church in Late Medieval Norwich, 1370–1532.* Toronto: Pontifical Institute of Mediaeval Studies, 1984.

Thompson, Sally. *Women Religious: The Founding of English Nunneries after the Norman Conquest.* Oxford: Clarendon, 1991.

Thomson, J. A. F. "Orthodox Religion and the Origins of Lollardy." *History* 74 (1989): 39–55.

Tristram, Ernest W. *English Medieval Wall Painting: The Thirteenth Century.* 2 vols. Oxford: Oxford University Press, 1950.

———. *English Wall Painting of the Fourteenth Century.* London: Routledge and Kegan Paul, 1955.

Vauchez, André. *La sainteté en occident aux derniers siècles du moyen âge, d'après les procès de canonisation et les documents hagiographiques.* Paris: École Française de Rome, 1981.

Verdier, Philippe. "Woman in the Marginalia of Gothic Manuscripts and Related Works." In *The Role of Woman in the Middle Ages,* ed. Rosmarie Thee Morewedge, 121–60. Albany: State University of New York Press, 1975.

Warren, Ann K. *Anchorites and Their Patrons in Medieval England.* Berkeley: University of California Press, 1985.

Watson, Nicholas. "Censorship and Cultural Change in Late-Medieval England: Vernacular Theology, the Oxford Translation Debate, and Arundel's Constitutions of 1409." *Speculum* 70 (1995): 822–64.

———. "The Composition of Julian of Norwich's *Revelation of Love.*" *Speculum* 68 (1993): 637–83.

Webb, Diana M. "Woman and Home: The Domestic Setting of Late Medieval Spirituality." *Studies in Church History* 27 (1990): 159–73.

Weinstein, Donald, and Rudolph M. Bell. *Saints and Society: The Two Worlds of Western Christendom, 1000–1700.* Chicago: University of Chicago Press, 1982.

Weitzmann-Fiedler, Josepha. "Zur Illustration der Margaretenlegende." *Münchner Jahrbuch der bildenden Kunst* 3, no. 17 (1966): 17–48.

Wieck, Roger S., ed. *Time Sanctified: The Book of Hours in Medieval Art and Life.* New York: George Braziller, 1988.

Williams, Ethel Carleton. "Mural Paintings of St. Catherine in England." *British Archaeological Association Journal,* 3d ser., 19 (1956): 20–33.

Winstead, Karen A. "Capgrave's Saint Katherine and the Perils of Gynecocracy." *Viator* 25 (1994): 361–76.

———. "John Capgrave and the Chaucer Tradition." *Chaucer Review* 30 (1996): 389–400.

———. "Lydgate's Lives of Saints Edmund and Alban: Martyrdom and *Prudent Pollicie.*" *Mediaevalia* 17 (1994): 221–41.

———. "Piety, Politics, and Social Commitment in Capgrave's *Life of St. Katherine.*" *Medievalia et Humanistica,* n.s., 17 (1990): 59–80.

———. "Saints, Wives, and Other 'Hooly Thynges': Pious Laywomen in Middle English Romance." *Chaucer Yearbook* 2 (1995): 137–54.

Wogan-Browne, Jocelyn. "'Clerc u lai, muïne u dame': Women and Anglo-Norman Hagiography in the Twelfth and Thirteenth Centuries." In *Women and Literature in Britain,* ed. Meale, 61–85.

———. "Saints' Lives and the Female Reader." *Forum for Modern Language Studies* 27 (1991): 314–32.

———. "The Virgin's Tale." In *Feminist Readings in Middle English Literature: The Wife of Bath and All Her Sect,* ed. Ruth Evans and Lesley Johnson, 165–94. London: Routledge, 1994.

❈ Bibliography ❈

Wogan-Browne, Jocelyn and Glyn S. Burgess. Introduction to *Virgin Lives and Holy Deaths: Two Exemplary Biographies for Anglo-Norman Women,* xi–lxiii. London: Dent, 1996.

Wolffe, Bertram Percy. *Henry VI.* London: Methuen, 1981.

Wolpers, Theodor. *Die englische Heiligenlegende des Mittelalters.* Tübingen: Niemeyer, 1964.

Woodforde, Christopher. *Stained Glass in Somerset, 1250–1830.* London: Oxford University Press, 1946.

Index

Aelred of Rievaulx: *De institutes inclusarum*,
23, 35–37, 48–49, 54–55; "De Sanctimoniali
de Watun," 49–50
Aers, David, 103–4
Agatha, Saint, 1–3, 6, 29–33, 36–37, 68–69,
73–74, 76, 78, 80, 86–87, 115, 127
Agnes, Saint, 1–2, 6, 26–27, 115
Allmand, Christopher, 157–58
Ambrisco, Alan S., 158–59
Amsler, Mark, 138
Anastasia, Saint, 10, 77–80, 99–100, 109, 111,
117
Anchoresses, 21–23, 34–57; as readers, 34–40,
56–57
Ancrene Wisse, 34–40, 49, 51–55
Anne, Saint, 4, 11
Apocryphal Acts of the Apostles, 7–8
Apollonia, Saint, 1–3, 7, 9–10, 92–93, 97
Armstrong, C. A. J., 128
Arundel, Archbishop Thomas, 175
Ashley, Kathleen M., 4, 98
Aston, Margaret, 105, 111, 121, 135–37, 172–73,
175
Augustine of Hippo, 13

Badby, John, 135, 175
Baker, John, 89, 92
Barbara, Saint, 1–2, 6, 147–51
Barron, Caroline, 159
Bartlett, Anne Clark, 54, 56, 128
Baxter, Margery, 137, 173
Beadle, Richard, 119
Beauchamp, Richard, 134
Beauchamp, Thomas, 83–84, 104
Beaufort, Margaret, 119, 128
Beckwith, Sarah, 12, 129, 164
Bede, 7
Bell, Rudolph M., 10
Bell, Susan Groag, 147
Bennett, Judith M., 106–7
Bernard of Clairvaux, 34

Bert, Robert, 170
Biscoglio, Frances M., 96
Bjelland, Karen, 71
Black Death, 107, 110
Blamires, Alcuin, 98, 138
Bloch, R. Howard, 99
Bokenham, Osbern, 4, 15–17, 70, 118–22, 140–
46, 150; Agatha, 127; Cecilia, 16, 125; Chris-
tine, 124–27; Dorothy, 119; Elizabeth, 142–
43; Faith, 127; Katherine, 16–17, 150, 180;
Lucy, 127; *Mappula Angliae*, 142, 145; Mar-
garet, 124–27, 144–45; Mary Magdalene, 11,
141–42
Boléo, José de Paiva, 10
Books of Hours, 12, 128, 145–47, 150, 154, 156
Bond, Francis, 92
Bornstein, Diane, 98
Bourchier, Isabel, Countess of Eu, 142–43,
145–46
Boureau, Alain, 69
Bozon, Nicholas, 18, 70
Braswell, Laurel, 72
Breviaries, 113
Bride of Christ, 59–61, 65, 113, 172, 179
Bridget of Sweden, 11, 17
Brieger, Peter, 90
Brigittine Order, 160
Brown, Peter, 7, 9
Brundage, James A., 58, 98
Brut, 159
Burgess, Glyn S., 18
Burgh, Beatrice and Thomas, 120
Burrow, J. A., 157
Burrus, Virginia, 7
Burton, John, 70
Burton, William, 73
Bury St. Edmunds, 134–35
Bynum, Caroline Walker, 10, 34

Caiger–Smith, Alan, 86
Campin, Robert, 147–50

Capgrave, John, 120–21, 143–44; *Abbreuiacion of Cronicles*, 175; *Life of St. Katherine of Alexandria*, 15–17, 115, 156, 167–80
Carleton, Thomas, 72
Carrasco, Magdalena Elizabeth, 29
Carthusian Order, 160–61
Catherine of Siena, Saint, 10, 17
Catto, Jeremy, 160–61
Cavanaugh, Susan Hagen, 70, 72
Caxton, William, 70, 129, 180
Cazelles, Brigitte, 18
Cecilia, Saint, 1–2, 6, 16, 19–21, 65, 74–76, 78–83, 85, 101–5, 117–18, 120, 122, 125, 132, 174
Cecily, Duchess of York, 128
Chaucer, Geoffrey, 4, 12, 15, 17, 70, 101–5, 110, 143; "Second Nun's Tale" (Cecilia legend), 65, 82–83, 85, 101–2, 120, 122, 132; "Wife of Bath's Prologue," 100–105, 111, 138
Cheetham, Francis, 92
Christina of Markyate, 19–23, 53, 59–61, 63, 178–79
Christine, Saint, 6, 17, 28, 66–67, 74–75, 80, 83–85, 87, 90, 108–9, 111, 124–27
Christine de Pisan, 12, 17
Clay, Rotha Mary, 21
Clemence of Barking, 17–18
Clergy: as authors, 11, 47–48, 50–52, 71, 120–22, 161; and laity, 64–65, 69, 81–82, 101, 134–35; as readers, 70–73, 101; and women, 11–12, 21–23, 47–57
Clifford, John, 73
Cloud of Unknowing, 163–66
Coakley, John, 51
Coens, Maurice, 9
Coleman, Janet, 121
Conduct literature, 12, 98, 128–29
Constance of Castile, 160
Constantine, 158–60, 168
Contemplative literature, 162–67
Copeland, Rita, 138, 140, 174
Crane, Susan, 101
Cross, Claire, 172
Curteys, William, 134

Damrosch, David, 34
Dauphine of Puimichel, 17
Davies, Stevan L., 7–8
Davis, Natalie Zemon, 110
Deanesly, Margaret, 70
Delany, Sheila, 119–20, 143–44
Delehaye, Hippolyte, 10, 77
Denston, John and Katherine, 144, 146

D'Evelyn, Charlotte, 11, 65, 70–71
Diana of Andalo, 51
Distaff, 94–97
Dives and Pauper, 85–86, 88, 109, 170
Dobson, E. J., 34
Dondaine, Antoine, 64
Dorothy, Saint, 17, 26, 28–29, 119
Doyle, A. I., 129, 180
Duffy, Eamon, 113
Dutschke, C. W., 86
Dympna, Saint, 6

Ebin, Lois A., 122
Edwards, A. S. G., 119, 140
Eggebroten, Anne, 35
Eleanor, Duchess of Gloucester, 70, 134
Elisabeth of Schönau, 17
Elizabeth de Burgh, 72
Elizabeth de Juliers, 73
Elizabeth of Hungary, 11, 142–43
Elkins, Sharon K., 21, 48
Elliott, Dyan, 60–61, 98
Engelbert of Nassau, 150
Eugenia, Saint, 6
Euphemia, Saint, 6, 87, 89
Eusebius, 9

Fabliau, 99–100
Faith, Saint, 127
Family, 5–7, 44–45, 58–63, 78–79, 133, 161–62
Farmer, Sharon, 81–82
Flegge, Agatha, 146
Fourth Lateran Council, 14, 64, 101
Francis of Assisi, Saint, 10
Fredeman, Jane C., 180

Gehl, Paul F., 27
Gender relations, 5–8, 31–33, 45–51, 56, 76–78, 86–101
Genet, J.-P., 158
Geoffrey de la Tour-Landry, 117, 132–33
George, Saint, 160
Gerould, Gordon Hall, 83–84
Gesta Henrici Quinti, 158, 161
Gibson, Gail McMurray, 97, 119, 121, 140–42, 146
Gilbert of Sempringham, 50–51
Gillespie, Vincent, 128
Gilte Legende (1438), 70, 156, 180
Glasser, Marc, 11
Goldberg, P. J. P., 106–7
Goodich, Michael, 10

❈ Index ❈

Görlach, Manfred, 11, 70–72
Gottfried, Robert S., 134
Gower, John, 143, 159
Grady, Frank, 158–59
Graham, Helena, 106
Gregory of Tours, 3, 20
Gregory the Great, Pope: *Life of Saint Benedict*, 3
Griffiths, Ralph A., 168
Grössinger, Christa, 96

Hahn, Cynthia, 33
Haines, Roy Martin, 175
Hali Meiðhad, 22, 34–38, 46–47, 57
Hanna, Ralph, III, 138, 172
Hardyng, John, 169
Harriss, G. L., 157
Harthan, John, 145
Head, Thomas, 59
Heffernan, Thomas J., 8, 72, 100–101
Der Heiligen Leben und Leiden, 9
Helmholz, R. H., 59–60
Henry IV, 135, 158–59
Henry V, 16, 156–61, 168–69, 177
Henry VI, 16, 134, 143, 167–70, 173–74
Heretics: virgin martyrs as, 136–37, 175–77.
    See also Lollardy
Hicks, M. A., 154
Hildegard of Bingen, 17
Hilton, R. H., 105–7
Hilton, Walter, 162, 174
Hirsh, John C., 129
Hoccleve, Thomas, 112–13, 139–40, 157, 177
Hogg, James, 161
Howard, Katherine, 144
Howell, Martha C., 106
Hrotsvitha of Gandersheim, 17, 77
Hudson, Anne, 121, 137–38, 175–76
Hughes, Jonathan, 162, 164
Humphrey, Duke of Gloucester, 134, 143
Hunt, John and Isabel, 142, 146
Hussey, S. S., 163–64
Hutchison, Ann M., 128–29
Hutton, Diane, 105–6

Idley, Peter, 132

Jacob, E. F., 135, 138
Jacobus de Voragine: sermons on the saints, 69. *See also Legenda aurea*
Jambeck, Karen K., 119
Jankofsky, Klaus P., 72–73, 100

Jankowski, Eileen S., 120
Jean de Cantebrigge, 70
Jean de Mailly, 64–65
Jenkins, Jacqueline, 117
John de Worstede, 72
John of Gaunt, 160
Jones, Michael K., 128
Jordan, Constance, 109
Jordan of Saxony, 51
Julian of Norwich, 17, 104
Juliana, Saint, 3, 6, 22, 25, 28, 68, 73–74, 86–87, 98–99, 115–16
Justine, Saint, 6, 28, 67–68, 77

Karras, Ruth Mazo, 107
Katherine Group, 14, 22–23, 34–40, 45, 50, 120, 180; *Seinte Iuliene*, 35, 43–45, 56–61, 99; *Seinte Katerine*, 35, 41, 56; *Seinte Marherete*, 35, 40–43, 61–63; sources, 40–45, 62
Katherine of Alexandria, Saint, 1–3, 6, 11, 15–18, 22, 37, 75–76, 79, 89–92, 94, 97, 102–3, 109, 111, 113–15, 150–56, 167–80
Katherine of Valois, 157, 160
Keiser, George R., 160
Kempe, Margery, 15, 17, 96, 102–3, 111, 138–40, 165, 173, 176, 178–79
Kendall, Ritchie D., 140
Kieckhefer, Richard, 10
Knighton, Henry, 111
Kolve, V. A., 109
Kowaleski, Maryanne, 106
Kurvinen, Auvo, 156–57, 180

Lacey, Kay E., 105–6
Laity: as authors, 82–85; and the clergy, 64–65, 69, 81–82, 101, 134–35; literacy of, 121–22, 137–41, 152–56, 166–67, 169–70, 172–75; piety of, 127–29, 145–46, 160–67; as readers, 57–65, 70–73, 79–82, 85–86, 118–22, 141–46, 163–67
Lancastrian apologetics, 158–60
Leclercq, Jean, 25, 27, 58
Legenda aurea, 65–71; Agatha, 68–69, Christine, 66–67; Juliana, 68; Justina, 67–68; Margaret, 122, 130
Legendaries, 64–65, 70–73. *See also Legenda aurea; North English Legendary; South English Legendary*
Legge, M. Dominica, 64
Lerer, Seth, 121, 141
Lobel, M. D., 134

❈ Index ❈

Lollardy, 15, 111, 121–22, 135–41, 157–58, 164, 169–70, 174–77; women in, 17, 172–73
Love, Nicholas, 118, 164–65
Lucy of Rome, Saint, 1–3, 6
Lucy of Syracuse, Saint, 7, 80, 86, 88, 109, 117, 127
Luttrell Psalter, 92–93, 97
Lydgate, John, 15, 17, 70, 118–22, 134–36, 140–41, 143, 150; Margaret, 119, 122–24, 130–33; Petronilla, 119, 124, 130, 133
Lyf of Seynt Katerine (circa 1420), 15–16, 156–67, 177–80

Maddocks, Hilary, 88
Makowski, Elizabeth M., 98
Margaret, Lady Hungerford, 150, 154–56
Margaret of Antioch, Saint, 1–2, 6–7, 11, 22, 24–25, 27–28, 33, 74, 89–97, 100, 108–9, 112–13, 116–17, 119, 122–27, 130–33, 144–45
Margaret of Ypres, 51
Margherita, Gayle, 58, 103
Marriage, 26, 46–47, 58–63, 98, 102, 161–62, 171
Martina, Saint, 6, 23–24, 27–28
Mary (mother of Christ), 131, 150, 165
Mary Magdalene, Saint, 11, 142–43
Mary of Egypt, Saint, 108
Mary of Oignies, Saint, 11
Master of the Saint Lucy Legend: Bruges Altar Panel, 1–3, 4, 10
McNamara, Jo Ann, 7–8, 48
McNiven, Peter, 135, 175
Meale, Carol M., 150, 154
Mertes, Kate, 128, 145
Millett, Bella, 22, 34, 52, 57, 72
Milosh, Joseph E., 165
Miracles, 66–67
Mirk, John, 112
Mockridge, Diane L., 40
Mone, Hawisia, 172–73
Moore, Samuel, 119
Mortimer, Ann, Lady March, 119, 141
Muller, Ellen, 147
Myroure of Oure Ladye, 129

Nationalism, 158–61, 167–68
Nevanlinna, Saara, 78, 157, 180
Newman, Barbara, 22, 47
Nicholls, Jonathan, 121
Noah's wife, 96, 100
Noonan, John T., Jr., 58
North English Legendary, 11, 65, 78–82; Anastasia, 78–79, 99–100, 111; Cecilia, 78–81

Northern Homily Cycle, 78
Novak, Maureen, 146

Oldcastle, Sir John, 136–38, 157–58

Pantin, W. A., 64, 128, 163
Paris, William, 104–5; Christine, 17, 65, 83–85, 108–9, 111
Parkes, M. B., 70
Paston, Margery, 60
Paston, William, 134
Patterson, Lee, 110, 135
Paul and Thecla, Apocryphal Acts of, 7–8
Pearsall, Derek, 134–35
Pecock, Reginald, Bishop of Chichester, 175–77
Perpetua, Saint, 8
Petronilla, Saint, 119, 124, 130, 133, 147, 149
Philippart, Guy, 64
Poletti, Gian Battista, 10
Politics, 4, 58, 134–41, 154–61, 167–70
Polton, Thomas, 158
Poos, Lawrence R., 145
Powell, Edward, 136, 157
Property, 12–13, 80–82, 145–49, 178–80

Queen Mary's Psalter, 86–87, 92–97, 109

Randall, Lilian M. C., 96
Rape, 6, 13, 19–20
Readers: men as, 17, 33–34, 100, 104–5; virgin martyrs as, 147–56, 170–74. *See also* Anchoresses; Clergy; Laity; Women
Reading practices: among laity, 128–29, 165; in religious communities, 27, 39–40
Reames, Sherry L., 69–70, 80, 82, 85, 101, 105, 113
Regina, Saint, 1
Revolt of 1381, 135
Richard, Duke of York, 143
Richmond, Colin, 127
Riddy, Felicity, 102, 107
Riehle, Wolfgang, 166
Robertson, Elizabeth, 22, 34, 47, 55
Rolle, Richard, 163–66
Romance, 178
Rosenthal, Joel T., 179
Rubin, Miri, 5, 12

Sadlek, Gregory M., 72
Saenger, Paul, 58
Saint Alban's Psalter, 21
Saints: modern, 10, 17 (*see also* Christina of Markyate; Kempe, Margery); nuns, 5, 11;

reformed prostitutes, 5, 11; transvestites, 5–6, 11; wives, 8, 11
Salter, Elizabeth, 84, 128
Samson, Annie, 72
Sargent, Michael G., 161
Saul, Nigel, 145
Savage, Anne, 34
Sawles Warde, 22, 34–35
Sawtry, William, 135
Scarry, Elaine, 12
Schirmer, Walter F., 119
Schulenburg, Jane Tibbetts, 3, 13
Sexuality, 5–12
Seybolt, Robert Francis, 70
Sheingorn, Pamela, 4
Shirley, John, 134
Shklar, Ruth, 103, 138–39, 176
Siger of Lille, 51
Silvia, Daniel S., 132
Smith, Richard M., 107
Social order, 65–66, 82, 98, 109–11, 127, 134–35, 138–41, 167–77
South English Legendary, 11, 65, 70, 71–79, 103; illustrations in, 115–16
Speculum Sacerdotale, 112–13
Staley [Johnson], Lynn, 105, 157, 176
Storey, R. L., 168
Stouck, Mary-Ann, 84
Stourton, William, 73
Strohm, Paul, 16, 73, 99, 106, 109, 158–59
Suffering, 3, 74, 87–89, 97–98, 112–15, 149–50, 178–79
Susanna, Saint, 6

Taavitsainen, Irma, 157, 180
Tait, M. B., 161
Tanner, Norman P., 141
Thecla, 7–8
Thomas, Lord Berkeley, 72–73
Thomas de Cantimpré, 51
Thomas de Roos, 72
Thomas of Cobham, 81–82
Thomas of Wottoun, 72
Thompson, Sally, 21
Thomson, J. A. F., 176
Thorpe, William, 137, 140, 175
Translation, 16–17
Tristram, Ernest W., 70–71, 90, 92

Underwood, Malcolm G., 128
Ursula, Saint, 1–2, 6, 113

Vauchez, André, 10
Verdier, Philippe, 96
Vere, Elizabeth, Countess of Oxford, 134, 142
Violence, 1–3, 12, 40–42, 73–75, 78, 86–89, 149–50. *See also* Rape
Virgin martyr: as model of conduct, 19–21, 73–74, 79–82, 97–105, 112–18, 122–33, 139–40, 152–56, 161–67, 178–80; as reader, 147–56, 170–74
Virgin martyr legends: exposition in, 25–27, 66, 122, 124–27, 141, 174; generic features of, 5–10; prayer in, 23–25, 66, 74–75, 122, 124–25
Visual arts, virgin martyrs in, 1–3, 29–33, 70–71, 85–98, 109, 113–16, 147–56; Agatha, 1–2, 29–33, 86–87, 115; Agnes, 1–2, 115; Apollonia, 1–3, 9–10, 92–93, 97; Barbara, 1–2, 147–51; Cecilia, 1–2; Christine, 87, 90; Euphemia, 87, 89; Juliana, 86–87, 115–16; Katherine of Alexandria, 1–3, 89–92, 94, 97, 113–14, 150–56; Lucy, 1–3, 86, 88; Margaret, 1–2, 33, 89–97, 109; Petronilla, 147, 149; Ursula, 1–2

Walleworth, William, 72
Walter, Lord Hungerford, 70
Warren, Ann K., 21–22, 37, 39, 52, 55–56
Watson, Nicholas, 34, 111, 164, 169, 175, 177
Wattun, nun of. *See* Aelred of Rievaulx
Webb, Diana M., 147
Weinstein, Donald, 10
Weitzmann-Fiedler, Josepha, 33
White, Joan, 173
White, William, 136–37, 173
Widows, 8–9, 179
William of Saint-Thierry, 27
Williams, Ethel Carleton, 86
Winstead, Karen A., 102, 113, 169, 174, 177–79
Wogan-Browne, Jocelyn, 18, 21, 58–60
Wolffe, Bertram Percy, 168
Wolpers, Theodor, 124
Women: and the clergy, 11–12, 21–23, 48–57; as readers, 17, 21–23, 33–35, 47, 50, 55–57, 100–102, 138–39; religious vocations of, 21, 48; social status of, 105–7
Woodforde, Christopher, 92
Wooing Group, 34–35
Wyclif, John, 105, 175
Wynter, Symon, 119–20